MORE ADVANCE PRAISE FOR
CHOOSING FAMILY

"[An] affecting memoir. . . . Insightful and reflective, this is a moving tribute to the power of chosen family." —***Publishers Weekly***

"In this powerful, incisive, and deeply personal memoir, Royster explores the beauty and challenges of creating family and the tenets of community necessary to sustain and nurture said family. With precision and heart-wrenching details, she calls into question everything one thinks about generational wisdom, queerness, partnering, parenting, and the consummate fear and the proportional courage that shadow it all. I savored every word." —**Cheryl L. West, award-winning playwright of *Fannie, Pullman Porter Blues, Before It Hits Home,* and *Jar the Floor***

"In her memoir, *Choosing Family*, Royster places herself in conversation with both familial ancestors and intellectual muses in order to make an honest reckoning of her own experiences as a queer Black woman and an adoptive parent. Aptly named, this book highlights the power of choice, particularly when it comes to building family and community of all kinds, and making meaning that serves the future while honoring the past."
—**Nishta J. Mehra, author of *Brown White Black: An American Family at the Intersection of Race, Gender, Sexuality, and Religion***

"This is the most beautiful love story I've read in a long time. Maybe ever. Royster describes and cultivates a love that moves across generations, across loss, across doubt, across every social construct of separation. This is an intimate, vulnerable, and wise ceremony. Royster dwells in the lessons of the small and large revolutionary choices involved in being a daughter, a partner, an aunt, a community member, and a seeker. I held it close while I read it. It hasn't let me go. This book is offering me new lessons on my own love stories. This is a story that can love each and every one of us, if we let it. This is a story that can offer us a more loving world, if we let it. Let it be so."
—**Alexis Pauline Gumbs, coeditor of *Revolutionary Mothering: Love on the Front Lines***

"*Choosing Family* is a joyful and compassionate memoir of the life of an extraordinary queer Black woman reckoning with her past as she creates a family of her own. But this is only part of the story that Royster captures in this deeply affecting narrative, which is, finally, a portrait of a world full of meaningful and lasting connections between individuals, living and dead, and the various cultures that produced them. A beautifully written work of personal reflection, *Choosing Family* is actually a guide to life for those of us who are interested in learning the meaning of resilience and finding happiness wherever we land. Beneath the many captivating scenes and magical moments in this book is a river of kindness that fuels Royster's perspective on the world and makes *Choosing Family* a delightful, warm, and sacred space in which any reader will find comfort, acceptance, and inspiration." —**Emily Bernard, author of *Black Is the Body: Stories from My Grandmother's Time, My Mother's Time, and Mine***

choosing family

choosing family

A Memoir of Queer Motherhood and Black Resistance

FRANCESCA T. ROYSTER

ABRAMS PRESS, NEW YORK

An earlier version of "Resetting the Table" was published as "Narrow Places" in the journal *Slag Glass City* 3, no. 1 (June 2017).

An earlier version of "Stories We Tell After Orlando" was published in *Feminist Studies* 44, no. 2 (2018).

An earlier version of "Changing My Mind" was published in *Untangling the Knot: Queer Voices on Marriage, Relationships & Identity*, edited by Carter Sickles (Portland, OR: Ooligan, 2015).

Library of Congress Control Number: 2022933891

ISBN: 978-1-4197-5617-7
eISBN: 978-1-64700-376-0

Printed and bound in the United States
10 9 8 7 6 5 4 3 2 1

ABRAMS The Art of Books
195 Broadway, New York, NY 10007
abramsbooks.com

This book is dedicated to my family, blood and chosen.
To my love, Annie
And to Cece:
You are our ancestors' wildest dreams.

And in memory of my mother,
Sandra H. Royster
(1942–1999)

Mom with the ancestors.
Sandy Royster at the Door of No Return, Gorree Island, 1990s.
Photographer unknown.

It is an act of love to participate in the resistance work of child-raising.

—Alexis Pauline Gumbs,
"m/other ourselves: A Black queer feminist genealogy
for radical mothering"

[We] must be as strong as our ancestors, and twice as fierce!

—*Fierce Love*, a 1991 play by the Pomo Afro Homos, Djola Bernard
Branner, Brian Freeman, and Eric Gupton

CONTENTS

PREFACE
LOOKING FOR SIGNS
April 2012

THE FRIDAY WE BEGAN TO think of ourselves as mothers started with a series of signs and wonders: a Banksy-style painting of a child lifted by a red balloon stenciled on the wall of a downtown construction site as we walked from the El; a toddler in a spring-green knit cap who popped his head over the back of our yellow booth at our favorite breakfast place, waving at us shyly. Chicago Aprils could give you anything—rain, hail, fog, snow—but the day was miraculously warm, with a steady sun.

I had an important meeting that morning with the promotion committee at my university to consider my application for full professor, and my partner, Annie, had come to hold my hand. Despite the years of hard work and preparation for that day—teaching, researching and writing books and articles, volunteering for hours of committee work—my mind was preoccupied with what I hoped would be a much bigger milestone.

Four months previously, Annie and I had turned in our photobook so that birth parents could consider us to become adoptive mothers. In that photobook, we tried our best to represent our strengths: two seasoned older women, one Black, one white, who loved each other and wanted to raise a child and to bring that child into our community of family and friends—our chosen family. We tried to present ourselves as we are: caring and goofy. We wore our hearts on our sleeves. Somehow, we hoped, the book would communicate our passion to become mothers. Then, three weeks before my meeting, we got a nibble. Our social worker, Wendy, showed us a photograph of a beautiful baby girl who had just been born, her face mostly cheeks and shining eyes. Her birth mother was considering us, among others. At a giddy breakfast brainstorming session, Annie and I gazed at the photo and came up with the name Cecelia, if we were chosen. (At first, I really pushed for the name Jesse. No one would mess with Jesse! I pictured her leaning against a brick wall, thumbs in the loops of her jeans. But in the end, it had to be Cecelia, graceful, ringing, and true.)

Before my promotion meeting was scheduled to start, we quickly ducked into Walgreens for last touches: a bottle of water, lip gloss, and breath mints. Standing in line, we heard Simon & Garfunkel's song "Cecilia (You're Breaking My Heart)" playing on the loudspeakers.

"That *has* to be a sign! We're going to hear something about the baby, for sure!" Annie called out, doing a little dance.

The promotion meeting floated by seamlessly. Afterward, we planned to unwind at our favorite café and meet up with our niece Allie to talk about her post–high school plans. At seventeen, Allie seemed to be growing out of the need to hang out with her aunties, so the chance to spend time with her that day felt like a good sign, too. We headed to the café, ordered our tea and coffee, and sat down to wait. In a moment, I heard my phone buzz in my book bag. I answered, expecting to hear Allie's voice.

"Francesca, where are you right now? Is Annie there, too? I've got some exciting news. Are you sitting down?"

I PUT WENDY ON SPEAKER, and over the din of the crowded café, we listened to the details. K., the baby's birth mother, was a single

African American woman in her thirties from a small struggling town just to the south of us. She was already raising several children, juggling work and school, and taking care of an ill mother when she found out she was pregnant and made an adoption plan. We had no clear information about the birth father. She had made an adoption plan with our agency for two children before this one and was almost sure that she was ready for us to be her new baby's mothers. Almost sure.

We whooped and hollered, hugging Allie, who had wandered into the middle of the excitement, and spent the next hours celebrating, texting, and calling our loved ones. But somewhere beneath our glee was caution. We had been told the statistics. As of that spring, there were seventy families waiting at the Sayers Center, the Cradle Adoption Agency's program for the adoption of African American children. Most of those families were between thirty-five and forty years old. Only 8 percent were older than forty-five, which we were. And only 15 to 20 percent of those couples were gay or lesbian, and most of them had been waiting for a child for three to four years. And, hardest of all to face, we were told that one in five birth parents change their minds about adoption.

Setting aside our worries for the moment, we spent the next few days preparing. We went to Target and piled our cart high with all the things that we knew we'd need in those first weeks of motherhood: diapers and wipes and onesies and formula. The agency required that we have a new car seat to take the little one home safely from the nursery when the time came. Friends began dropping off stuffed animals and toys at our home and our offices on campus. And we made our first visit to the Cradle to meet the baby, to hold her, to feed her bottles of milk, and to imagine ourselves as her mothers. It was irresistible not to.

But then, a week later, Wendy sent us an email that began: "We've run into a wrinkle. But please don't give up."

Wendy wrote that K. went to a graduation party for a cousin and told her extended family for the first time that she had recently given birth and was in the process of making an adoption plan for the baby. They begged K. to reconsider and promised to support her if she kept the baby. K. told the social worker that she needed more time but for us to keep close.

We had chosen the Cradle because it offered a program that focused on African American children and on open adoption, a process in which parents and birth parents work together to shape family. But this also meant that we'd have to live with the possibility that the parents who chose us might change their minds.

At first, we didn't tell anyone about the potential change of plans. We were afraid if we said it out loud, we might lose the baby. But slowly we admitted the truth.

Our friends Laurie and Erica cooked meals for us. Annie's sister Laura instructed us to keep working on the baby's room. "That baby is coming. You've got to be ready," she said. Allie reassured us, "I'd need more time to make this decision, too. She needs you to hang on for her." Our friend Misty reminded us that we needed to hold ourselves with tenderness as we waited. Lourdes and Amina encouraged us to lean into our teaching while we waited.

We spent our evenings wrapped in each other's arms on our red velvet couch, eating animal crackers and watching old episodes of *Friday Night Lights*, trying to breathe. Finally, I broke down and called my father.

"It hurts so much," I told him.

"That's how you know you're her mother," he said.

THE LAST DIRTY DREGS OF salt and ice from the late April snowstorm that had sent the city into the doldrums had finally melted, and the newborn onesies that we bought on impulse were already too small. Annie and I stood on the stone stoop of the Cradle waiting to be buzzed in by the nurses. Against Wendy's advice, we continued to make visits to the Cradle to see the baby as we waited for K.'s decision, unable to bear the thought of the baby waiting without us. Going to see the baby was what we did then, instead of sleeping in, grading papers, or sneaking off to a matinee. The building, with its lead glass windows and imposing turrets, reminded me a little bit of Hogwarts and a little bit of the convent that Maria waited to be sprung from in *The Sound of Music*.

"Ready?" Annie asked me.

Together, we traveled through the dark maze of meeting rooms and offices, the business part of the building closed for the weekend. We walked by the fire extinguisher and the bomb shelter sign, by the framed photos of babies and toddlers who had once waited in the nursery, too. Their faces had become increasingly familiar with each visit.

In the nursery, we washed our hands and nervously helped one another into surgical gowns that opened in the back. We were asked to wear these over our clothes, a task that was also beginning to feel like a ritual. The gowns were faded, washed and dried many times, and had a distinctive smell. I let myself breathe in that smell: a clean, artificial, and inexplicably pink smell, a cross between baby powder and bubblegum.

I remembered the breakfast we had made for each other that morning: scrambled eggs with grated parmesan cheese and potatoes fried hard with onions and garlic. There was the smell of dark coffee and some lingering incense from the night before.

"I wish she could get used to our smells," I said to Annie. "I want her to think of us as home."

A schedule of the baby's daily activities was posted on a nearby bulletin board: feedings, bathing schedules, and playtime. With each week, the activities became more complex. The baby was now almost a month old, and the nurses would start taking her outside so she could see the world beyond these two rooms. I imagined her taking in these new things, her young mind already growing—without us. I yearned to point out to her the colors that were beginning to emerge from the winter grays and browns: the tattered yellow heads of forsythia, always the first Chicago flower, now joined by brave knots of buds.

Sucking on her green rubber pacifier, the baby that we wanted to be ours looked up at us as if she knew us, her dark eyes asking the question: "Now? Now?"

THIS IS A STORY ABOUT losses as well as miraculous gains. This is a story about beginning motherhood in the second half of our lives. So it's about sore backs and knees, about making mistakes when we thought we should know better, and about the unspoken worry that we might not live to see our grandchildren. But it's also a story of second chances and rebirths. This story is set in Chicago in the first decades of the twenty-first century, so it reflects the gentrification, racism, continued homophobia, and transphobia taking place in that city. But it's also about making sense of the past and about creating home right where we're planted. This is a story about building a chosen family, which means trusting friends to love you like family. This is a story about queerness and, because of that, it's about yearning for the world that we want to have, but don't yet.

I am writing this in a time of reckoning, when protests for Black liberation in the wake of the violent deaths of George Floyd, Breonna Taylor, Tony McDade, Ahmaud Arbery, Nina Pop, Tiara Banks, Jada Peterson, Remy Fennell, and so many others have demanded that the nation and the world face the continued history of white supremacy and the urgent need to change it. I am writing at the time of the coronavirus pandemic, which has reminded us all of the fragility of human life and of our own social safety nets. It has also forced us to face the uneven playing field of access to health care, food, and shelter, those very basic and essential aspects of survival. This uneven playing field is also relevant to the role that adoption plays in our society. Motherhood has been one way to change the narrative of the disposability of Black life. Through the nurturing of one small life, we're also putting into the world a model that we think the world needs: to care for one another, to see one another fully, to connect, to feed our imaginations with new stories. By writing this story of Black queer motherhood, I hope to join with others around me who seek to change the script. We are rewriting the story, claiming the joy that the others—society, our family sometimes, even our own inner voices—said wasn't meant to be ours.

This is our story.

PART I

BLUEPRINTS FOR A QUEER FAMILY

1

EVOCATION

A Gathering of Mothers

DEAR MOTHERS, HELP US MAKE a way out of no way.

In this time of waiting, I reached beyond death to call on the mothers of my family, those shapers of my history who embraced the gathering of kin as their life's work, often against the odds of laws and propriety. These mothers, sometimes bigger than life, sometimes movingly human, have taught me how to bring my whole self, even with my flaws, to the work of loving and making a home. From these women I learned an ethos of family that includes chosen as well as blood relations, that's both fierce and vulnerable—and sometimes a little wily. We needed these mothers as we waited for an answer.

I have been without church, without a practice; after a childhood of on-again, off-again visits to the Catholic and Baptist churches of my family and friends, I have become more of a do-it-yourselfer, drawn most to the West African conception of ancestors who shape everyday life. When I call on my mothers, one part in memory, one part in prayer, I find affinity with the Yoruba religious tradition of the orishas, the spiritual deities who are intermediaries between the human and the divine. The orishas are associated with aspects of nature, like rivers and fire, and have both virtues and flaws that help keep them relatable to human worshipers. I find in these deities a blueprint for the deep spiritual presence that my mothers manifest for me now and for the passionate ways they cared for their families, struggled against racism, and lived out their passions in their own lifetimes. As with so many things in my life, there is no neat mold for me to follow. I've had to—and I've chosen to—craft my own path. I don't fit the models that were given to me in childhood. There are pieces of those I still carry with me, but there is too much that I feel compelled to reject—or which feels compelled to reject me.

In the shape of the orishas, I have found a world that mirrors and deepens my own. A world of hidden power and of female strength and open sexuality; a world that makes space for both peace and rage. I see the orishas everywhere: shaping my favorite films, like *Daughters of the Dust* and *Black Panther*, in the music of John Coltrane and the trickster scowl of Grace Jones, in Black folktales and in my favorite novels by Zora Neale Hurston and Toni Morrison. And in her book *Ezili's Mirrors: Imagining Black Queer Genders*, Black feminist critic Omise'eke Natasha Tinsley writes evocatively of Ezili, the pantheon of water spirits of Haitian Vodou, that for many models gender and sexual nonconformity as expressed through all kinds of creative outlets, from the insurgent spirit beyond Haiti's first slave uprisings to Beyoncé's *Lemonade*. I want these tools to help me understand whom I come from and what kind of mother I now want to be.

YEMOJA: MOTHER OF WATER, MOTHER of all orishas, Patroness and Protector of children and fisherman. Her symbols are river stones, cowrie shells, multistranded necklaces of crystal, mermaids. Her colors are blue and white and coral. Orisha of the Yoruba people of Nigeria, Benin, and Brazil, Mama Yemoja is associated with the moon, water, and feminine mysteries. She is the protector of women.

She governs everything pertaining to women, childbirth, parenting, healing. She oversees deep secrets.

MY GREAT-GRANDMOTHER CILLIE'S HOUSE WAS a place of delight and warmth, where we stayed when we visited Chicago from Nashville. It was a place where as a child I listened for Santa, confusing him with the lights of passing taxis on the ceiling. Cillie's kitchen drawers seemed to have an endless series of renewable candies, chewing gum, and bendable straws that I imagined were always present, not yet realizing that she put them in the drawers just before we came to visit.

Lucille—Cillie—came to Chicago as a girl from New Orleans in 1914. Her mother, Mattie, was of mixed race, and her grandmother was a white Irishwoman. According to family legend, when Cillie was a little girl, a white woman, a stranger, slapped her, and her mother, Mattie, beat the stranger down. Mattie and Cillie had to make a hurried escape to the North while her white grandmother stood on the front porch with a shotgun, fighting off the Klan. This is the kind of story that feels like a movie—and yet it echoes the experience of "making a way out of no way" that's shaped my family and that of many Black people who fled the South. In making a home in Chicago's Black Belt, they found a new set of challenging circumstances: cramped living conditions, unemployment, and racism. Still, Lucille and her mother were able to create a new life for themselves, both cleaning houses. Eventually Lucille was able to craft an urbane city womanhood, which included membership in the local Black women's club movement and dating. In her late teens, she became pregnant with my grandfather, outside of marriage, and though she never shared the details of my grandfather's birth with me or my mother, she named her child after his father, John. I don't know why this part of her life was shrouded in secrecy, but I do know that my grandfather was the apple of her eye.

When my grandfather was a boy, Cillie married her first husband, J. Alphonso, who was part of a prominent Black Chicago family. Alphonso adopted my grandfather, and they lived in a six-flat owned by his family at 3210 South Indiana Avenue. This was in the South Side neighborhood poet Gwendolyn Brooks nicknamed Bronzeville for the gleaming promise she found there. It was the center of Black life and culture in Chicago from the earliest waves of Black migration, until the city was forced to integrate in the 1970s.

From the beginning, Cillie and J. Alphonso's marriage was volatile. When Cillie's father-in-law died, the house was lost to the bank, and the already tenuous marriage went down for the count. Against the codes of her New Orleans Catholic upbringing, Cillie divorced.

It was her second husband, Johnny, who was the great-grandfather I knew. He was a jovial longshoreman who unloaded the steamboats that shipped products down the coasts of Lake Michigan. He was tall, handsome, midnight-skinned, ten years Cillie's junior, and quick to smile. Together, somehow, the two of them managed to buy 3210 back from the bank and hung on to it all the way through to the 1970s, patching pipes with electrical tape, bringing in friends to help with the plumbing and maintenance, and financing the mortgage by renting rooms to boarders. They always had a dog to guard the house. In my time, the dog was Jackson, an affectionate, brown, overweight Labrador retriever for whom Cillie would fry fresh liver and eggs every morning.

Like the other mothers in my life, Cillie modeled for me how to make a way out of no way. She always found a seat for others at her table. Over the years, Cillie's and Johnny's boardinghouse served as a refuge for blood and chosen family, including streams of friends and friends of friends from Louisiana and the Mississippi Delta as well as blood family in need, including my mother.

To me, Cillie's household reflected the spirit of queer family in the fluid shape of its membership and the permeability of its borders, stretching always in the face of political and economic troubles, as well as troubles of the heart. As Black scholar and writer Imani Perry describes Black chosen family, "We bind where law fails and rules miss."

Were any of the boarders who lived at Cillie's queer? I imagine the possibilities:

Vera slips her swollen feet out of her dusty flats, and she hears a group tromping through the front door, laughing and teasing one another. When they enter the kitchen, she takes in first the food-stained aprons and smell of sweat and onions and old frying oil. They tell a story of hard work, but work that might be had, nearby. There are two women, both in variations of work uniforms, white dresses gone gray with washing. A slim man in a mostly unbuttoned work shirt and a porkpie hat makes his way to the refrigerator and helps himself to a Schlitz.

One of the women pulls out a kitchenette chair and stretches her legs out in front of her, rolling her stockings down long, lotioned legs. The woman's dark brown skin is silky, her face untouched by makeup, and when she smiles, she has deep dimples. Vera can't tell if she is fourteen or forty. Vera sneaks a look at her hair, which, freed from her hairnet, is cut in a short poodle and seems to have its own tight, natural curl. The back of her hair is shaved short and close to the scalp. Vera has never seen a woman wearing her hair like that back home, and she shivers a little, imagining the delicious feel of clippers on the back of her neck. The woman catches Vera staring and smiles a slow smile.

"OK, Tilly, it's your turn to deal," the woman says, pulling a deck of cards out of her pocket and handing them to her.

"I don't even know what you're playing. And my name's not Tilly!" Vera says, frustrated at her twang.

The man removes his hat and smiles, and a gold tooth winks.

"Don't worry, she calls every cute girl that. Some chick who broke her heart once. Or vice versa." He pulls up a chair to the table, too. "Come on and play with us, sweetheart. The name of the game is Spades. And what do you take in your coffee?" He pulls out a metal flask, even though it was only 4:30 in the afternoon.

AS BLACK LESBIAN FILMMAKER CHERYL Dunye says at the end of her film *The Watermelon Woman*, "Sometimes you have to create your own history." This very queer practice of making a history that's been erased or lost, and making a fierce love out of it, is a way of writing as well as loving. I imagine a queer family made up of friends and near strangers from another time in order to see myself and my desires in the bits of materials I've found: census records, photographs, and the fragments of family stories, told and overheard.

My family was queer without ever claiming the word. That queerness has less to do with sex and more to do with loving—and creating, in spite of struggle. Cillie had been given the message that community was earned through obedience, but she made community through disobedience—her son out of wedlock; her divorce and remarriage; her resistance to the bank's grip on her home. In the face of an economic catastrophe that told her she should think narrowly and fend for herself, she did the opposite—she put out links, made connections. She built a circle of kin that was creative and nontraditional. She took what she'd been told was not hers to take and gave what she was not in a position to give. The reward, I'm sure, was thousandfold.

More than material delight, her house was proof that my family withstood all those external struggles by forging new connections. In the 1940s, Cillie took in my mother, Sandy, her granddaughter, when her parents separated and my grandmother was

Cillie sitting pretty. Lucille Williams, Southern Illinois WPA camp, early 1930s.
Photographer unknown.

struggling to find work. She did this out of loyalty to her son and
her love for my mother, but by doing so she ended up sustain-
ing her relationship with her daughter-in-law as well, despite the

divorce. Marriage, its rise and fall, did not dictate how Cillie made her family. The rent from those boarders in the 1940s and 1950s, strangers and relations, kept the bank at bay and contributed a new, if ever-changing, set of relationships and connections for the rest of the family. I've seen their impact on my mother's thinking of family, and on my own. When I was growing up, my mother took in family and friends, as a way of buffering one another against hard times. For a time, in the 1970s, my teenage aunt lived with us, as she fought with her parents about whether to join the army. Friends like my parents' musician friends, Eddie and Maria, came to visit at Christmas and stayed until spring. My mother's best friend, Nadine, came to live with us when I was nine and my mother was recovering from cataract surgery. And, in turn, Annie and I have taken in family and friends when we felt as if we had "too much house" for ourselves alone.

Cillie also showed me the secret to re-creating the world that you're missing within your own walls. Her house was the house of my first queer imaginings of a world beyond a world. Cillie's house has acted as a conduit to a past that was still unknown, to past lives that Cillie and Johnny and my mother didn't always talk about directly but were present in ritual and sometimes in story: Cillie's Louisiana childhood hinted at in the smell of her red-eye gravy, in her love of Louis Armstrong, and in her love of blue, the color of water. Her house has been a way station for migrations from South to North, her own as well as that of others.

I've often dreamed about her house, where I am roaming her blue hallways. Sometimes, these dreams are about loss. In one dream, I push open the heavy door that led from the dining room to the kitchen and discover a beautiful, sparkling contemporary kitchen, all in marble and stainless steel. But then I realize that I work there, and I find in my arms a heavy tray of dirty dishes, the remnants of someone else's finished meal.

In another dream, I am roaming the house, and I open the door to water, which floods the house, floor to ceiling. All of the things I have known in the house, the neat blue-and-white braided rug, the little figurines of jazz musicians twisted out of black wire, the Brach's turtles candies that Cillie kept in a flowered porcelain candy dish, are all washed away now, lost, the wood of the beautiful house warped beyond repair.

I travel through dark empty rooms until I find my great-great-grandmama, Cillie's mother, Mattie, who died before I was born. I bring her a potted ivy plant, and she guides me to sit on her lap, and I do, even though she is old and sick and in a wheelchair, and I worry about hurting her legs. But she holds me tightly to her—her arms have unexpected strength—and we sit in the cool, watery sunlight of a Chicago winter morning.

We are made up of stars, Mattie whispers to me in my dream. *The light that we see from the stars has already happened, because it takes so long to travel back to us. Starlight has traveled 680 years to reach us. That light that we see on a starry night is 680 years old. By then, 680 years ago, Europeans had already arrived on the coasts of West Africa. We are shaped by this violent coming together. But we are also made up of stars.*

FOR GENERATIONS MY FAMILY HAS struggled to make a home against all odds and has made that home in ways that sometimes aren't recognized by authorities like census takers or social workers, ways that aren't reflected in the pages of *Ladies' Home Journal* or even the Black striving images of *Ebony* magazine. My mother, a poet and lifelong lover of the arts, wrote about this experience of growing up in the spirit of making a way out of no way, and the uncanny ability of her grandmother and great-grandmother to create a sense of pride and culture in the face of violence and erasure, in an essay she published in *Chicago* magazine in 1990:

For me, growing up [in the 1950s] in the shadow of the University of Chicago, the subtleties of discrimination were just that. In the early days, my blonde and blue-eyed friend, Pam, shared with me her life, her secrets, and her room loaded with books and toys and specially designed child-sized furniture. (I shared *my* room with my siblings.) Many years later an invitation to my high-school graduation party inspired only a formal regret with no personal response from this beloved friend from my childhood.

The stories of late-night visits from the Ku Klux Klan and narrow escapes from the consequences of disrespectful treatment toward whites, told in hushed tones by my grandparents, were the mythology of my Southern ancestors. My reality was the surety that no one was better than I. Were not family resources pooled to provide piano lessons, dance lessons, drama lessons, and regular visits to a paid beautician? My library card had already seen ten years of service when I entered high school, armed with art and literature and a fresh hairdo. I knew where my favorites were at the Art Institute. I knew a relevé from a plié. Thanks to the great Katherine Dunham and her research, I learned in those years that the ballet and modern dance I loved, as well as the twist, the Watusi, and the Boogaloo, had relatives and ancestral ties all over the world.

This is where African American families share much with queer families—in our mutual associations by mainstream culture with excess and disobedience, as well as our resistant joy, pleasure, and pride. African American families, too, have been left out of the privileges of heteronormativity, together with norms of class and norms of whiteness. Even as the outside world has shamed the LGBTQ community, African American families have been seen by that same world as excessive: too fertile, too big, too poor, too loud, too funky, too spread out, or too cramped together in the narrow spaces where we've been planted. As African American queer theorist Cathy J. Cohen suggests, "Who, we might ask, is truly on the outside of heteronormative power? Maybe most of us."

The Spirit of Yemoja, nurturer and protectress, riding out storms and flood, links Big Mama Mattie to Cillie, Cillie to my grandmother and to my mother, Sandy, Sandy to me. The mothers are the buffers of loss, even in illness, even in death. The houses might be lost, flooded, and invaded, but the mothers create the center, the resting place. And they accomplish this through a strength much larger than their individual wills. These mothers teach Annie and me how to lay claim to our destiny, to tell a story of joy for ourselves and our family and our community even when joy isn't part of the story we've inherited.

OSHUN: THE DEITY OF THE river and fresh water, luxury and pleasure, beauty and love. She is connected to destiny and divination. In the diaspora, Oshun is associated with deep yellow and gold; in Nigeria, white and yellow; and in Trinidad, pink. In Brazil, Oshun is a symbol of melancholy, as well as sweetness, and is identified by weeping.

MY GRANDMOTHER GWEN, OR NEE Nee, as we called her, made her own wedding dress, and later, my mother's. She was a wonderful craftswoman. Once she showed me a photograph, a triptych from a photo booth, from her teen years when she first met her first husband, Cillie's son John. She was wearing a velvet suit jacket, with a fine cloche with a veil tilted jauntily to the side, and my grandfather was wearing an army uniform and had a thin mustache something like Clark Gable's. They were both dashing, but my grandmother looked shy and young next to John with his confident grin. That courtship would lead to marriage and then divorce, but showing me the picture Nee Nee smiled, her slightly crooked finger hovering to the top of the photo, and said, "I made that hat!"

Like Oshun, Nee Nee loved beauty and filled her world with beautiful things that she sewed, cooked, collaged, and sometimes occasionally "liberated" from others. Her creativity is for me a sign of her resistance and a model of claiming joy despite the world's story for you. She herself was beautiful but didn't seem to see herself that way. Nee Nee had wanted to be a doctor but did domestic work for most of her life, first in the homes of rich white people on the northern suburbs, and later, as a janitor for two South Side Chicago public high schools, Simeon and Chicago Vocational School. She took great pride in this work and bragged that she could wring a rag so tightly that it would disintegrate under her fingers. With these professions, she was probably never truly seen as a "woman," let alone a "lady," but just as a worker. She resisted this imposed narrative by claiming luxury and glamour for herself and her children, adorning herself and her home with fine, beautiful, "worldly" things that often sprung from her own imagination or that she found in others' castaways.

At the end of every school year, she would bring home the books and pencils and notebooks that the students left in their lockers—"liberating them," she called it—and distributed them to her children and grandchildren. Over the years, she built a fine library made up of these liberated books, as well as ones she'd find at garage sales and thrift stores: thesauruses and dictionaries, science and math books, foreign language books and cookbooks, the classics of British and American literature, a whole set of the *Encyclopedia Britannica*, as well as books about Black culture and Black nationalism gleaned from festivals and neighborhood bookshops, such as *The Crisis of the Negro Intellectual* and *The Spook Who Sat*

Nee Nee created a beautiful life in the midst of her everyday struggle.
Gwendolyn Harvey, Chicago, Illinois, 1972. Photographer unknown.

by the Door. Nee Nee was very proud of the library, as well as her kitchen, which gleamed with spices and huge, industrial-sized cans and jars of dried goods—also liberated from the high school cafeteria, perhaps. When I write, I often do so with her in mind, what she might like to read were she alive: stories about everyday survival, complicated stories where she might also see herself as the heroine.

Studying at the (televised) knees of Julia Child, Paul Prudhomme, and Jeff Smith (aka The Frugal Gourmet), Nee Nee was an inventive cook, a master of the basics of French cooking, the Cajun *and* the Creole cuisine of New Orleans, the Tex-Mex of her native Waxahachie, as well as good old South Side Chicago soul food. Nee Nee loved the idea of food she'd read in books, so it was at her house that I tasted my first (Brer) rabbit and my first mouthwatering madeleine (though at the time I thought of the children's book, not having yet encountered Proust).

Sometimes Nee Nee's special talent in creating luxuries out of seemingly nothing could radiate beyond the family. She might trade a little of her knack with the hot comb for a few of the Christmas oranges and grapefruits that her neighbor Nel got each December from her sister down south in Florida. Or she'd design one of her spectacular birthday cakes (trains with orange gumdrop wheels, or a carousel cake with yarn zebra and monkey) for timely help with a dripping faucet or dead pilot light from the building's maintenance man. Once in a while, she'd venture to one of the specialty bakeries or spice stores in Bridgeport or Little Italy near Maxwell Street, the white ethnic neighborhoods bordering her own. Sometimes her savvy and perhaps her lemony skin helped her navigate those "do not cross" zones for Black Chicagoans. But sometimes she ran into trouble, where shopkeepers were slow to serve her, or worse, when they paid her too much attention, with questions, wandering eyes, propositions. Back at her bus stop, she'd seek safety in other dark faces, when she could find them. We all knew that men, women, and children had been beaten, chased, and worse for crossing these invisible geographic lines in Chicago. Not so far into the past, a Black teenager had dared to swim across the invisible line of Lake Michigan's segregated 35th Street Beach (just a few miles to the east of the Bridgeport neighborhood), and his beating and drowning led to the 1919 race riots. This story was notorious, but smaller humiliations and erasures could eat away at your sense of what is possible, too.

When I was growing up, it was not uncommon to come over for dinner and find it in the trash can: a brown-roofed meatloaf, still pink at its cracked center and still steaming at its broken seams.

A golden lamb cake, face crushed to the side. Golden oodles of egg noodles, still bare, the cream for the stroganoff now curdled in the fridge. This was because Nee Nee and my stepgrandfather, James, whom I called Gramps, had been fighting. They both worked hard, and on the weekends cooking was their place to create peace and loveliness, but sometimes also a place to express anger. Where some couples fought around the dinner table, Nee Nee and James fought while cooking. There was a romantic energy around them that I could sense even as a child, an energy that could fuel both creativity and pain.

I remember looking in my grandparents' bedroom after one of those fights, when I was eleven or twelve. Light from the back window filtered into the room, so that I could barely see the black-and-white TV with its sound turned down low and Rex Humbard preaching to his flock. Nee Nee and Gramps were in their robes (matching, monogrammed) and appeared to be asleep on top of their covers, each curled tightly away from each other at the edge of their bed, so that you could see the gap where their two twin beds had been pushed together underneath the comforter. Gramp's clothes were strewn wildly on his side, as if removed hastily, while Nee Nee's slippers sat neatly by hers. It was then that I began to put together the ways that passion and anger worked together for my grandparents. I noted a freshly poured glass of her favorite Fresca and gin on Nee Nee's nightstand, the ice cubes still not melted. The smell of a lovely spaghetti sauce, now forgotten, lingered in the air. I take this memory now and turn it into a prayer to remember the ways that we can hurt each other sometimes even when we start out with good intentions. Even at our own tables, we can go hungry.

In the summer after eighth grade, when I was lonely and ready to abandon my fair-weather junior high friends for some better high school ones, Nee Nee taught me how to cook. And while she couldn't help me sort through my loneliness, she did explain to me the chemistry of yeast, how important it is to capture the heat from its promiscuous hunger under a clean white kitchen cloth; how bread must be battered in order to rise again, but must also rest or it will be broken. She taught me how to tell a turnip green from a mustard green, and how important it is to have both the acrid and the sweet in your pot. She taught me how to clean the shit from chitlins, too, running and squeezing her fingers along the pale, limp skins, and I decided then and there that I had a limit to the amount of shit I would take, even though it might taste tender with the right care, even when there's hot sauce.

As I prepare to become a mother, I think about Oshun's dance between superhuman strength and loss; pride and shyness; creativity and desolation that was also my grandmother's. I think of my grandmother's struggles for a life of glamour that went against the grain of the stories available to her, and how vulnerable that life was, too. Our visions of utopia can be tender. They are worth protecting, however fragile.

OYA: IN YORUBA, THE NAME literally means "She Tore." Oya commands winds, storms, and lightning, death and rebirth. Attributes of Oya include great intensity of feeling, sensations, and charm. She is said to control the mysteries that surround the dead. Her color is red. Her symbol, a copper sword.

MY FATHER'S MOTHER, GRACE, HAD her own kind of glamour. She wore her hair in a Billie Holiday upsweep until her death in the 1990s. She always wore earrings, usually clip-ons of gold or red beads, even when she was in the hospital, embattled by Parkinson's and a failing heart. And she often wore bright red lipstick and, despite the hard work that she did for most of her life, had well-tended red nails.

She was the grandmother who lost us for a time, whose rage kept us away.

Grace was the lightest of all of my grandmothers; her mother was white, a Polish immigrant who married a Black man against the will of her family and set up housekeeping on the West Side of Chicago in a mostly Black neighborhood. My father tells me that when he was a kid visiting his own grandmother, the siblings who were lighter skinned, like he was, got to play out front, while the others had to stay inside or out back. I bet each child felt ashamed, no matter which spot they were given.

Grace rebelled against her mother's preference for light over dark by marrying my grandfather Maurice, a milk-chocolate-brown man and a jazz drummer who loved books and worked many jobs, including a stint in the navy during World War II. Grace and Maurice raised a house full of children, most of them darker than she was—eight altogether. But I often wonder if her mother's conflicted ideas about Blackness haunted her. I always thought Grace wore red to set off both her pale skin as well as her full lips, to highlight her combination of dark and light.

Grace seemed to pay a big price for her rebellion, and over the years, she lost her sparkle. Sometimes I try to imagine her when she was young, playing cards with friends or doing the Lindy Hop with my grandfather between jazz sets in the 1940s. But I know that she already had two children by then.

I have Grace's eyes, as does my father, large and round and so dark brown they seem to be black—eyes that always give us away, whether we're sad or anxious or excited or have a fever. Sometimes, I wear glasses to shield my eyes when I want to keep others at bay, but Annie knows this trick and peeks behind my glasses when she thinks I'm coming down with a fever or have had a bad day. Our eyes slant downward a little and are protected by cushions of darker flesh from below and heavy black brows from above, though my grandmother plucked her brows until they were gone, drawing new ones in. "Doe eyes," I liked to think of them when I was younger and vainer. "Polack eyes," my father once joked when I was in high school, a comment that embarrassed me and also made me wonder about the battles he saw reflected in my eyes.

When I was growing up, I thought that the reason my father moved into his grandmother's house when he was a teenager was because his family was too poor and too large to take care of him. Everyone struggled on both sides of my family, but life on my father's side seemed to be the harshest economically.

But now I know that my father was raised in a household that felt violent. He'd watch his father hit and verbally abuse his mother, and then, perhaps because he was his father's favorite, his mother would beat him, sometimes calling him by his father's name. My father took a job at age twelve, working with his father at a drug store, and then as a janitor, and then moved out by the time he was seventeen, living with the same Polish grandmother who relegated some of his siblings to the backyard. But he decided that if he stayed home, he'd never make it to college. If he stayed home with his mother, he'd never stay alive.

My father didn't speak to his mother for a long time. But after my sister and I were born, he attempted an on-again, off-again reconciliation with Grace. On those childhood visits, we would sometimes come over for fried chicken and spaghetti dinners and sit at the table in the kitchen and sip iced tea afterward. We would always leave early, certainly before the sun went down.

I never saw my grandmother's violence firsthand, but sometimes she'd stare at us hard when we spoke, even though she'd say something mild, like "Imagine that." Sometimes when she'd set things down on the table for dinner, they'd land a little louder than necessary. When she hugged me hello or goodbye, it felt like she had the heaviest hands in the world.

When we'd stand up to say goodbye, Maurice would quietly slip my sister and me a folded twenty-dollar bill. Grace would run up to us on our way out the door and say, "I'm sorry. I'm so sorry," buttoning our coats, her eyes asking forgiveness for something that I didn't yet understand.

My father has filled in some of Grace's story for me, including the harsh struggles to make ends meet in a household with eight children. Despite the three jobs that Maurice often worked, she sometimes had to borrow from friends and neighbors to cover the household debts. Maybe every Black mother living in the 1940s and 1950s had a secret history, the struggles that she hides from her children the best she can.

My father told me some of Grace's struggles, but he also remembered that whenever Grace cooked chicken when he was a kid she would always take the stingy back and neck, leaving the meatier pieces of the bird for her husband and children. He remembered sitting as a preschooler with her in the kitchen while she cooked and did the dishes, and they'd clap and sing together to the country music on the radio that Grace loved, to the disdain of her more urbane neighbors and her jazz-loving husband. Grace divorced Maurice, and then, two years later, remarried him, whether out of love, or fear, or financial expediency, I'm not sure, but after their remarriage they had separate bedrooms. They remained married but separated until Maurice died.

After my grandfather's death, Grace's curiosity for life seemed to be reawakened, and she talked about traveling outside of the country or even just Chicago, though she never had the chance. She'd ask my mother about her trips to Haiti and the Caribbean, eyes gleaming. Or she'd ask me about what I was learning in college. Before her body wore down too much, before the second heart attack that felled her, she quit smoking and took up cycling. I remember watching her wobbling down the sidewalk in front of her house on a bright red fat-tire bicycle, giggling as she worked to keep her balance.

When I think about Grace, I say a prayer of mercy for the hurt that she carried with her to her grave and the hurt my father has not quite recovered from. And I realize that maybe it was mercy that Grace never quite got from the world. When I think about Grace, I also consider the mistakes that I'll surely make as a mother, the tough lessons of the world that I might not yet know, and I pray for the powers of protection or maybe second sight, the ability to see forward and backward. Grace.

IBEJI: THE NAME OF AN *orisha representing a pair of twins. In Yoruba spirituality, twins are believed to be magical. In African American revisions of Yoruban spirituality, the concept of twinning can include the joining of the living and the dead; the unification of spirit and body; the reconciliation of inner and outer selves lost to slavery.*

IN THE ENTRYWAY OF MY father and my stepmother Phyliss's house, there's a big sepia photograph of a woman with a gentle, almost sad smile. Her head is tilted slightly to the left, and she wears her hair in a cute pile of curls on the top of her head, something like Betty Grable. Unlike Betty, though, her dress is dark, plain, and unfettered by ornament. Even if a photographer posed her, you get the feeling that this tilt of head was her own, everyday gesture, a tilt of empathy. When I asked them who the woman is, recognizing already that half-smile, that tilted head and kind eyes, they told me that it's Phyliss's mother, Earnestine, who died when Phyliss was young and whom my father never met. Although Phyliss is bustling and determined, this woman appears still and soft; where Phyllis is modern, the woman in the photo is delightfully old-fashioned. But when I look at the photo squinting my eyes, holding myself a little queerly, I see that they are twins. I see that same core sweetness. The steadiness. The loving empathy of their Christian practice. The eyes that say, "I am willing to ride this road with you." That same listening tilt of the head.

My father has told me that he's adopted Earnestine as his mother, just through this photograph. It had that powerful an effect on him. When he stopped speaking to his own mother, he went looking for new mothers, women to confirm his own sense of the world as having steady streams of kindness that could be tapped when thirsty. And he found it in this photo. It probably helped that this photograph looked so much like the woman who is the love of his life. My dad and Phyliss still hold hands after thirty years of marriage. That photograph represents a psychic source, a way of being in the world of the mother who has shaped the woman with whom he shares his days.

Phyliss Royster and Mama Earnestine, St. Charles, Illinois, 2022.
Photograph by Philip M. Royster.

And Earnestine is a twin, perhaps, to that other mother whose home he left, in grief and determination, eventually to create this new one.

When I pass that photograph of Earnestine in the hall of my father and stepmother's house, I give praise to the powers of reinvention. I know that we can heal from our losses in our families and in our deeper histories, sometimes reaching beyond our own bloodlines, sometimes reaching across generations. I bring Earnestine into the home I am building in my own heart to remember that sometimes it takes the next generation to return to the sites of our struggles, to create something new. To try again.

MOTHERS, GIVE US STRENGTH TO face all truths.

2

QUEER ROOTS

When the World Is Not Enough

I'M A NORTHERN AFRICAN AMERICAN, born in the now defunct Michael Reese Hospital on Chicago's South Side Lake Meadows neighborhood. But like many Chicagoans, I can trace my roots to Black migrations from Mound Bayou, Mississippi, Waxahachie, Texas, and New Orleans. Ancestry.com has given me a little more to go on, with bloodlines from Nigeria, Ireland, and Great Britain, but for the most part, that's where the concrete details of my genealogical history stop, wiped out by the violent technologies of chattel slavery.

There are places and stories in my history that are unknown to me, stories suppressed and records lost and purposely erased, the product of slavery and the continuation of racialized and gendered violence. I've had to re-create my sense of Southern history and identity from stories: my great-grandmother's recipe for red beans and rice and hot-water corn bread, the music of the Neville Brothers and Buckwheat Zydeco that my mother loved, my grandfather's passionate love of blues and jazz and classical, too; the comfort found in caring for trees, watering and turning the earth that I learned from my father.

I've thought about the ways that my family must have struggled with the feeling that the world wasn't enough for them. I've hoped that they didn't always feel when they failed that their failures were only their own. With that pain often came rituals of comfort found in food, music, worship, each other. I've seen comfort as well as resistance in their efforts to stretch the boundaries of family and home to neighbors and friends in need, funding ballet lessons and new shoes seemingly out of magic, making gourmet dishes from recipes clipped out of the *New York Times* with the finely chopped onions grown in kitchen gardens and those huge blocks of yellow government cheese. In those efforts to create something possible out of the impossible, I've seen the DNA of what a family could be. These are the queer family roots that shape my own vision of family.

As Darnell L. Moore puts it so powerfully in his 2018 memoir, *No Ashes in the Fire,*

> We have always been here. Black queer, transgender, and gender nonconforming people loved and fucked on some racist master's plantation. We wrote theories debunking white racist supremacist ideology. We, too, were architects of Black liberation, women's justice, antiwar movements, and the Black arts. We are the unnamed Black sisters, brothers, and nonbinary people who lived queer theory before it was popular among those in white academe.

The very aspect of us that makes us feel strange, not quite fitting into the dominant world, is also a source of powerful feelings: loss, grief, and also desire. In one of my favorite passages by the late queer writer and theorist José Muñoz, he writes, "Queerness is that thing that lets us feel that this world is not enough."

That story of making queer family that I see in African American culture feels much more solidly to describe who I am than the popular images of gays and lesbians marrying and raising children that I occasionally see in popular culture. For example, on my way to work, traveling through a neighborhood wealthier than my own, I pass by a billboard of a new advertisement from Tiffany & Co. that shows two young men—white, ridiculously handsome, so similar in their gym-muscled good looks they could be brothers—gazing into each other's eyes. They sit together on a stoop of what could be gentrified Brooklyn, their Brooks Brothers blazers and natural fiber sweaters keeping them warm. "Will you?" the caption reads.

As the LGBTQ community has become a target for advertising everything from Tide to vodka, the meaning of gay or lesbian or queer has been simplified. In these advertisements, we're either strivers, hoping to be recognized by straight culture as "just like them," or we're "fabulous" consumers, proponents of a "gay lifestyle" fueled by a lot of disposable income.

Occasionally we are portrayed as parents: stylish Daddy and Papa, instructing the working-class parents of *Family Circle*, or the tragically pale and beautiful childhood friends who become lesbian lovers and then just like that, parents, with a towheaded kid in the backseat, selling Renault sports cars. They have "a passion for life," the ad copy tells us.

At my first job in State College, Pennsylvania, where I was not quite out, the only recognizably queer spaces I had access to were bars. My queer life then was new and was made up of a cycle of less-than-successful trysts, followed by self-imposed isolation, binge reading *Curves* and *Girlfriends,* which featured fabulous lesbian lifestyles and haircuts, at home on my couch with my cats. It seemed from those magazines that there was one way to live an authentically queer life. But I knew that I had to make my own way, drawing from a river of strength that ran deeper.

3
BECOMING US
Our First Nine Years

IN THE LAST YEAR OF the twentieth century, when I was thirty-two, I took an assistant professorship at DePaul University, moving back to Chicago to be nearer to my family and with the hope of building a strong queer, creative, activist community that fed my work. I had lived hundreds of miles away from them for my entire adult life, although I always came home for Christmas and at least part of the summer.

I was at a small party given to welcome me to Chicago and DePaul when a woman walked into the room, and I knew that I wanted to know her. There was something in her buzzing energy, her agelessness, and her sense of humor—the combination of sarcasm and empathy—that drew me to her immediately. This was confirmed by everyone at that five-person party, who clearly liked and admired her. Annie was wearing a bright blue T-shirt and bright red Levi's rolled up a bit above the ankles. She removed her bike helmet to reveal a mop of slightly mussed, curly dark brown hair. She quickly pulled a black fisherman's cap from her backpack and slapped it on top of her head, tilting it to a jaunty angle. My heart gave a little flutter.

Annie broke into a smile as she described biking at breakneck speed the several miles from the Lake Front to Elsa's home.

"I don't usually exercise at all. That was only my third time on this bike! I ran all the stop signs and red lights." Annie confessed to me later over our first coffee that she rushed because she had heard about my coming to the university and wanted to meet me. I had heard of Annie, too. At queer-related community events and gatherings, whenever I told anyone that I would teach at DePaul in the fall, people told me about Ann. And they always said, "You'll like each other." They were right.

I concocted a scheme for everyone at the party to write their emails and numbers in my journal—to "network." Annie was the only one who I called, for a coffee in three days' time.

For the rest of that summer, Annie and I hung out with each other almost every day at one of the many summer fests, museums, and bookstores. We'd get together sometimes before noon, moving from coffee to museum to lunch, one activity segueing into another, until it was already nighttime. Or, we'd find ourselves walking from neighborhood to neighborhood and would get lost. We never ran out of things to talk about.

When it was time to introduce Annie to my mother, we were both nervous. I had come out to mom a few years before at the IHOP on Halsted in Boystown, not far from her apartment.

"I figured as much," she told me, pouring her trademark three creams and three Equals into her coffee, her body relaxing into the plush pleather. She seemed relieved that *this* was my big news. "When I was your age, I already had you and your sister and I was working on my divorce. So I knew there must be more happening than you were letting on," my mom said. "I figured you'd tell me in time." Mom met my eyes, and I smiled back shyly. She had a way of defusing drama like that, with a smile. When I was nine and I stole five dollars from her pocketbook to buy Jolly Ranchers and Bubblicious for me and my friends, all she had to ask was whether I had something to tell her, and the confession came pouring out of me. In my twenties for Christmas one year she gave me an electric blanket with "his and hers" settings, an unspoken acknowledgment that my male roommate and I were also bedmates. The conversation at IHOP was easy after that.

I hadn't introduced her to any of my partners for all of this time that I had come out. Introducing Annie felt like a raising of the stakes. Deep down, entangled with the happiness of new love, I worried that I was being disloyal to my mother. One of the big reasons that I had moved back to Chicago was to spend more time with her. But over the past few months of Annie's and my courtship, I was less available for our impromptu dinners.

Annie and I stopped at a café near Mom's office to rehearse what we wanted to say. Fortifying ourselves with iced teas, we searched for the right words to tell her about our serious feelings for each other. And that we hoped our families could join together. "Should we call each other partners? Lovers? Girlfriends sounds so frivolous," I said.

"I don't think I'm ready to tell your mother that I'm your lover," Annie joked. I grabbed Annie's hands, cold with September air-conditioning and nerves, and held them to my cheeks.

We arrived at Mom's office, weaving through the maze of cubicles to find hers. Mom worked at the Chicago Cultural Center, a library that had been converted into a free arts and performance space by the city, and my mother did everything from planning the calendar of programs to writing the grants to fund them to ushering in audience members. You'd know her cubicle by her full and messy desk and by her "Wall of Fame"—her shrine of photographs of famous and not-so-famous loved ones: an autographed photo of Hugh Masekela with his trumpet; a snapshot from an interview that my mom gave with Spike Lee, Mom's arms around Spike's shoulders, kissing his head. My mom treated her work like family. There was a wedding photo of Carolyn—once Mom's intern and now a longtime family friend; a photo of Mom arm in arm with Mayor Harold Washington, her first boss. My sister and I were there, too: receiving our college diplomas, and on a cruise with Mom to the Bahamas. Mom also had no compunction about posting photos that I wished could have been left private: me looking like I just woke up wearing only an extra-large concert T-shirt, which I was pulling to cover my knees; my niece Allie wandering around without her diaper; my sister blow-drying her hair, not quite ready for the prom. These photos remained up despite our protests.

Mom looked up from her desk, smiling expectantly. I flanked Annie, giving her a squeeze.

"Mom, this is Annie! We're on our way to go and eat lunch. Want to come with us?" Annie's hand shot out, ready for a handshake.

"Oh, Annie. So good to see you, sweetheart, but I'm sure we've already met."

"I, I don't think so," Annie said, a little confused. I felt embarrassed, at first. Was my mom just trying to rush us past this awkward moment? Or maybe Mom shared my own sense of feeling already connected to Annie.

"No, I'm sure we have. You're so familiar." Mom got up and hugged Annie and then me, and then sat down to continue her paperwork.

By making Annie family before we could ask her for it, my mother included Annie in her mental wall of fame. In the months that followed, Annie was treated the same way that my sister and I were, part of my mother's inner circle, which meant that Annie was included in her somewhat raunchy jokes, gifted random finds from Nordstrom Rack, and asked to help bring up the chairs from the basement for Thanksgiving dinner.

Annie was with me the night that I received the call that my mother had died.

It was December 1999, and we had just come home from an all-Black production of *The Nutcracker*. We chatted as Annie made tea and I tidied up the breakfast nook.

"I don't think I ever remembered how frightening those rats were," Annie said. "Were they like that in the old version?"

"I think they changed the mice to rats to make the show seem more 'street.' But I've always thought that *The Nutcracker* was already pretty scary, all those toys coming to life."

We were brainstorming Christmas gifts when the phone rang. It was my sister.

I hadn't learned yet to dread late calls.

"Mom's gone," Becky said. My mom was on a trip to Brazil for a music conference, and we had all been nervous when she left because it felt so far away. I thought that Becky meant that mom was sick, and that we had to figure out how to get to her. My mind began racing with the logistics. Pack a bag? Call for help? How to get to her quickly?

"No, Frannie. She's gone."

Suddenly, I was watching myself from a few feet above. I was watching myself doubled up on Annie's kitchen floor crying, and Annie was holding the phone for me. She was crying, too, and that was how I knew that everything had changed.

Annie caught and held me in my free fall of grief.

On a walk by the lake a few months after the funeral, Annie took a Polaroid photo of me, the soft colors of pink and blue and sandy brown already fading. I am looking across the water. I am waving my hand to her, but I'm also turned partly toward the water. It's as if that lake water was the ocean. I can barely look at that photo now, but Annie has kept it in a small frame on her desk. That, too, is a memory of our courtship.

IN 2006, SEVEN YEARS AFTER we first met, Annie and I were walking through a large public park in Beijing, lingering a little behind our tour group. We were both struck by how many people were out enjoying the scenery, even in the middle of this overcast early summer day. There was something about that Beijing park that reminded me of home, that scrappy way that Chicagoans turn up in shorts and picnic baskets as soon as the snow's melted. Nan, a psychology professor from our group, offered a toddler and his big sister a few pieces of hard candy. The toddler dropped his sister's hand, eagerly stumbling toward us, and Nan snapped the photograph of the child sticking his hand out, begging. "So darling," she cooed, as his older sister glared. I burned with embarrassment at Nan's boldness, as I was also embarrassed by the American flag on her T-shirt. But some part of me also felt torn. There were many photographs I wanted to take, too, but held back: the elderly group practicing tai chi in the park, their arms slicing the air in unison; the man in a worn army jacket bent lovingly over his mahogany *ruan*. His elbow poked out of a hole in his sleeve as he bowed the mournful notes out of his instrument, eyes closed. I was moved by this everyday beauty, but I wanted to tread lightly as an outsider. I suspected that I'd never be here again, and part of me wanted to take these faces home with me to remember. How do I manage this mixture of delight and discomfort in my own skin?

Annie and I were on the first week of a three-week faculty development trip to China, sponsored by our university. In those lusher and plusher days of the economy, faculty were invited to propose coursework or research interests where we could engage with China, and then travel there to lay the groundwork. I was interested in Black performance and, by accident, I stumbled on a reggae band playing in our hotel. The band was made up of musicians from all over the diaspora. I was interested in how they negotiated their Blackness with audiences who were both curious about them but also sometimes ignorant of them.

On this trip, especially as we moved in public spaces, I became more aware of myself as an African American woman, as someone clearly from the West, and as a lesbian, sometimes all at once. I was at least a head taller than most of the people I saw, and at least three shades darker. My hair, a short, curly Afro, was often eyeballed skeptically, maybe both for its kink as well as for its shortness, and I took to wrapping my head in soft, colorful scarves. Being a tourist in a place where I felt so visible made me even more aware of when I held back from the world and when I dived in.

I was used to being stared at, both in Chicago and in small towns in the United States, but I wasn't always sure how to read people's responses to me here. As I paused at a busy intersection in Beijing, I was nudged at the small of my back by someone in the crowd. "Keep it moving," I read that touch to say. That nudge, as much impersonal as it was urgent, was the first time that anyone besides Annie had touched me on this trip.

Left on our own for a few hours in Shanghai, Annie and I entered a small crowded shop on Nanjing Road. We were searching for gifts for our collective nieces and nephews. Our heads bent together, we whispered over a display of small satin robes. As Annie held up one of the robes against my shoulders and chest, caressing the smooth fabric, a saleswoman swiftly walked over to us. She was dressed in what might be one of the robes over a sleek Black turtleneck, and she glared at us over a pair of stylish reading glasses, eyebrows raised. Annie spoke up: "We're looking for something for our niece. She's six." Annie pulled out a photograph of a little African American girl striking a womanish pose in ballet tutu, hands on hips. "Oh, no," the saleswoman said, "she's too big for anything that *we* have." The woman wrinkled up her nose, as if at something smelly, then pulled the child's robe out of Annie's hands, smoothing it gently and putting it back on the rack. She didn't offer any other suggestions. I turned my attention back to the other brightly colored satins and silks on the rack, but Annie took my arm. "Let's get out of here," she said in a loud whisper.

On that trip, Annie and I leaned on each other more and more as we navigated these unfamiliar spaces, deepening our bond even as we revealed our crankier, travel-addled, less flattering sides. That was another kind of risk—to be your most hunger-humbled, messy self away from home and to rely on this single loved one to get you through it. Annie learned to tell from my tone and the flash of my eyes when I was having difficulty making a decision because my blood sugar was low. She made sure that I followed my diet to control my diabetes, checking on my medical supply and making sure that others in our tour group didn't eat up all of the low-cal, vegetarian food that I had arranged for the trip. I knew that Annie had trouble sleeping in new places, so I'd whisper a recap of our day as we bedded down in each new sleeping place, stroking her temples until she finally closed her eyes. So far away from home, we were becoming home to each other. This new context sharpened our partnership, and the assurance that we'd protect each other and stick up for each other whatever came our way.

Our flight back to Chicago was more than fifteen hours. Annie and I were huddled together like hamsters, our fears around public displays of affection tossed aside for the expediency of sleep. We were exhausted by our big journey. I woke up with the strong need to pee, and I reluctantly untangled myself from Annie's warmth. Because of the time change, I wasn't quite sure what time it was any more. In Shanghai, the last city on our tour, it was the middle of the night. To accommodate that, the plane set the cabin light to a dusky twilight. We were up above the clouds, and outside the sky was gray and indeterminate. A few stubborn readers had their overhead lights going, but most were in deep sleep, snoring under blankets and coats, curled awkwardly in too-small seats. I headed toward the back of the plane. There was a short line. I got behind a woman who was carrying a small child still wrapped in a blanket, a girl. The child faced me over her mother's shoulder, and even in the dim light I could make out the softness of her face, sulky lipped, cheeks flushed with sleep.

She looked three or four years old, with long legs that wrapped around her mother's hips. I smiled and thought to myself, "Surely you are big enough to walk." And as if she could hear me, she looked at me defiantly, frowning a little, before closing her eyes to doze again. Her mother jiggled her to readjust her weight, and then pat her back in slow rhythms. I imagined what this might feel like, to carry a child already big enough to reach half your own height. To comfort. I felt an urge then to nestle the top of a small head beneath my chin, to feel another's milky breath. To know that possessive hold of a child, claiming my arms and hips, a hold so different from a lover's; to experience that miraculous ability that mothers have to keep holding, despite shaking arms, their already-walking child, against odds and often in uncomfortable spaces, such as airplane aisles and grocery store checkout lines; to carry a child up and down stairs to the bathroom in the middle of the night. As I watched the mother and child, I wanted to be of use in that deep and fundamental way.

I was outside my everyday life in this interstitial moment between day and night, between countries, half asleep and half awake. I thought I heard crying, not from the child in front of me, but from somewhere deep in the pit of my chest. I had a feeling of warm light coming out of my chest, rays coming from all directions, and for a moment I couldn't see the face of the mother and child because it was so bright. It was the middle of the night, but we seemed to have struck the sun.

Was that really how it happened? I wasn't someone who tended to have mystic visions. Why did this homely vision—baby, bathroom, airplane aisle—open up a new space in my head?

I walked back to my seat, holding that light within me, waiting for the right moment to share it.

Our lives together—mine and Annie's—were already so much more than I had ever expected: gentle, loving, fun. We worked too hard, maybe, sometimes reading and grading papers together deep into the night, but we did it together. Annie was my favorite person in the world. Her generosity and her compassion for other people, as well as for me, had already changed my rulebook for how to engage with the world. Could we stand the risk to change ourselves and maybe lose what we'd created?

IT WAS RAINING LIGHTLY AS I stared at a window of children's shoes, remembering. Those bright patent leather Mary Janes were the kind I begged my mother to let me wear to school instead of sneakers when I was in kindergarten. They make them in red and blue now. Over there were the baby shoes, so small, the soft leather bottoms still sturdy enough for little feet to walk in. It was only when a gust of a late April wind pulled the umbrella out of my hands that I was reminded to keep walking, late for class.

For a few months after our trip to China, the urge to have a baby receded to the edges of my thoughts as Annie and I chased tenure, took care of our nieces and nephews, traveled, and lived, but as soon as I hit my forties, it came back raging. It feels trite to admit it, but like so many women, right at that age—not quite a young woman anymore, not yet old—I began to feel a yearning and a kind of possessed, manic interest in babies. What was I? Some character from *Sex and the City*? My friends and I made jokes about what we called the "Breeder Starbucks," the one not far from our campus that had more double strollers than others, and yet there I was doing double takes at every infant I passed on the street.

This felt doubly weird because I was a lesbian who identified as queer. To call oneself queer, especially as an African American woman, was to purposefully court contrariness and unconventionality. We're not supposed to yearn for those things like motherhood and family, at least not in the same way that the cooing women at the Breeder Starbucks do, right? One of the things that I'd loved about being queer is the freedom to create my own circles of kinship, and those circles aren't beholden to a biological clock.

I have always felt myself guided by a queer sense of time. Queer writer and thinker Jack Halberstam has written about the concept of queer time as one that is shaped around cycles of friendship and collaboration outside of the reproductive time line of marriage, babies, and death. Queer time ages you differently and offers a more fluid sense of life's meanings and relationships, shaped by "strange temporalities, imaginative life schedules, and eccentric economic practices," as he puts it. For me, that has meant not overlooking what's unsatisfactory about life as it's usually lived and trying something else. I've watched my friends, gay and straight, struggle to keep a sense of creativity and risk in their art and their teaching as they age and become responsible for others, maneuvering the weight of domestic life. I've watched my friends with children as they struggle to balance childcare, home care, activism, scholarship, and each other. Would I be losing that commitment to queer time if I had a baby? And how would I convince Annie to join me? For the first time, I had to think about these questions not just for myself but together with someone else.

I've debated these things also knowing that queer women, coupled and single, have children all the time. Even if we were in the midst of a so-called gay baby boom in the past decade, influenced by changing marriage and adoption laws, lesbians and queer women have been having babies all along: through marriages, through platonic arrangements with male friends, with turkey basters, or, much less visibly, through adoption. Despite the sense of the newness of queer families that one might get from mainstream popular culture, we have been having and raising kids for generations. Some of my favorite lesbian and queer feminist sheroes were also mothers. For example, in *The Argonauts*, memoirist Maggie Nelson chronicles the erotic charge of pregnancy, parenthood, and change, together with her partner, Harry, who is in the midst of a gender transition. Together, they are exploring how both transitions shape desire, identity, and self. But more than forty years earlier, Black lesbian feminist poet and activist Audre Lorde had also entered the institution of parenthood queerly, raising a son and daughter, first with her bisexual husband, Ed, then with her white lesbian partner, Frances. Audre and Frances raised their children as an interracial couple more or less "out" and in the conservative community of Staten Island in the 1970s—something I find miraculous, even if it was not without complications and pain. Lorde's experiences as a mother very much shaped her approach to community and art and to political activism as a form of caregiving. So many of my favorite queer of color thinkers and artists—Cherrie Moraga, Alice Walker, Rebecca Walker, Meshell Ndegeocello—have been boldly redefining what it means to mother all along.

I felt in my own bones this desire to mother, but what about Annie? I didn't want to do this without her, but I was pretty sure she didn't want to be a parent. She said all the time that she didn't want to risk becoming her own parents, who carried with them deep rage and unpredictability that was sometimes taken out on their children. Annie grew up feeling a great contradiction: a strong sense of family loyalty and connection, and the underlying presence of violence. It was Annie, though, whom I wanted to make a home with, with whom I felt the most comfort in my own skin. I wanted to take that comfort and share it.

For a while, I found myself split between the lovely present of love and work and a future self who would be a mother. I found myself changing on the inside, wanting more and more a different ordering of my life. Wanting a different sense of life's work by nurturing another life. Bringing those selves together meant bringing Annie into the vision. That, however, would mean asking her to change her daily routine, her relationship to money and time, in effect, to change her whole story of herself as a woman committed to resisting norms. Could I ask her to change for me, to revise her life and maybe also her politics? I had already convinced her to abandon her queer ritual of going to the movies and having Chinese food on Christmas with her best friend, Lourdes, in favor of spending the day with my extended family. Could I ask her to take a risk with me that was even bigger? Sometimes it felt easier to just imagine a life alone so that I could avoid being told no. But still that possibility of new joy glimmered.

Those questions in my head grew louder as I went on sabbatical. It was the spring of 2008. I was forty-one years old, the same age as my grandmother when she had her last child and almost twenty years older than my own mother when she had me. I was working on a new book on queer life making and music. As I read and researched one life, I found myself reflecting on my own and the shape I wanted it to take. Most of me was afraid of drastically changing the course of my life, and I was also worried that I would lose Annie if I did. But freed from my classes and other departmental obligations for several months, I felt ready to ask some hard questions.

Sitting cross-legged on my bed, old photos spread before me, I felt my heart beating a little faster. It had become a ritual when I was by myself, after I had done my writing for the day, to open up my old trunk that I stored in my closet and find the photographs and the letters, to try to remember myself then and to imagine what might have been. I studied the faces of my old boyfriends together with my younger self, squinting my eyes to imagine what combination a baby might have taken: those eyes, that dimple, skin somewhere in between. What would have happened if I had just married the first person I fell in love with, in this case, a man? If I had had a child then, that child would already be a teenager, maybe even already an adult. What would my life have been like, being a mother for my whole adult life?

Annie was in the bathroom brushing her teeth when I blurted out, "I feel so restless and distracted, Annie." What I wanted to say was, *I want to have a baby.* But I was afraid. I didn't trust myself. Was this just a flurry of hormones? The restlessness that spring always stirred up in me? A baby had never been in our plans for the future.

I walked into the bathroom. "I feel like I need to figure some things out," I said. "Maybe we should take a break."

I said it fast but also conversationally, like it was continuing something that we were already talking about, even though we weren't.

Annie was smiling at first, but then she turned off the water. She wiped her mouth on the red towel very deliberately.

"What are you saying? Do you want to break up with me?"

This wasn't going the way I hoped it would. This conversation was moving way too fast. I panicked then, my heart saying, *No! No!*

But I breathed deep and said, "I don't know. I'm confused." *Stubborn! Just say you're sorry!* an inner voice said. *Take it back.* But I said, "I feel like we have a lot to think about. I feel like we need to figure out what we want our lives to look like."

Annie started crying, and then so was I, and we held each other in the bathroom like we were both drowning, which we were. Then I went to my apartment, which was just across the driveway from hers. Once I was inside, that's when I cried loudest, howling, even scaring my cats.

We took seven days.

We spent time in our own apartments, though still coming together at night, not talking about it, sleeping back to back. It was like we were underwater, exploring the depths in our different directions, tied by the same oxygen tank. We still ate our meals together, a little glassy-eyed, conversation stilted, like some old couple who have forgotten why they stay together. One night, we went to eat at a neighborhood diner that features healthy meat: grass-fed beef, free-range chickens. It was a lovely night, June spring rapidly turning into summer, and Christmas tree lights were on in the outdoor dining area. The air was moist, temperate, lovely. Everything screamed romance, but I felt hollow. I tried to fill my gut with food, ordering a hamburger that I could barely swallow.

Before this fork in the road, our arguments, if you could call them that, were more like little bursts of feeling: misunderstandings, irritation, impatience, pain leftover from the past. Sometimes one of us might draw back if we were feeling vulnerable. Our fights never lasted longer than thirty minutes, and they ended in kisses and tears and talking through. But this was different.

I knew I wanted to stay together, but I also wanted more. It felt like something was holding us both back from getting closer. Work, writing, politics, worries about our families, everything took priority over the time we spent together, and the very things that we shared in common were beginning to create a wall between us, keeping us from moving deeper, taking fewer risks with each other.

This was as difficult as the first grieving weeks of my mother's death. I saw in Annie's face how much she was suffering, too. But I felt that this was the work that we needed. We needed to face the possibility of being apart, of losing each other, in order to find out where to go next.

4

CHANGING MY MIND
Rethinking Marriage

FOR MOST OF MY LIFE, I'd thought of myself as "not the marrying kind." Even before I knew I liked women, I was queer on the idea of marriage. At first, I thought that what scared me was the idea of walking down the street and being seen as a couple *only*, my own self disappearing. That's what was captured for me in the phrase "man and wife." But as I looked deeper, I saw that what scared me was the idea that I could live day by day with someone, entangle my life with someone else's, let my body, my things, even my ideas and dreams meld with another's, and be wrong. Remembering my parents, I'd mostly chosen to turn away from that prospect of loss. But to my surprise and joy and fear, I felt myself deep in it: There was Annie, whom I wanted to be my partner for life. And, the image of a child kept coming to me. Our child. In other words, risk of the deepest kind.

The home that I thought I lost as a child is still with me, stones that I carried within the pockets of me, stones that were still jagged and stones rubbed smooth with time. Stones that weighed me down. Where did they fit in this new, changed picture of my life?

It was the summer of 1973, a year of Afro puffs and Michael Jackson showing us how to do the robot on *Soul Train* and Minnie Ripperton with baby's breath in her hair hitting the whistle notes.

My parents had been separated for a year, soon to be divorced. That summer, my father took my sister, Becky, and me on a road trip from our home in Nashville to visit him in his new home in Albany. Thus began a ritual of spending summers with my dad that would continue until we entered college. As we moved from Tennessee northward, red and orange and blue-gray cliffs of clay and limestone hugged the highway, jutting out from beneath the buildings and concrete, from beneath the grass and trees. I wanted to slow down the cliffs as they whipped past us, as if I wanted to slow down the whole trip. I wanted to take the orange cliffs with me and keep them, even though I suspected that they were in the category of things that couldn't be kept, or even touched, like baby birds that had fallen out of their nests. But when I asked my usually careful father if we could stop to climb them, he surprised me by pulling the car over to the side of the road. We emptied the paper bags that held our car snacks of popcorn, red pistachios, and peanuts, and filed out. Other cars sped past us. My father kept a lookout for crazy drivers and police cars from the bottom of the embankment as my sister and I climbed the wall of stones. We selected a few of the smallest rocks to keep, as most of them were too big for us to carry. We put them in the back of the car, along with our suitcases, and joked about them as our treasure.

I loved that drive from Tennessee through Kentucky and Ohio and finally New York and reveled in the beams of attention I soaked in from my father when it was my turn to sit in the front seat, listening to the mixtapes that he made for each of us, cracking and feeding him pistachios until my fingers were salted and flamingo pink with the dye. When I got home from the trip, I held the red cliff rocks, still warm from the car's engine, and listened over and over again to the first song on the tape my dad made for me, Willie Bobo's soulful rendition of the samba tune, "Dindi," from his album *Lost and Found*. Bobo, a Puerto Rican percussionist who died at the young age of forty-nine, was one of my father's favorite singers, and his voice, deep and resonant, somewhere between folk and blues, seeped into my skin as I listened:

The sky, so vast is the sky
With faraway clouds wandering by
Where do they go?
Oh, I don't know. Nobody knows.

Like a secret code, like the cracks of hidden crystals, Willie Bobo's voice, smooth and then broken with feeling, said out loud what I was not supposed to admit, the sadness free floating like clouds that I tried to keep hidden from my parents.

I thought of the conversation just a year before in my parents' bedroom, of how we were all crying and how messy it felt, all of

We have our father's eyes. Philip Royster, Rebecca Royster, Francesca Royster, Chicago, Illinois, 1970. Photograph by Leonard Fancher.

our faces wet and twisted with feeling. I made a joke to stop the tears: "When you get your divorce, will I still get my allowance?" We all laughed, and *that* became the story that we'd all tell afterward of the divorce, forgetting the way we were all coated in the wetness of our sadness. When Willie Bobo's song got to the part where he sings, "I'll come running and searching for you like a river / that can't find the sea," I felt like wailing. Instead, I mouthed the words quietly to the ceiling, learning then my habit of letting music speak for my feelings. I hoped that my father chose this song because he mysteriously knew what I was feeling and because he was missing me, too.

The year before my parents separated, when I was five, I started to get adult-sized headaches that made me cry and clutch my head on my nursery school cot. My teachers, Miss Dozier and Miss Mayer, asked if everything was okay at home. I let myself cry then and told them that I thought my parents were going to get a divorce. They chuckled and tried to reassure me. Miss Mayer pressed her hand on mine. "Plenty of kids worry about that. And lots of times they're wrong. It's all going to be okay," she told me. They were older than me, and so kind. But I knew that change was coming.

Strange that in most of my memories of my parents, they were separate from each other, even before they were divorced. I remember harried breakfasts and dinners and Christmas, of course. Our house was often filled with guests then: family, students who couldn't afford to go home, musician friends of my father's passing through. Perhaps this busyness created a kind of subterfuge. And, we'd also go hiking and on car trips all together. But mostly I remember them doing things with my sister and me or being busy with their own things. I remember listening to music with my father in the living room, sitting on the cushions or going through his record albums: Celia Cruz, Patato & Totico, Eddie Palmieri. He played the congas along with teaching English and writing poems, and music was his passion. I remember sitting and listening while he played his drums along to the music in his earphones. My sister and I would sometimes go with him to the park to play his drums, and we'd proudly help to carry his instruments. I remember bringing lunch to him up in his study while he was writing, enjoying that quiet time with only him.

But my mother was my more frequent companion in those preschool years; I did just about everything with her, so my memories of our time together are of everyday things. Eating apple peels as she made a pie, playing on the floor in the kitchen as she washed dishes under a huge FREE ANGELA DAVIS poster above the sink, one of my parents' shared political commitments. There was Angela Davis mid-yell, fist-raised, and beautiful, so articulate about the struggles she faced, a gift I've always wanted to learn from her. My mother sometimes combed my hair into a big Afro just like Angela's. My mother was gentle with the comb, and patient, and she made me laugh even as she pulled and tugged.

Small details let me know that my parents were not the centers of each other's lives any more: the tandem bicycle that my father bought so that we could ride together as a family was more often than not used by my father to take my sister and me on rides. Becky's short legs strained to pump the pedals from the second seat while I enjoyed an unsteady ride from the kid's back seat. Meanwhile, my mother was at home or running errands. The waterbed that my parents decided to try out, festooned with Indian print spreads and requiring intensive upkeeping rituals, was finally abandoned, sometime after my sister and her friend Sherry accidentally made a hole while playing on it and tried patching it with a Band-Aid. I watched friends of my mother and father split, as if forming camps, with overheard whispers between my mother and her friend Pam.

During these months, we started to hear the word "divorce" with regularity in the arguments between our parents. One afternoon, that year that led to their separation, a big thunderstorm left us without electricity. It was in the middle of a Saturday afternoon. My sister and I had been so busy playing in our room that we hadn't noticed how quiet the house had gotten. For a while, we could just hear the rain and the occasional thunder. We didn't know where our parents were. I wandered over to my parents' room. The door was closed, but I went right in. They were taking a nap together, all wrapped up in the sheets and a big flowered quilt. It seemed strange to me that they were taking a nap in the daytime. My father's arms and legs were curled around my mother protectively. My father was wearing his blue robe, the one we got him for Christmas, but my mother was naked underneath, her brown body curled up tightly beneath him. She slept with her hands folded underneath her chin. I stood there for a few minutes, taking in the pleasant smell of their room, sandalwood and just washed sheets. My father's eyes opened. He put his fingers to his lips. "Shhhh."

"We're bored. We want to go outside. It's stopped raining."

He whispered, "Yes, okay, okay. Your mother is sleeping. Stay close to the house."

Outside, it was sort of like a holiday. All of us kids in the neighborhood were there in open slickers and rain boots. The sun came out and everything—the leaves on the mulberry bushes, the sidewalks, the metal gates that surrounded the housing complex—were wet and sparkling in the new light. My sister and I played for hours, no parents coming to take us shopping or to lessons or to clean our rooms. It was as if the loss of electricity had stopped everything for a while.

I LOVE YOU MORE EACH day. Dindi yes I do. You know I do. I'll let you go away, if you take me with you.

THE MORNING THAT WE LEFT my father, I woke to the feeling of dread and the smell of wet cardboard: sweet, dusty, a little like the smell of the first day of school and that bouquet of chalk and bologna sandwiches at the bottom of the lunchbag, bananas browning in the heat since morning. It was raining outside, and I saw through my bedroom window that there was a moving van pulled up to our front door. The door was open, and a man carried a large yellow Mayflower crate, which held the top of our glass dining room table, padded in a blanket. My mother was following him with instructions. She didn't have her bra on yet, even, just her nightgown and an unbuttoned robe wrapped around her, because the moving van came early, or we overslept, and I felt embarrassed for her soft body, exposed to the men. I was wearing my nightgown too, and I felt like crying, but like my mother I kept any tears tight in my chest. The men, muscled and loudly chewing Juicy Fruit and already working up a sweat, were loading all of our things, packed or unpacked, into the van, and my father was nowhere in sight.

In those first years of the divorce, when I was seven and eight and nine, our changing family felt to me like watching those Tennessee cliffs whip by from our moving car. My eyes would try to focus, to keep things from moving and shifting, but they always failed. My father soon got a girlfriend, Cindy, who kept her hairbrush and clothes and birth control at his new apartment. She helped him rearrange his furniture from the way my sister and I did it when we helped him move in. She remained part of his life those first years after the divorce. My mother met Pat the Cop, a gentle man who would come over after dinner and let me put his hair in barrettes, even though he wore a holster and—when he wasn't in our house, and under the watchful eyes of my mother—a gun. Even the mixtape that my father had made me eventually wore down. Willie Bobo's voice grew slower and slower, until the tape caught, garbled, whined, and suddenly stopped, a tangled mess of magnetized plastic. Angela Davis was long freed, but for a while, I gave up on the power of my voice to stop things from changing. So, I grabbed onto rocks and pebbles, shells and driftwood, jamming them in my pockets, and then arranging them in neat rows on the windowsill of our new apartment.

Leaves and mud and minerals welded together through time. The sand and dirt came off as I rubbed them, and I liked to imagine my own sweat and oils joining the history on their surface, maybe someday to be found by somebody else. The rocks had been around for thousands of years, longer than we had, longer than the apartment we lived in together for almost all of my six years in a red brick-and-wood building with walls thin enough to hear your neighbors. It was faculty housing for Fisk University, where my father taught. Longer than my father's next place in Albany, New York, a high-rise he jokingly called Menopause Mansion. It was populated with older unmarried women—women who never married, women who left their husbands for another life, women who were left, and women who weren't the marrying kind. My father was very popular there—he was still young, only thirty-five. The women would eye him in his white painter's pants and snazzy caps, and maybe he appreciated the attention. There were only a few men, that I could see, and they did not seem to be linked to anybody else, either. When we would visit in the summers, we were often the only children at the pool.

As I grew into a teenager, I shaped myself into a vision of those unlinked women. I kept my deepest passions on the periphery of my vision, distracting myself with school and work, and also with boys, but knowing already that there was more to who I was, more to explore. For those years, my most passionate friendships were with my girlfriends. These were loyal friends with whom I would spend time every day and would miss profoundly when they weren't with me. We'd write each other letters and postcards during our summer breaks and send each other care packages. We'd cry and get jealous and confused over each other, but sometimes there would also be great, unaccounted for joy.

I put off coming out to my mother for years after I had figured out that I was at least "lesbian with a small 'l.'" My mother always had "her boys"—the men from work and from the AIDS ministry at her church, as well as friends who turned to her for empathy, guidance, and fun. (She loved to go dancing.) Her world had always included gay friends, but I feared that she would see my queerness only as a reflection of herself, an accounting of her choices and mistakes. But while my mother's gay friends were a visible part of her circle, she also connected deeply with women friends, who became part of our everyday lives for months, even years at a time. There was Elizabeth, with her short, curly gray hair, commitment to macramé, and a voice that was husky and earnest. She cooked dinner for us often after my parents' divorce. My sister and I were sent to watch TV and play with the Tinkertoys she kept in her den while she and my mother talked, heads together. There was lean, funny, irreverent Billie, the daughter of a notorious Black Chicago socialite family. She hid out for weeks on the couch of our apartment after she left her husband. Kenya, the singer who introduced me to Minnie Ripperton, and who lived with us for a while in those early post-divorce years and cared for us once for a whole summer while my mother underwent some serious eye surgery. They were not my mother's lovers, at least as far as I know. But these women were trusted intimates, partners of a sort, and my mother leaned hard on their friendships.

Thirty years since my parents' divorce, and more than ten years after my mother's death, I found myself thinking hard about family, my past, and the future. What did I want to keep, what I could give up as lost, and what did we need to reinvent? With my mother's death, I felt like I could ask my father about their marriage and not feel disloyal. So I invited my father for an interview about home. We sat on the couch in his day room, in the large house he built with Phyliss, whom he had been committed to for more than twenty years. I set up the tape recorder on my iPhone and he set up a video camera, the fancy one that we all chipped in to buy him for his retirement from teaching. Before the interview, he made us both double-decker "Dagwoods"—Morningstar Farm soy burgers, cheddar cheese, lettuce, tomatoes, hard-boiled eggs on raisin bread—the huge sandwiches, named for the comic book character, that he made when my sister and I visited him after the divorce. He wore his Afro shorter and neater now, gray overtaking the black, but he still had a respectable head of hair. Before we began our conversation, he filmed a test shot. I could see in the miniature image caught in the camera how alike we were. We both had the same heavy eyebrows and unconsciously worried expression. We were both sitting with the same slightly off posture, haunted by sciatica in our lower backs. Both academics, we've faced the same occupational hazards and the same addiction to chiropractors. Our legs were crossed in just the same way, one toward the other. When one spoke, the other nodded softly, as if to say, "Go on."

I asked him about our home for that six-year time that we lived together, his memories of his childhood home, and his knowledge of my mother's household, too, since she was no longer with us to explain.

"You were both so young," I said. "Eighteen and nineteen. Mom used to say that you had to have Grandmother co-sign the marriage license—that she was really married to her, too."

"Her house was a hell," he told me. "And so was mine. We shared that. When I was growing up, my mother beat me, called me by my father's name. The last time she tried, I caught her hands. I wouldn't hit back, but I wanted her to know my strength. I was fifteen years old, and I had trained as a boxer. My hands were strong. I had to show her how strong I was. She told me to get out. She kicked me out. And your mother, your mother didn't feel safe at home."

I flashed on my own feelings at my grandparents' house. The love there, but also that feeling that anything could happen.

"Your mother loved our family. She loved building a home together, making decisions about your schooling and your hair and what we should eat. We'd never argue about that—it was like we were of the same mind. Even after the divorce. She loved our family. I just don't know if she loved me." When he said those last five words, he was laughing, rocking his legs open and closed. But his eyes were wet.

I thought about the love letters that my mother showed me from my father when they were courting. They'd all start out, "My Cherie Amour." She'd giggle as she showed them to me, shaking her head at my father's foolishness, his willingness to wear his heart so openly on his sleeve. But she still kept the letters.

There's a photograph of my parents' wedding that I've kept. The wedding was held in my great-grandmother Cillie's powder-blue living room, in her house on 3210 South Indiana Avenue, the family hub. It was 1962, before I was born, and my sister was just a small sea creature living inside the bride's belly. The photo is a little off-center, as if it were taken slightly from above. My mother and father are standing close and leaning forward, laughing, looking as if they are about to blow out candles on a cake. They look flirtatious, as if they've just jostled each other, as if someone might have pinched someone else under the table, as if they just found themselves at this wedding and, somehow, one of them is wearing a suit, the other, a veil. They look like they are used to doing things together, facing the goodwill and hope and high expectation of all of the relatives assembled in their best in the dining room. They look like they like each other very much. My father is wearing a white tuxedo with black trim, his hair cut very close to his scalp with a part shaved into the side. His cheeks and forehead look very smooth. My mother's cat-eye glasses are a little askew, and she is smiling widely, showing even her top set of teeth, which she never did because she thought they were too small for her mouth. Her hair is pressed into a flip, a style she abandoned for her own natural kinks just a few years later. I don't know who took this photograph—maybe another relative, maybe Cillie herself, but because of the poor exposure, everyone else and everything else is blocked out. So it's just them, suspended in time, laughing.

Studying that photo, I envied my parents their innocence as well as their affection for each other, even knowing that they would eventually lose both. For so long, I had assumed that the loss of that innocence outweighed everything else. But what that photograph told me is that maybe the risk is worth it.

AFTER A WHOLE WEEK OF reflection, I told Annie what I wanted. Annie was in her living room, sitting on the red couch that would eventually become our red couch, and which lived in her apartment and was sometimes mine. I went down on my knees. I lay my head in her lap, afraid to look at her, as I told her exactly what I wanted:

"I know it's boring, but I want a baby. I want a house. I want you and me together, figuring it out. I want a little garden where we'll picnic and blow bubbles."

I looked into Annie's face, as vulnerable as my own.

"Yes, I want that, too. But I'm scared. "

We decided then that we were both willing to try.

5

THE LITTLE HOUSE
Making Home with Queer Joy

OVER THE YEARS, AS WE traveled to the airport from our apartments, heading west and away from the lake, crossing from city into suburbs, there was a house that Annie and I would always pass. It was a cozy little blond-bricked bungalow, a bit down and out, with paint peeling around the edges. It looked almost exactly like the others on that block, set apart only by some plaster swan planters out front. For some reason, we found the house comical. It looked so ordinary! Annie and I embraced it, and every time we'd drive by, we'd honk at the little house and laugh. "There's our house," we'd giggle to any passing cars. We made this joke every time we were about to leave town, this not-so-handsome house that we couldn't imagine ourselves living in. We never saw anyone coming in or out of the screen door. The house was so Chicago, down to the slightly scorched lawn it sported in August and the attic add-on made with white linoleum siding. And I loved Chicago, despite my complaints. Just beyond the crush of other almost identical houses that continued down the block, you'd see a Walgreens, a Dunkin' Donuts, and a Chicago-style hotdog stand with two hotdog cave people flexing their muscles on the roof. It felt like it could be anywhere, but at the same time it also felt like a very particular somewhere. And just maybe as we passed by and honked at the house on our way to the airport and somewhere else, it reminded us of the possibility of being anchored.

Once Annie and I decided that we wanted to build a family, we thought that the first step should be to buy a house together. This forging of a space together came to our minds first, even before the idea of marriage, probably the reverse of the way our parents would have thought of it. We would give up our Frida-and-Diego lifestyle of separate-but-joined condominiums in the same building and meld our lives physically and financially. We'd look for a house with a yard, rooms for our studies, and a bedroom for a little person, the one we referred to in those in-between days as "the munchkin." Neither of us had great family riches to draw from. Both of us were guilty of giving our extra money away to the organizations that we cared about instead of squirreling it away. I was used to buying myself treats with anything left over, mostly books and CDs, and Annie frequently loaned money to her friends and family. But we decided that we could live with each other's financial habits and weaknesses if we set aside an account for the things that we were committed to together. Setting up a house fund gave clarity and commitment to our new decision. Saving up for our dream made it real in a material way, shaped by space and time and geography.

When we began looking for a house together, we were told by our realtor that there was no way that we'd find what we wanted at a price that we could afford: a single-family house with yard not far from Lake Michigan and with a train line close by to take us to school every day. We didn't want to live in the suburbs, and we wanted to be near cafés and communities of color.

We found what would become our house by accident, on our way to visit a friend who lived in the neighborhood: a small, brick-and-stucco bungalow shaped like a little triangle. The stucco was painted that 1950s salmon pink that hipster diners sometimes use, but this house looked like it wasn't trying to be hip. It looked like a house that a little kid would draw, with two eyes for windows, a door for a mouth, and a beard made of homely boxwood hedges—something like the house in the 1940s children's book *The Little House* by Virginia Lee Burton, the one about the house that stood steadfast while the world changed around it. When we walked through our house for the first time, we felt immediately at home—even in the basement. The house wore the evidence of the lives that had lived there before: floors that had seen many feet, someone's initials carved into a wooden panel in one of the bedroom closets, the backdoor screen scratched by someone's dog who clearly wanted back in. The last owner had hooked up his or her own internet and phone system, creating a squirrels' nest of wires that peeked out from the corners of the ceiling. The smaller bedroom in the remade attic was a Barbie fantasia, complete with pink-and-blue Barbie wallpaper and powder blue carpet. Down in the basement, you could see the base layer of solid red brick beneath the stucco, almost one hundred years old. The house had been built in 1917, together with others on the block, to house workers from a nearby electric company, and each house was a variation on the same plan. (A random fun fact: Edgar Bergen, Swedish American ventriloquist, vaudevillian, and father of Murphy Brown, lived here during his tween years, when the neighborhood was populated mostly by Swedish, German, and Jewish immigrants.) We could live here, too, we thought. We could join our dirt with their dirt. We could make ourselves at home. Fingers crossed, we put our bid in immediately.

We bought the house and moved in, and a few months later, feeling properly settled, we decided to take a trip together, a trip to New York City. And it was then, driving to the airport, that we realized that we had bought our own Little House, or at least its twin in terms of its layout, just like the one that we always passed and honked at in kindly mockery. When did our sarcasm for the little house turn to affection? And when did our view of this very common, very American way of declaring commitment change with it? Maybe deep down, we had always loved the house and yearned for its cozy everydayness. But how strange it felt to now see ourselves in this cozy domestic picture, two stick figures holding hands and traveling up the walk.

IN HER 1993 PHOTOGRAPH "SELF-PORTRAIT/CUTTING," queer artist Catherine Opie presents her own broad, bare back, which has been decorated with a passionate vision of domesticity. Carved into her flesh, still dripping blood, is the image of two stick figures: two girls standing hand in hand in front of a house with a cloud floating above them, a child's vision of coupledom. In this and other Opie photographs from the 1990s, her own journey as a queer artist negotiating domestic life is captured in her self-portraits of her own exposed body. Her stories of trauma, risk, and transformation are recorded in the flesh work of tattoos and scars. In a later work, "Self-Portrait/Nursing," Opie portrays herself breastfeeding her baby, the keloid scars from an earlier cutting shaped in the word "pervert" still visible on her chest. Her face is serene, a Madonna and child made more, not less, complete with the scars, tattoos, and other evidence of queer life and well-lived desires on her body. In both photos, Opie dramatizes the process of being changed by the intimacies of making home and family. These works are evidence of collaboration and queer family, in the same way that the baby who is suckled by her changes her relationship to her bare body, making it possible, perhaps, to bare it to us. Just as she has been changed by the person who carved the domestic scene on her back, a carving that necessarily had to involve another hand. And yet these photos also insist that Opie is intent on doing things her own way, queerly. She is still the author of herself, challenging us to fit her neatly into any ready-made narratives of normal.

For Maggie Nelson, Opie's 1993 self-portrait is puzzling, a narrow imagining of family or perhaps a sign of the unavoidable lure of heteronormative acceptance. Nelson sees in its portrait of family and home an eerie echo of California's Proposition 8 posters, which set about to ban same-sex marriage in California. Although approved in the 2008 election, it was later overturned by federal courts. In her memoir, *The Argonauts*, Nelson describes passing the signs supporting the proposition that same autumn that she was building her own queer household, with her transgender partner, Harry, his son, and eventually, with a child she would give birth to:

> Throughout that fall, yellow YES ON PROP 8 signs were sprouting up everywhere, most notably jabbed into an otherwise bald and beautiful mountain I passed every day on my way to work. The sign depicted four stick figures raising their hands to the sky, in a paroxysm of joy—the joy, I suppose, of heteronormativity, here indicated by the fact that one of the stick figures sported a triangle skirt. (*What is that triangle, anyway? My twat?*) PROTECT CALIFORNIA CHILDREN! The stick figures cheered.
>
> Each time I passed the sign stuck into the blameless mountain, I thought about Catherine Opie's *Self-Portrait/Cutting* from 1993, in which Opie photographed her back with a drawing of a house and two stick-figure women holding hands (two triangle skirts!) carved into it, along with a sun, a cloud, and two birds. She took the photo while the drawing was still dripping with blood. "Opie, who had recently broken up with her partner, was longing at the time

to start a family, and the image radiates all the painful contradictions inherent in that wish," *Art in America* explains.

I don't get it, I said to Harry. Who wants a version of the
Prop 8 poster, but with two triangle skirts?

Maybe Cathy does, Harry shrugged.

I hear in Nelson's snarky response to Opie's photograph my
own fears around having a child, partner, and home—the fear of
being boring and unhip; perhaps the fear of cooptation by politi-
cians who want to squelch difference, protest, and resistance into
some nostalgic, white supremacist vision of cultural order—"the
way we *never* were," as scholar Stephanie Coontz puts it. I agree
with Nelson that Opie's photos speak to the gravitational pull of
normality that queer families face. Yet there's something in the
passion of Opie's representation of her yearning for queer family
that also challenges heteronormativity—a passion I also find in
Nelson's own ecstatic descriptions of breastfeeding in *The Argonauts*. It captured a desire that we were building for ourselves that
year. To me, Opie's self-portrait and its public display of queer joy
challenges heteronormativity. Indeed, I'd argue that fighting for
and claiming queer joy is even more pressing when the bodies on
display are not white, and when those bodies have been born from
histories of violence and trauma. And if those joys come in the
everyday shapes of a home, a partner, and a child, we should grab
it. I echo Black queer scholar and activist La Marr Jurelle Bruce,
who writes:

> For far, far too long, I regarded joy and peace of mind as
> glinting treasures propped on some distant and potentially
> ever-receding horizon toward which I'd dutifully march or
> trudge with no assurance of arrival.

Now, rather than prop joy on some remote mountain cliff, I find and snatch it here where I tread. I cram it into my pockets, fill my mouth with it, cradle it in my arms, wrap it around my shoulders, secrete it in my sweat, carry it with me. It's surprisingly light stuff.

There is risk for us as queer women in an interracial household: the risk of losing your earlier, edgier, critical self; the risk of isolation, caught between worlds; the physical vulnerability of homophobic and/or racist violence against us in being public in our private joy; and the risks of the internalization of homophobia and racism. But there might also be joy to make our own.

As Annie and I moved toward creating our home and future life together, we brought to it hope and excitement in the face of these risks, for the promise of togetherness, of comfort and serenity and support; the opportunity to nurture a little one into a terrific new adult; the commitment to letting ourselves be changed, knowing the risks before us. And possibly, too, of changing the minds and views of the people who see us. Like Opie, for Annie and me to take on this vision of domesticity has meant altering our lives in ways as passionately felt and sometimes as painful as if we were carving it in blood. But there is also something in the ways that we were altering the ideal of family that still felt queer, at night as we readied ourselves for bed, bearing our flesh and our worries to each other, examining our scars, and nurturing our hopes for the future.

6

ADOPTION

And the Arithmetic of
Loss and Gain

ONCE ANNIE AND I COMMITTED to having a child, the decision to adopt rather than for one of us to give birth came easily and was in keeping with our own sense of queer community. Queer people, especially queers of color, often have to step in to care for one another when our blood family disowns us, neglects us, or fails to see us. This family relationship might look like older generations of lesbians looking out for baby dykes in lesbian culture, like Audre Lorde describes in her biomythography, *Zami: A New Spelling of My Name*. For young Audre, it's the friendship of older Black dyke sisters Vida and Pet that help her weather the challenges of being Black and poor in 1950s Greenwich Village dyke culture. In one memorable scene, Audre and her girlfriend Muriel are about to steal some fruit from a corner store for their dinner, until their older friend Vida drives up and catches them in the act: "'Scared you good, didn't I?' her voice changed, earnestly. 'Well, I'm glad. You all better stop this jiveass shit before next time it isn't me. Come on, Pet's in the car, let's go for a ride.'" Or, queer parenting might look like the platonic family in Black and Brown House culture that Marlon Bailey documents in his amazing book,

Butch Queens Up in Pumps, or dramatized on the wildly successful FX series, *Pose.* These relationships of care, Bailey explains,
sometimes overlap among parent, child, sibling, and lover. Bailey
quotes Tim'm West, a poet, activist, teacher, and former member
of the house of Ninja in New York City, who testifies that "for the
majority of people who entered the house scene when I did in
the late eighties—and of course houses precede me—it is kind of
an alternative social network for those who have been ostracized
from their family or didn't have people in their communities who
could understand their sexual identity."

And, as African American fiction writers like Toni Morrison,
Gloria Naylor, Colson Whitehead, Yaa Gyasi, and others have
documented, informal adoption, absorbing family, and extending
family beyond bloodlines has been part of African American world
making and survival since the days of slavery, an antidote to the
voluntary and involuntary family separations that have haunted
us: grandmothers mothering their grandchildren; uncles and aunties who step up to care for their nieces and nephews; neighbors
and teachers and ministers stepping in, sometimes with or without
the sanction of law to parent, sometimes under strain, but parenting the best they can. I see this logic of care in the queer family that
Morrison describes in her 1973 novel, *Sula,* a portrait of the Black
community of Medallion, Ohio, in the first half of the twentieth
century. Eva, matriarch and owner of a rooming house something
like my great-grandmother Cillie, takes in and ensures the care for
three unrelated boys, all of whom she names Dewey:

> Among the tenants in that big old house were the children
> Eva took in. Operating on a private scheme of preference
> and prejudice, she sent off for children she had seen from
> the balcony of her bedroom or whose circumstances she
> had heard about from the gossipy old men who came to play

checkers or read the *Courier*, or write her number. In 1921, when her granddaughter Sula was eleven, Eva had three such children. They came with woolen caps and names given to them by their mothers or grandmothers, or somebody's best friend. Eva snatched the caps off their heads and ignored their names. She looked at the first child closely, his wrists, the shape of his head and the temperament that showed in his eyes and said, "Well. Look at Dewey. My my mymymy." When later that same year she sent for a child who kept falling down off the porch across the street, she said the same thing. Somebody said, "But Miss Eva, you calls the other one Dewey."

"So? This here's another one."

Morrison's narration reveals the ways that Eva's adoptions of these boys, even in her eccentricity, are recognized as acts of care and responsibility by the rest of the community. Eva's act of taking in children is part of the fabric of support in this community, a safety net that the outside world fails to provide. Morrison's novel speaks to the ways that chosen family has always been a tactic of survival for groups of oppressed people.

In addition to the cultures that we came from, Annie and I found that our bodies confirmed our decision to adopt rather than to give birth. Annie had already completed menopause, and while my diabetes has always felt under control, I feared it would present a significant risk factor for a birth, especially when combined with being over forty. At forty-one and fifty-one, we felt clear that our bodies might not be up to the task of pregnancy, even assisted by technology—though we certainly knew mothers in our age range who had given birth successfully. Besides these physical realities, though, we both agreed that there were already plenty of children on this earth to mother. We were both more interested in gathering kin than making a baby.

Strange, but even as a child I played house with a circle of adopted dollies. While my friends were busy shoving doll bodies underneath their T-shirts to simulate pregnancy (as well as socks in the bras that they stole from their mothers' dresser drawers), in my imaginative play I would skip the birth part to get to the mothering part. I loved the story of adoption, even as a young person. It made sense to me. Maybe this was because my mother bought me an assortment of multiracial dolls. Adoption became a part of my play, an explanation for the role in my life of these babies who didn't look like me. I admired the idea of adoption even when I was young, and I thought that there was something powerful and even heroic about caring for a child who needed to be cared for, whatever the circumstance. I would act out dramas with my doll where I was a paramedic, rescuing my Tamu doll from a burning car and then raising her as my own, a plot possibly stolen from the TV show *Emergency!* with Randolph Mantooth and Kevin Tighe. Or I would find my blonde Littlest Angel doll abandoned in the woods and would take her in and raise her as my own, my little Mowgli.

The desire to carry a child in my belly was never one that grew beyond the level of mild curiosity, though I loved playing with dolls and babying my stuffed animals and caring for my cousins and younger friends in the neighborhood. By the time I was seventeen, I had decided that I would never marry, interrupting the conventional narrative of adulthood of career, marriage, and then children. Even though there were boys—and girls—whom I loved, I didn't recognize myself in the images of married people around me. I found the happy nuclear family on *The Cosby Show*—the stable Black family of the moment—unconvincing. Maybe I was more like Laverne and Shirley, or Mary Richards's best friend, Rhoda, my lovers the satellites to my adventures with my women friends. This seemed to be reflected in my own family, too. My mother seemed so much happier and fulfilled not married, and after their divorce, my father took several years to find his soul mate. I also knew early that I wanted a professional life, to be a psychiatrist or a writer or a teacher, and I worried that early parenting could make that life more difficult, though many have done it.

But I think that my lack of interest in becoming pregnant also reflected something deeper about the way I felt in my body, as well as the way I saw it in response to dominant standards of femininity. When I was in graduate school, I once dreamed that I gave birth to a bucket of Kentucky Fried Chicken. In the dream, I remember feeling shocked, amused, and a little proud of what I had produced. Afterward, I took my bucket to a family picnic, and I was disappointed as I watched my family members picking through the chicken pieces, looking skeptically for a part that they recognized and wanted to eat. This surreal dream of motherhood (and cannibalism?), creepy in the ways that dreams can be, may well have been a fever dream induced by eating too close to bedtime, but it also spoke to me of the ways that I often experienced my body and desires as different, strange, and sometimes misunderstood by others, including my family.

We get our family by volition, by happenstance, and sometimes by force. As Annie and I talked through different kinds of adoption, we considered our own place in history, as queer women, as professional and middle-class women who had already accomplished many of our career goals, and as a multiracial couple, African American and white. The ability to choose to mother—as Annie and I were setting out to do—and the luxury to do it with intentionality, following our own sense of timing and with the economic and psychic resources that we needed, is something that is comparatively rare. I thought about my younger self, worriedly checking the calendar in fear that I was pregnant after a spontaneous tryst, or borrowing from my jar of pennies so my checking account wouldn't be in the red. I thought about weekend getaways that I was able to take without stress, only pausing to make sure that my cats had an extra bowl of food, or some of my more self-indulgent purchases that only meant I'd have to eat lower on the food chain until payday.

These choices were marked by my privileges as a middle-class professional, with only my own mouth to feed and a safety net of parents who could and would help me out if I ever were in crisis. On the other hand, that privilege, as an African American woman, has always felt precarious. I think about the struggles of the enslaved mothers who were my ancestors, attempting, often to no avail, to hold on to their children and to keep them safe from sale or being worked to death. I think about my grandparents, making choices and sacrifices to keep food in everyone's bellies and a roof over their heads, sometimes choosing to take in and raise family members rather than rely on the state's foster programs. I think about the mothers, too, all over the world, in any place that has faced war or famine or genocide. My ability to choose to mother is not disconnected from a history of mothers all over the world who face a narrowing of options as a result of systemic racism. As the reproductive justice organization SisterSong has argued, "the right *not to have* children, the right *to have* children under the conditions parents choose, and the right to parent the children one has in a safe and healthy environment, are human rights threatened by ongoing systems of inequality." For those reasons, Annie and I were reflective about the path we chose to adopt.

There were several ways that we could adopt and a few paths that were closed to us. We could foster to adopt locally through the Department of Children and Family Services. We could explore international adoption, though most countries were closed to same-sex couples and couples of different races. We could adopt through a private agency. We considered all three at some point. The fostering process was the most familiar to me. I had images of the benefits and challenges from my own study, reading works by scholars like Dorothy E. Roberts and Patricia J. Williams, both Black women who have studied the structures of racism that shape adoption and who have also chosen to adopt at a later age. The benefit of fostering to adopt is that it would be the most politically direct—helping a child who has been left to "the system." I had read that many children, especially children of color, reach an age when they're considered "unadoptable." I wanted to make a difference in this injustice, but I also wanted a baby. I wanted to be at the very beginnings of a little life, to shape it, nurture it. Annie had her hesitations about fostering, too. Annie felt that fostering was a way of participating in a system that unfairly punished women by taking away their children and that spread mass incarceration through this country, devastating families and communities. Could we become mothers in ways that didn't make the lives of other women worse?

We both agreed that we would adopt an African American child, though our reasons may have been understandably different. Both Annie and I were aware of the ways that Black children have been left behind in this country, in adoption and beyond. We felt like we had a lot to offer. And for me, I felt a pull in terms of a feeling of community commitment and restoration. I didn't feel like I had to adopt someone directly from my "bloodline," produced out of my own body or blood family. But I loved the idea of continuing the good work of raising the African American community, restoring the loss that I felt is part of the continuing effects of the slave trade. After struggling as a Black girl in a white supremacist world, I wanted to love and nurture a little Black girl, to see her, to make her feel visible, to help her shine in a world that was still not quite worthy of the task. This history of loss is part of my own fierceness around mothering. I imagined a girl child, browned and beautiful, basking in the love we could give her. I imagined her confidence growing like a dandelion in the concrete against the negative pressures of this still racist, still sexist world. Maybe she would see us as a new way to be a woman. Maybe our quirkiness might attune us to her own, to help us raise up her own individual spirit, rather than squelching it. I imagined the joy that we could give her, as parents who had lived full lives already and who had already made some mistakes, lost and gained love. Maybe our lessons of everyday joy and spirit that we learned later in life could be hers now—her legacy.

I was compelled by the possibility of international adoption, particularly from Africa. Cheryl, Annie's friend from graduate school, had adopted two beautiful girls, one after the other, as a single mother. She did so after years of being a social worker. She spoke frankly to us about the challenges and gifts of adopting and would continue to be a resource, a spiritual fairy godmother, again and again in this process. During one of our visits to her beautiful Seattle apartment, in the midst of a rich, wide-ranging conversation that traveled everywhere from writing and collecting art to the politics of identity and the examples of injustice that keep repeating all over the world, Cheryl pulled me aside and said in a whisper, "I think about all of those children who have been orphaned by AIDS. I wonder, what's going to happen to them. You and Ann would be great mothers. What do you think? You have so much to offer a child. Do you have room in your heart?"

Cheryl's question haunted me. Could we make a difference in something that feels so vast? I knew that we could bring so much to any child's life, particularly our love, bolstered by our education and economic stability. But would this be enough in some eyes? My hesitancy around international adoption was informed by pragmatism. South Africa is currently the only African country to allow LGBTQ couples to adopt, and this is barred from foreigners, according to scholar Samantha Moore. And, according to the organization Considering Adoption, as of this writing, the only nations that allow LGBTQ foreigners to adopt are Brazil, Chile, and the Philippines. If we were to attempt such an adoption in South Africa, we'd have to hide who we were to accomplish it.

Besides, I yearned to make a difference in my own backyard. Here in Chicago, I knew many Black children faced violence, hunger, and lack of access to education and health care. I have watched and grown up with children who had been lost between the cracks right here in my own city. Kids with wonderful imaginations, with talents. I've watched some of my friends who have survived neglect in their families, watched them fight and sometimes win to keep their own spark. But often that meant finding a surrogate family, or even one person who can step in to make the difference. All children deserve love and someone to see and nurture the spark in them. I knew from my own friends, my own family, that Black children get left behind more often in this country. That knowledge is, in the end, what drew me to the children who I knew most, the children who are right here.

ONE SUNDAY DINNER IN 2010, we sat down with my dad and Phyliss and my stepsister Tara to talk about our plans to adopt, exploring the different options together and asking for their support. They were supportive and encouraging, telling us that they thought that we would make excellent parents, that we are loving and have a good way with children, reflected by our relationships with our nieces and nephews. We left the house, heading back to Chicago, feeling buoyed and restored. But the next day, Tara called to talk about her doubts about the foster system. She is a committed social worker focusing on children. By that time, she had spent fifteen years as a case worker in the trenches of Catholic Charities and the Department of Children and Family Services. On the phone, I could picture her with hands on hips. Her tone was knowing, a little weary, but also passionate.

"What you need to understand about the foster care system is that you're taking a child away from their family, and most of the time they really don't want to go," she said. "Even if they've been abused or neglected. Even if their family has fallen apart, they're holding on to something in their minds, that first family that they've lost."

But I had known people who had worked through that loss, hadn't I? I had friends who had themselves been fostered and who thrived in their new families. I also knew friends and members of my family who had lost or were threatened with the loss of their children. I had witnessed the effects of the upheaval, knew the loyalty of children to their parents, sensed the weight when they felt like they had betrayed them. And then, the joy for all of us when things worked out, habits kicked, lives rebooted. The chance to start again.

Tara was right—fostering would be hard. It could still be our journey, but there were challenges that I hadn't considered. I yearned for clarity—that *we* would be the mothers. If, after living with us for months or even years, a child that we adopted went back to another home, I would be devastated. I could survive it, but would that fear of loss keep me from being as open and loving as I would need to be to mother?

As Annie and I started talking to friends and acquaintances who had adopted in the area from private agencies, the Cradle kept coming up. The Cradle has been a part of Chicago's adoption history for a long time. It was founded in 1923 by Florence Dahl Walrath, a white Evanston woman who originally got involved with adoption by helping her sister who had lost a child at birth connect with a family ready for adoption. In its early days, some of the Cradle's most famous adoptive parents confirm a culture of whiteness, with a flavor of aspirational class consciousness and celebrity, including Bob Hope, George Burns and Gracie Allen, Al Jolson, and Donna Reed. But in the 1970s, that shifted. African American football player and adoptive parent Gale Sayers, together with his wife Ardythe Bullard, founded the Gale Sayers Center, which is dedicated to meeting the adoption needs of the African American community, including seeking out Black adoptive parents. This aspect caught our attention the most.

We were also interested in the fact that the Cradle approaches adoption through a lens of openness that runs deep. The birth mother, or in a few cases, birth father, or both, choose the adoptive parents through a series of introductions: an online webpage, a book, and a one-page stat sheet. Depending on what the birth mother (or family) wants and needs, prospective parents might meet with the birth parents. Or, they may never be in direct contact. The program offers medical, social, and psychological support for the birth mothers through the time that they gave birth, with some structures of support that would remain afterward. Mothers could be young, or older, we were told. They might be married or not. They may have become pregnant by choice or not. With the help of a birth counselor, social worker, and lawyer as intermediaries, birth parents negotiate what kind of contact and connection they'd like to establish for the child after adoption. Adoptive families might receive cards and letters from a birth family. There might be occasional visits, or there might be just an initial exchange of a photograph and story. In the trainings, adoptive parents are encouraged to make the reality of adoption a part of everyday life for their children as early as possible, including sharing information about their birth parents' medical and family histories and likes and dislikes, if known, and creating a story of their child's adoption, allowing for more complexity as children age.

While this idea of openness was exciting to me and seemed the most politically palatable, it also scared the hell out of me. I worried about confusion about who would be the mother, or a mother or family stalking our child, trying to get her back. My fears were shaped by films like the 1995 *Losing Isaiah*, which portrays a Black mother, Khaila, played by Halle Berry, who, while struggling with an addiction to crack, loses custody of her child to a good-hearted white social worker, Margaret, played Jessica Lange. In recovery, Khaila struggles to get him back. Watching the film again, I teared up as I heard Khaila testify in court that it was her love of her son that helped her kick her addiction. And at that moment it seemed right to me, given the unequal history of things, that Khaila should get Isaiah back. But then who wouldn't be moved when the social worker rips Isaiah from Margaret's arms when it's time for him to be returned to his birth mother? Over Isaiah's screams of "Mama! Mama!" Margaret tells the social worker, "He needs the light on to sleep!" The mothers end up with an ambiguous plan of cooperation, charted outside of the system. But where was I in this story? If nothing else, adoption meant facing head-on the pain of loss from all sides, but particularly a child's loss of his or her birth mother and family. I had to reckon with the arithmetic of those losses, as well as what we would gain as a new family.

At our first adoption workshop at the Cradle a few months later, after coffee and cookies and introductions led by two social workers, we were startled when told to remove our wedding rings, or whatever we considered a valuable possession we had with us. One half of the room is asked to walk their possessions over to the other side, giving them to the strangers sitting there. We are asked to then go back to our seat. Those of us who have been given the rings and other possessions are asked to hold them in our hands, taking in their beauty. We are asked to think about why they are valued by the people who gave them to us. Are we're asked to sit with the fact that the people who gave them to us feel their loss. The other half of the room, those of us who have given our valuables away, are asked to sit with that feeling of loss of control and to imagine the grief we might feel if we never got our things back. There were all kinds of couples in that room, mostly heterosexual couples, but a few lesbian and gay couples; a sprinkling of people of color among white people. But all of us were rocked by this exercise. We all shared the same nervous laughter as we gave our valuables away to a stranger. This exercise, though imperfect, gave us the chance to think about adoption from the perspective of openness. One of the hallmarks of this approach to adoption is that it is meant to identify the grief and loss of adoption, as well as the gift of it.

We knew that we had months of work ahead of us to get certified to be foster parents, which was the next step while we waited to be chosen. We had to get the house ready, inspect for places where a little person could hurt themselves, fix those weird banisters on the back porch where a child-sized head could accidently get stuck. We had to get a lawyer! We'd have to work out our mutual parenting style. Work through a few demons. Both of us planned to go back to counseling that year. We'd have to spend a lot of alone time with each other, soak up this time together. We planned a trip to San Francisco for later that year, a getaway alone that might be our last for a while.

Annie and I had to face the experience of the unknown, of being chosen at a time that had little to do with our own preferences and of having our lives turned upside down. Or else not being chosen at all. From conversations with other queer friends who had survived this process, we knew that this could be a bumpy road, with hidden rejections and tensions, bringing up issues of sexuality, class, and respectability. The myth of Black queer people as being out of but not necessarily a part of the Black community still had some people under its sway. We'd have to face the fact that for some Black birth parents, our motives, our knowledge about Blackness, and our stability would be questioned just because we were queer.

FOR A WHOLE NINE MONTHS, from February through November of 2011—the length of time that it would take for a child to be born from conception—Annie and I completed workshops and trainings offered by the Cradle: Adoption 101, Preparing for Openness, Conspicuous Families, workshops on the nuts and bolts of paying for adoption, including tax write-offs, workshops on bonding with the child that we weren't sure we'd ever face. We had couples counseling sessions, where we discussed our parenting styles, our fears and expectations. We visited some of our most difficult experiences as children in our families, including divorce and conflict, thinking out loud with a stranger how we might approach them differently. We attended meet and greets on weekdays and evenings with past Cradle families, never quite knowing how long our wait to be parents would be.

Becoming an adoptive parent at the Cradle required an amazing amount of preparation. In the CPR training, I remember pumping the chests of eerie toddler-sized manikins, putting my mouth to their strange, stiff mouths. I had to face the question: what would I do in a life-or-death situation? Could I handle having this young life in my hands? Could I act quickly and remember what to do? I learned at least two crucial lessons about myself from those sessions: first, that I had inherited a set of lessons about being the "baby" of my family, not quite in the driver's seat, and to be a parent, I had to get comfortable being a decision maker in a new way. But I also had to learn how to share this responsibility. I would not be parenting alone. I had to learn how to act on a dime while also working with Annie and acting as a team. I would have to trust Annie—and myself—in an entirely new way.

As we planned and waited and trained and hoped, some of my straight friends and family commented on how different our process was from theirs. "Too bad all parents don't get to go through a training to become parents," my college friend Paige commented. She herself was without children, living out a deliberate choice to be an active auntie to her three siblings' children while also dedicating herself to her work defending clients facing the death penalty. She was also learning the piano, running and biking competitively, teaching herself how to bake bread and make flipbooks, and spending quality time with her boyfriend in their cute Arts and Crafts bungalow in Lawrence, Kansas. Friends who had their children biologically admitted sheepishly how easy it was for them to get pregnant, some when they wanted to, some not. "It's the raising of the kids that's the hard part," my friend Michele said wistfully as I reported our progress at the department coffeemaker.

I found myself thinking about my parents, their own circumstances of becoming parents. My parents married young, not quite a shotgun wedding since the pressure to marry came from themselves and not from their parents, my sister born a mere five months later. For the first years of their marriage and parenthood, they drew a lot from my grandparents for childcare, parenting advice, and emotional sustenance. Did they feel prepared? They were so young, still shaping their life's goals. In those first years of parenthood, my father drove a city bus by day and studied and went to school at night, eventually the first person in his family to go to college and earn a PhD. My mother dropped out of college to care for us and to support their homelife and returned to night school to finish her education when Becky and I were teenagers.

But even though they didn't have the compressed process of training to become parents that Annie and I sought, overseen by a staff of social workers, certified eventually by the state, I am convinced that they wanted to be parents. They saw in my sister and me the chance to build the homelife that each of them wanted, and there was passion in the ways that they chose books and toys and activities and clothes, the themed birthday parties with the magician lady, and, despite our pretty meager means, a few years in a private school. Even more, I knew that they wanted to be our parents, that they loved us as people, not just as responsibilities. I knew this by the way both of my parents spoke to us. Not quite the lefty sixties parents of some of my friends (we did get grounded, and a few times, a spanking; we were not allowed to call them by their first names or drink wine at dinner), they nonetheless treated us like we were intelligent and loved. They asked our opinions about things. They let us choose our own clothes, and after the age of five, do our own hair. They encouraged us to do the things we loved, however goofy (for me, to make our old shoes into planters, listen to Prince or AC/DC; for my sister, to read romance novels taken out from the library or thrift stores daily), and to think about our life's work that way. These things I would bring with confidence to my own parenting. Whatever mistakes they made—and in my child's eyes, they did make mistakes, including divorcing, being interested in their own dating lives, treating themselves to new clothes or record players without asking us (imagine!), occasionally drinking and smoking pot, choosing odd friends, spending too much time at board meetings instead of hanging out with us, not always buying the right style of penny loafers or real Izod shirts (the ones with the real alligator, not the fake fox shirts like JCPenney's)—they were willing to talk about them with us. Sometimes the mistakes were bigger: moving so that we had to change schools, choosing girlfriends or boyfriends who were unkind to them or occasionally unkind to us, sometimes being preoccupied when we wanted to talk, or else peppering us with questions when we wanted to be left alone. Even during those difficult years of fighting before the divorce, or that lonely, financially rough period afterward, I knew that my sister and I were their ultimate priority, helping them to make the changes that were harder to make on their own behalf. We were their checkpoint, the measure of whether or not they were being true to themselves.

My mother's and father's mistakes—and their willingness to talk about them—have helped make me who I am, in terms of both my fears and my strengths. My fear of conflict has shaped my diplomatic skills, and my experience of losing a home in ways that felt sudden has made me also deeply invested in building home, coziness, safety. But also my friendship with my mother, both of my parents' transparency, and their willingness to admit their times of struggle have given me the energy to keep moving too, to make decisions knowing that I can and will make some missteps. Their mistakes together with the good lives that they built with us, their children, have given me a kind of optimism that has never left me, even as I face my own struggles to become a parent.

7

THE BACKYARD
Our Last Summer Before, 2011

DEEP SLEEP. RAIN-SOAKED AIR. COTTON *sheets and the weight of blankets on your legs. The first weekend of summer and time is elastic. Maybe this will be your last summer free to sleep in like this, time only your own to fill. Hope for that. The Japanese maple after a night of rain sparkles, reminding you of all the life happening while you've been sleeping. Clean off your desk. Make a pile of library books to return, crack open a new journal. Write by hand until words turn to sentences. Then type the words to make them solid, marveling at the movement of your fingers. Later, walk the eight blocks to the lake that edges your city, side by side with your girl, arms swinging, hands sometimes touching. Imagine as you walk the blue of underwater, and a flash of sun as you turn your head to breathe. Your muscles will burn today from this movement, reminding you that you are alive.*

Make arugula salad with fennel, lemon, garlic. Make curry with plantains. Your mouth will burn with cumin and paprika and turmeric and chili and garlic. You will cool it with the easy laughter between friends. You will cool it with the mint that Jen and Choua have brought from their garden, which you will drink iced and with lime. Grateful for Annie's smile and this easy company.

Another day this summer, Laila stretches out on the blue church pew in our backyard. The pew is big enough for a medium-sized family to sit together, but Laila, lying down, reaches almost to the end. She smokes Spirit cigarettes and waves the smoke away with faint coughs and apologies. It is her incense, along with her rose-water soap and lemons and the garlic from the meal we've made together. She sips and talks and laughs, telling story after story.

As the afternoon ages, your next-door neighbors Susan and Jack, middle-aged sister and brother, poke the green egg-shaped cast-iron smoker on their deck, the kind that your grandmother made wonderful barbecue with. You sniff the smoky air, your eyes tear up with nostalgia, and you wish that your grandmother was still here to be a part of this new shape of your life. Their deck, a half story higher than your fence, gives a full view of your backyard, and so they give a little wave and linger a little to chat, even though we're having a party. As they tend the tomato vines roping from old industrial-sized tin cans, they appear to be listening to your chatter. You wonder what they think of this party of women, all the colors of the rainbow, laughing loudly at our own inside jokes. Your houses are so close together that you share your lives whether you want to or not. You know when Susan's sons or Jack's daughters are in town for a visit. They all share the same sweet, melancholy smile, the same piercing blue eyes. You know what furniture they've decided to put out for the junk trucks that roam the neighborhood in search of metal: an old recliner, a hospital bed, and a large panda that no one will pick up until it becomes so soggy with rain that someone finally puts it in the trash can. And they know things about you, too: when your family is coming to visit, how often you weed your garden plot, the jumbled state of your garage, the rat traps that the pest control people periodically check. You wonder if they know when you and Annie are making love, especially if you've forgotten to close the windows, but you try not to think about that. You wonder if they know that you are both changing, expanding, making room for another to join you.

On our street, you look out for one another's place, keeping an eye and an ear on things when the other goes out of town. And when the ambulance was called for Jack, because the pain from his bone cancer became too hard to control, you and Annie rise out of sleep, called by the flashing red lights, to come stand outside with the rest of the neighbors. The night air blew your pajamas around you, and you could do nothing but watch and smell the linden trees, witnessing and remembering.

You run into Daisy on Devon Avenue. Daisy lived with you and Annie for a while earlier that spring, when life with her dad and his new wife became overwhelming. He disapproved of the candles she burned in her room. You miss having Daisy around the house, with her quiet but determined presence and the way she helped make the "too much house" feeling go away. Still, you all knew it was time for her to make her own home. And, besides, now you see her many mornings on her way to work at the daycare around the corner. Today she is wearing a yellow sweatshirt and yellow button earrings and matching yellow flats, all scored, quite possibly, from the Value Village Thrift Store down the street. Her walk is dainty and fairylike despite the rough cracks in the sidewalk. Seeing Daisy is an omen that it will be a good day. Later, you see yellow finches back at the bird feeder, and you are sure that Daisy brought them. The birds have come back after being chased away by the neighborhood cats and by the aggressive Chicago squirrels who have found a way to trick food out of the squirrel-proof feeder.

You plant carrots from seed this year. You put out trellises for green beans. You are warned that the squash will take up too much space, but you plant them anyway. You dig and dig past the grass and violets, and before you hit sand, because this land was once on the lakeshore, and before the water receded, you discover a hidden world of worms. You add new soil and drop in the seeds. You plant tomato seedlings, too, and watermelon seedlings. You plant small trees and bushes on the edges of the back and the front yards, so they can keep the hostas and the irises and the orange and yellow lilies company later this summer. Susan warns you that you've planted them all too close together. You've never grown a garden before and don't know any better, and you want to be sure that the garden is crowded with plant bodies and with color, because you and Annie love a good crowd. You are not sure yet which lives will take, which will grow, so you try for them all. As you wait for any news of the baby, you and Annie keep your eyes open for spears of green poking out of dirt, for seed husks dropped from curling seeds, and then blossoms.

8

DOING THE LIMBO
The Winter Before, 2012

WE ARE AT THE BREAKFAST table on a chilly Chicago Tuesday, when we hear our social worker Wendy's voice on our answering machine, a voice as familiar as that of a favorite aunt who knows how to get a rise out of you.

"Well, ladies, I see that you both have birthdays coming up soon. You're not getting any younger, so let's get your profile in, please!"

We groan. Yes, we are dragging our feet a little in completing our profiles, the web-and-hands-on narrative with photos that will "sell us" to a prospective birth mother. Now that the adoption training is over, the letters of recommendation from our favorite family members secured, and the home inspection completed and approved by the state, all that's left is to be matched with a birth family. You'd think that would be the easy part—we are bursting with anticipation of the baby—but this stage, putting on paper all of our strengths as well as specifying conditions we might not be able to accept, in a way that is animated and eye-catching and yet also somehow authentic, was very hard for both of us. We know that we have a lot to offer as potential parents: we're college educated, we own our house, we're tenured at our university, we are surrounded by blood and chosen family members who want to be involved in this baby's life. But we wonder whether the unique selves that we have to offer will translate to eyes outside of our own inner circle of friends and family.

During our training, we had the chance to look at other families' successful profiles, and we saw many attractive photographs of smiling, irresistibly wholesome potential parents. Some had children already. Some had pets. Almost without exception, most were white heterosexual couples. The brief biographies managed to be breezy and charming, never betraying the anxiety that we felt.

With some deep breaths and a little more coffee, we realize that Wendy is right and that perhaps her nagging is proof that she thinks we'll make good parents—even if she did seem unsure of what to do with us at times. She has admitted that she hasn't worked with many LGBTQ parents in the past. Over the course of our conversations and interviews with her, she warned us that birth mothers were searching for security for their children, with the implication that we might not be seen as such sure bets. (Even though in our families, we were the problem solvers, a source of stability and fun for our nieces and nephews.) Wendy warned us that some birth parents might be alarmed by older parents because they worry about their child's futures. Or, they might fear that being part of a multiracial family or a queer family would exacerbate the ostracization that being adopted already carries. At the heart of our procrastination is that we share some of Wendy's fears. How do we reassure someone we don't even know that we are well equipped to raise their child, even knowing the potential bumps in the road ahead? How do we connect when we may not even have a chance to meet them in person?

Truth be told, we had been working on our profile, gathering photos of ourselves, of our friends and family, of our home, of the beautiful mural that we painted together with my sister-in-law Laura and our nieces to welcome the new baby. But we are stuck. Should we sweeten the story that we're telling about ourselves—posting our most flattering, youngest-looking photos? Or do we present ourselves as we really are, loveable warts and all?

Even if adoption doesn't rely on a biological clock, there is a focus on one's physical viability that is based in realities: one's sustained energy even with very little sleep, one's ability to pick up a squirming toddler, one's ability to carry the deadweight of a sleeping child from car to bed. My airplane vision of the mother and child now feels so far away. It is beginning to feel like maybe it wasn't going to happen, that time is slipping away from us. Maybe we should set our minds on another, more attainable goal: writing a book together, maybe, or a big trip. But nothing would match the vision of the three of us that has emerged and taken hostage of our brains and hearts over the past year.

So, a few weeks before my forty-second birthday, we pull an all-nighter or, at least, a middle-aged version of an all-nighter, stretching from after dinner to one o'clock in the morning, and we get the profile done. It feels a little like writing a shared college application. We decide against slick for a homey, scrapbook style, with bits of fabric and jewels and flowers around the edges. We include photos of ourselves that may make us look a little younger, and yes, a little more active (how many times did we hike the Indiana Dunes, after all), but that still attempt to capture our true bond and our sense of connection with our families and community. We show ourselves in our motley, unprofessionally landscaped backyard that is overblown with black-eyed susans, blowing bubbles. We include photos with my nieces and Annie's nieces and nephews, with our siblings and my parents, and the multiracial youth group that drops over every now and then for brunch. We include the lyrics to "This Little Light of Mine" (Tina Turner's version is one of my favorite songs,) and, in the spirit of openness, changing the "mine" to "ours," to convey that we see in this adoption an investment in what's best for this child, her light—shared by her birth family and us. As we work into the night, we lean into one another's skill sets. I rely on Annie's solid sense of how to work the technology and the layout, while I offer suggestions to shape the story we are telling. We each add the quirky details that might help us come alive to someone who doesn't know us: our collection of stuffed animals that we keep in the backseat of the car; our shared love of Ferris wheels. We gobble bowls of popcorn as we work, a team fueled a little by panic but also by inspiration. As we work together, we begin to convince ourselves that this just might work. The family that we were inventing isn't only in our imaginations. And it doesn't require us to abandon the selves that we've always been. It's a continuation of the lives we've been living all along.

When I look at my journals from winter 2012, I note my state of squirrel brain: teaching two classes, directing a small academic program, editing a journal special issue, and writing an essay. My writing is jittery and distracted. But at the core of my thoughts is always the impending adoption. On one page, I write a list of required textbooks for the next quarter, and next to it, I write "Maybe! Maybe! maybe!" In another entry, I observe a couple in front of my favorite café battling to push a stroller uphill against the wind, and I imagine Annie and I doing that, too, sciatica and fading upper body strength and all. The next day, I sign up for a personal trainer. My journal includes my to-do lists, including researching the demographics of our neighborhood school and finding a Black pediatrician. No matter what else I'm writing about, my mind circles back to "The Munchkin," or "our little one," already a part of my circle of loved ones.

On those pages, I worry some about my professional life and how it would shift once I become a mother: the exhaustion and distractedness that comes from juggling too many balls in the air; the double standards about missed student appointments or stalled research or sloppy teaching for faculty of color. At that time, I am the only tenured person of color in my department, and the pressure to represent on all levels feels high. I think about one of my male friends at a nearby university. He and his partner were once considering adopting a child but ended up putting it on the back burner permanently. He has been wildly successful in his career, and as I watch his star rise, I wonder to what extent not becoming a parent has to do with it. I know that in the eyes of some, having a child will mean putting my career on the back burner, too. But I'm willing to live with that.

Soon after we finish our profile and send it into the ether, Annie and I take a night off to go to POW-WOW—Performers or Writers for Women on Women's Issues—a gathering of Black and brown folks that had been happening for several decades that includes music, dancing, poetry, and food. It's there that we see in action what we have to offer a child: love, community, collective joy. The gathering is one part open mic, one part feminist consciousness-raising session, one part cruising spot as women of color "in the life" from all over the city get together to talk, share poetry, organize, and flirt. Butches, femmes, kikis, trans women and men, baby butches and femmes, elders—this has been a spot to see and be seen, to feed ourselves with one another's company and rejuvenate from the rest of the month. POW-WOW has also been an important spotlight for lesbian and queer writers and performers based in Chicago, from poets C. C. Carter and E. Nina Jay to performers Sharon Bridgforth and Omi Osun Joni L. Jones to leaders in the community like Jackie Anderson and Mary Morton. For a while, POW-WOW had a permanent location at Mountain Moving Coffee House. After it closed, POW-WOW traveled itinerantly to different spots around the city, and that experience gave each gathering a sense of its fragility, pushing all the more the importance of showing up and showing out. This night, with its sound and movement and laughter and beauty, is the perfect event to bring us out of our period of self-scrutiny. It was our first time there, and it came right on time.

The night begins with music and then poetry, as we write erotic poems collectively. First, members of the audience shout out chosen words from which we all craft our poems, words like "gurrrrl," "car wash," "juicy," and "sweetness." Then some of us take turns reading our poems out loud, the audience roaring in approval with fists raised. Some of us dedicate a poem to the cutie across the room, some to our partners sitting at our sides, some to ourselves. Then C. C. Carter gives us "The Herstory of My Hips":

> for these were my great grandmother's
> and my grandmother's
> and my mother's hips
> and now I am heir to the throne—my crown?
> these hips of course
> and I will proudly pass them on to my daughter
> for her dowry.

Afterward, we celebrate our bodies by dancing to disco and house and, if we can stay awake late enough (we can't), feasting on fried chicken and biscuits run over from the spot around the corner. I soak in the company of so many queer Black women in one room—something that is rare, even in Chicago—taking in the spirit lift that I needed after so many months of scrutiny and the occasional feeling that I am losing something of myself and my queerness. That night, under the pressure to be seen as viable parents, we are both craving a little community, and maybe a little raunchiness.

Annie and I bend over backward. Our movements are synchronized, and we are sweating with the effort, soaking our carefully chosen dance outfits, as we attempt to clear the stick in limbo. This was as hard as we've ever worked, harder, maybe. But we are not lonely in our movements. Even strangers in the crowd are family. The women in the crowd are bending and arching too, making circles with their hands to usher us forward, and our bodies arch in response as the stick gets lower, and lower. We make graceful circles with our arms and hands, too, belying our effort and our sweat, Chaka Khan's strong soprano thrilling in the background:

> I can cast a spell of secrets you can tell
> Mix a special brew, put the fire inside of you
> Anytime you feel danger or fear
> Then instantly, I will appear.

Our thighs quiver with the effort as we bend deeply, as we lower our arched torsos under the stick, as we sing "I'm Every Woman," these beautiful women, all colors, clap, stomp, and cheer as we clear the stick, our chins just grazing it, our feet planted firmly. We have been changed and moved by the women's cheers and by the beat.

9
AND NOW WE ARE THREE
Spring 2012

WE MUST HAVE CONVINCED SOMEONE, because our daughter came home to us. On a drizzly, gray day in May 2012, we drove the two miles from Rogers Park to Evanston to pick her up from the nursery and take her home, our tiny Honda packed tight with the car seat firmly fitted by Officer Diaz, who warned us that from that time on, our own legroom was irrelevant. We videotaped ourselves on the drive so that some day our child can see us on that day and witness our magical transition from free women, unencumbered, to parents. As I watch the video now, it's clear to me that the transition had already happened. You can see it on our faces: We share the same wide-eyed, joyous, stunned look, like we've just been lifted by a sudden, unexpected wind. Neither of us could keep from smiling.

Before we could take our daughter home, we gave her one last meal in the Cradle nursery. The blue-and-white bottles of baby formula donated by some hospital were weird and squat and medicinal looking, but she sucked them down anyway, emptying three of the bottles at one feeding. She had already grown since we first met her and was too big for the terry cloth pajamas from the Cradle that she wore. We had gotten better at holding her over the past few weeks, more confident, but we still had to focus ourselves single-mindedly on the task. Annie giggled as the baby inched her way up past her breasts and chest to rest her head on Annie's shoulders to burp. My hands shook as I gently folded our

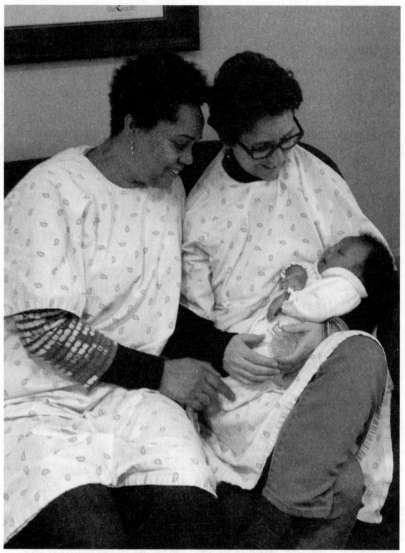

And now we are three: Francesca Royster, Ann Russo, and Cecelia Royster-Russo. The Cradle, Evanston, Illinois, 2012. Photographer unknown.

daughter's legs into the new yellow-striped, duck-footed pajamas that we brought with us, one of the many things we purchased on faith that this would all happen. It had been hard, but there we were, making a future together in the face of loss.

Her birth mother had given her the name Angella, a name that is both beatific and that of a fighter, both graceful and original. Angella with two *l*s. Angella with one, two fists, upraised. And we chose Cecelia for her first name. Cecelia, patron saint of the healing power of music and of breaking and broken hearts. Cecelia, whose name echoes for me Lucille, whom we called Cillie, my New Orleans–born great-grandmother who so enjoyed music and doting on those she loved. Cillie, whose pork chops with red-eyed gravy healed the sick, or at least the homesick. Cillie, of stylish shoes and weekly beauty shop appointments and a deep-dimpled smile. Cillie, of healing hands that smelled, now I know, of lemon balm. Honoring the past, we named her Cecelia Angella. But honoring who she was right then—small, beautiful, quick—we called her Cece.

We heard a ringing voice announcing that Cecelia was going home over the intercom, followed by a bell, summoning us all to the sitting room. Annie and I carried Cece in her car seat (so unbelievably heavy!). As we entered, we saw another family leaving, one that we recognized from our parenting classes, a cherubic blond couple wearing the same jubilant smile we had, carrying their little brown baby boy, whom they'd dressed in a blue-and-white onesie and soft Cubs hat. We watched the couple awkwardly and laughingly maneuver the car seat out of the front door and into the unknown. "Congratulations!" we called out to them. "Good luck!" they called back.

And then it was our turn. Our social worker, Wendy, ushered us to sit on the overstuffed striped couch as the ceremony began.

Women of different colors and sizes and ages circled around us, peering into Cece's car seat. Some, including Wendy, had tears in their eyes. They were the volunteer huggers, the nurses, the social workers, the administrators, and the fundraisers. In short, everyone who had worked on the process. We posed for photos, shook some hands, and got some hugs. Then, they waved goodbye to us, too, as we walked out the front door and into the unknown.

Our joy, the fit of our particular child in our arms and the sense of the rightness of our choice to become mothers so late in our lives together, despite our questions and struggles, felt both fated and intentional—a sign of a fierce love within us and beyond our powers. I understood more than ever that adoption is both a coming together and a rupture, a separation from one family to another. But still, there must have been some kind of magic at work in the relationships that brought us all together. These included the folks at the Cradle and our own families, blood and chosen, who listened and encouraged us, gave us bags and bags of gently used clothes, helped us to buy the right car seat and maneuver the many belts and buttons to install it. There was magic, too, in Cece's birth mother's decision, in her choosing us for reasons that we will never fully know. Magic, and her birth mother's own logic, connections that we didn't fully understand, and a kind of grace, be it fate, karma, or the hand of the ancestors, led to this moment.

In addition to any of the otherworldly forces that may have been at play, I hold fast to the idea that we have a kind of responsibility to create community with the people around us, and they to us, even as we navigate the different and often difficult social forces that bring us together in the same room. Those are bonds that don't have to be of blood, or region, or profession, but of what we do in the world, a shared fight. With our coming together, there is a refusal that the world is in freefall, that our connections, however they began, can have an impact on the world. Cece's very life, her vitality, and the decision that she come home to us to be our child, are a reflection of that community.

Annie says that when she sees Cece, she sees a new dream of motherhood, the possibility of being a different kind of mother than her own, a motherhood shaped by intention and a life lived resisting history.

When I look into Cece's eyes, I find traces of my own lost family and self. To me, she's the embodiment of all there is in my own family story that has been lost or purposefully erased. Not just the way that her eyebrow lifts mischievously the way my mother's did, or the way that her nose, round and shiny in the middle like my own, makes me always want to tweak it. But in her deep-brown, sun-kissed, African face.

I write this knowing that Cece may have to fight not to hear her own story only as one of loss: the loss of a birth mother whom we know only through occasional emails; the loss of a father whose story is still cloudy to us; brothers, sisters, cousins, and grands lost. Hers is also a story of gains and unexpected twists of connection: the gaining of double mothers and home and a chosen family waiting breathlessly for her arrival. The gain of a future community of others who have been adopted like she has been or who have been raised by same-sex or interracial parents, who are other Black girls born and raised in this troubled but also beautiful century.

PART II

THE THREE OF US AND MORE

10

BINGE-WATCHING CECE
Spring into Summer, 2012

FOR ALL THE WAYS THAT adoption is about choosing and training, preparing and planning, waiting and hoping, there is still no way to know what it is *really* like to be a parent until you finally are one.

Annie, Cece, and I sat on the red velvet couch in our living room, and it felt like we'd been in the exact same spot for the past week. It was like we were binge-watching a new show, except that the new show was the three of us. Cece was finally our daughter, after studying and waiting and being certified and scrutinized, after visiting her and falling in love with her. Love at first sight. We were so busy, so full, we hardly had time to look back at what we missed.

Cece was tall for a baby, and at six weeks old, she was too big to fall between the cracks of the cushions (one of my early fears), but she *was* squirmy enough to work her way to the edge. When we held her, she knew how to inch her way up to the warm space between our shoulder and neck. Her cries were strong, but it was rare for her to get to the level of a howl, because we were always right there to help her with what she needed: more milk, a burping, the comfort of our arms. Her brown eyes had lost the blue of newborns. They were bright and alert, with eyebrows arched like birds that gave her face, still soft and formless otherwise, an inquisitive look. Cece had a head full of kinky-curly hair, black and shiny and luxurious. Her velvety skin was the brown of a lucky penny whose color only deepens and burnishes the more you hold it.

While she slept, she snored comically loud for such a little body. When we heard her snores our first night home, we immediately called Phyliss, who's a nurse. Phyliss reassured us in her typically calm way that it was normal for infants to snore and even wheeze. But how would we know? Despite being dedicated aunties and godmothers, the reality was hitting hard that we were actually mothers.

We were transfixed by this little person and also grounded by her, anchored to this planet in a way we'd never experienced, to the rhythms of sunup and sundown marked by her body, though it's true that we hadn't had much sleep those first few days. One morning, there was bright light streaming through the windows, past our neglected plants. It was early May. While Cece snored, the world was busy outside, following its own Chicago rhythms: the Metra commuter train, speeding down Ravenswood Avenue, had slowed from its rush hour schedule. I could hear the sounds of the moving trucks from the business around the corner making their way down our narrow one-way street, and the rattling of their empty beds told me they had already completed a morning's run. The laughing children on their way to school were long gone, and we could now hear the sparrows roosting below our roof eave and the chattering of a squirrel in the crabapple tree outside our window. I reflected that this might be one of the few times in my busy, crammed-to-bursting adult life that I had time to sit in the living room in the middle of the day and just listen. I remembered, then, to breathe.

I looked at Annie's face, as familiar to me as my own reflection. Despite the differences that others might see in us from the outside, she was home to me. That day, her forehead was shiny from the lack of a shower, and her dark, curly boy-model hair was flattened to one side, just like my Afro was. Her hazel eyes, behind her smudged eyeglasses, were content, if sleepy. We were both wearing our pajamas, fading flower nightshirt for her, David Bowie T-shirt and pajama pants for me, even though we were expecting our friend Michele to come over any minute.

FOR THIRTEEN YEARS, ANNIE AND I had been together, driving in our car, reading side by side at cafés, crammed together in a hammock in El Salvador, prepping for classes at the dining room table, cooking food for parties, dancing and eating, and fitting our bodies together to sleep and to love. During those years, our days had been shaped by the university where we both worked, a medium-sized university right in the middle of Chicago's North Side, at once private and urban, Catholic and more or less liberal. We considered ourselves lucky to be out as a couple at work, to even occasionally give each other a quick goodbye kiss in the halls without getting fired or harassed. We were lucky to have offices right across the street from each other, which meant that most days we got to spend our commutes together.

From the first days that we met, we sought ways to spend the most time together. Back when we had been together for three weeks at the most, we decided to take a plane trip to Boston to visit some of Annie's oldest friends, and, perhaps, also to show off our new, in-love selves. Our friends thought we were crazy to travel together so soon, and there were a lot of jokes about U-Hauls being next, but we ignored them. We had already found our rhythm. We had figured out how to sit together in silence or, more likely, how to keep such a lively conversation going that we almost missed our plane.

In this new terrain as parents, we had to shift and relocate ourselves. We were and still are finding our rhythm. In the brief moments that we had away from the baby, we found ourselves a little shy with each other:

"Is it cold in here to you? I'm cold. Do you think Cece needs another blanket?" I asked her.

"I feel just fine, but if you think we're cold, let's turn up the heat," Annie said, although she and Cece were sweating.

"Thanks. I think I'll make some coffee. Oh, wait, I've got to pee."

Annie got up, and then sat back down on the couch, reaching over to pick a little green baby blanket lint out of my hair. She kissed me. "Wait, I'll make the coffee for you."

We were still searching again for the rhythm that had brought us together, that place of safety and contentment that we called "our bubble." Surely there was room for one more little person, so precious to us already, who was more dependent on us than anyone else we'd ever known. And maybe there would be room for others, too, friends and neighbors, in our bubble of safety. Maybe we could all fit, find a way to float together.

When I used to think about becoming a mother, which I did from time to time when I was single, I'd always picture just me and a little curly-headed kicker in a baby pack navigating a playground somewhere. Annie told me soon after we met that she never imagined being a mother at all. Deciding to mother together was a big act of faith for both of us. We were not religious people. But we both believed in other people, in community. And in each other.

Our contemplation was interrupted by Cece, who was beginning to squirm and cry—what we were learning was her hungry cry. Annie picked Cece up and set the baby on her knees so that they could look into each other's eyes. Annie made a goofy face, babbling nonsensical sounds. The baby stopped crying immediately, absorbed by her mother's face. One of our early discoveries as a couple was that we made the same face when we were trying to get our siblings to laugh at the dinner table when we were growing up, both of us the family crack-ups and peacemakers.

I got up to make more milk. I fetched a new bottle from the dishwasher, measured out the powdered formula, warmed a little water in the saucepan, tested a drop on my wrist to make sure it was room temperature, and then combined and shook. This process was beginning to feel automatic. I wondered what it would feel like instead to just put my child to my breast. It seemed simpler. But this way of making milk was a loving act, too, homey in its bustling business. Thinking about that, I let my hips sway a little as I moved from dishwasher to sink to stove, feeling a little more in my maternal groove.

Our friend Michele had offered to come and watch Cece so that we could go for a walk. It would be our first time alone together since the baby came home. From the time Cece arrived, our house had been alive with visitors and with this new sleeping, waking, eating girl. The idea of being alone with Annie made me giddy, and also a little nervous. Michele was a friend from the English department, a colleague. Our friendship had deepened by sharing each other's writing. Michele read some of the first writings where I was figuring out this need to become a mother, the writing that brought me to this moment. Michele is a great storyteller, funny and thoughtful. She manages somehow to both take things seriously and laugh at herself. She is a mother, too, calm and full of the everyday wisdom that one needs.

I heard a scratch at our screen door, and my heart gave a leap as I gave myself a mental check over: uncombed hair, worn jammies, no bra. But there was no time to change. And besides, I really wasn't the main event—Cece was. I often felt self-conscious about being seen in my pajamas by my friends. Even when I lived in the dorm in college, I often wore sweats rather than my pajamas when hanging out with friends in their rooms, self-conscious of my body that always felt too vulnerable to me in its undeniable womanliness; it was so expressive of the self that I wasn't sure I wanted known to all. But becoming a mother, I was peeling off those fears. Friends had brought over freshly baked bread before we'd even brushed our teeth. They sat on our unmade bed with us as we changed Cece's diaper. I was learning to appreciate those unexpected shows of generosity and community—sometimes from people whom I didn't know well, or even those whom I didn't know at all. We received bundles of washed and neatly folded baby clothes from a network of anonymous neighborhood moms we never even knew existed. It made me wonder what other acts of everyday kindness in my neighborhood had been invisible to me before.

I knew already what a gift it would be to have a little time alone with Annie, but I wasn't sure if I was ready to leave Cece yet.

"What if Cece forgets us?" I whispered.

Annie smiled, adding, "Or what if she doesn't miss us at all?"

Annie jostled my shoulders, getting me to giggle. I knew that I was being ridiculous, but I was addicted already to Cece's weight in my arms, the heavy damp feel of her head in the crook of my elbow. But what about that world outside? Meetings, our students, parties, the neighborhood, the *New York Times*, the movies we hadn't yet seen? What if when we left the couch, we'd forget about the warm feeling of that little body in our arms and get caught up in the joys and worries out there? And what about the feeling of just being the two of us, the way we never ran out of things to talk about, wandering the neighborhood with conversation so good we forgot where we were going? Would that come back?

What if we were tempted to just keep walking?

Thinking about leaving Cece reminds me of my mother's dream about quitting smoking. In the dream, Mom's smoking cigarette after cigarette, chatting and puffing away with pleasure. Mom said she started smoking when she was fifteen years old because she needed something to do with her hands. She wasn't able to stop until she was forty-five and had suffered her first stroke. In my mother's dream, in the middle of inhaling with the smoke and menthol burning in her lungs in that bad-good way and her heart starting to race a little, she remembered that she's already quit. She had already endured going cold turkey and survived the months of cravings but had now blown it. In the dream, she started crying, missing her lost new self, until she woke up. Then, wide-awake, she remembered that she quit and laughed with relief that she hadn't lost the person she'd worked so hard to become. I had this fear, too, that just as we were in the middle of making our family, I'd blow it somehow.

Michele let herself in and dropped two large plastic bags of baby clothes and toys on her way to the couch. She had been another constant supplier of baby goods that week: how-to books, lullaby CDs, bibs, crib sheets, and a crib itself (with a miraculously intact set of nuts and screws), all leftover from her son Andrew. She gave us both brisk hugs and immediately started talking to Cece. Somehow she managed to sound sensible, even as she asked Cece if she could eat her fingers.

Michele sat down on the edge of a rocking chair. "How are you two? Are you going bonkers yet?" Her smile was open, and she was animated as she updated us on happenings on campus and how Andrew was surviving kindergarten. I was reminded with a wave of dread that in just another week, we'd both have to go back to classes to finish out the term. Our university didn't yet offer a paid maternity leave for anyone who hadn't given birth the old-fashioned way—and that included fathers and adoptive parents. We both felt unfairly overlooked. (The university has since changed its policy.) Luckily, summer was coming, and I had a research leave that would last through the following winter, if we could make it to June. But it was only May. At that moment, it was hard to imagine myself teaching again. I hadn't read a book in days. And the world outside seemed too fast, too bright.

We started down the sidewalk toward the busier Clark Street. And we were a little bewildered by the everyday activities of our street. Two men made loud, joking conversation, slapping hands. There was construction on the sewer pipes a few doors down, jackhammers chewing through the sidewalk. The bright glass on car windows flashing past us was blinding. Streetlights, not yet lit, seemed impossibly tall. We were children in this world, and we were aware again of our own breath, the feel of air on our skin.

As we walked toward the lake shimmering to the east, I remembered the first time I saw Annie, tanned from being at the beach all day with her family, who were visiting from down state. That day, I heard a voice in my head whispering to me in a matter-of-fact tone accompanied by butterflies, "You're going to be in each other's lives. It's just a matter of how." I felt those butterflies again.

Annie gently took my hand.

11
SNAPSHOT
Summer 2012

THE WOMAN AND THE BABY are standing, not sitting, at a wooden booth in a crowded restaurant. The booth is full of graffiti. It's not clear what time of day it is. The image is a little blurry, but you can see the expression of the woman pretty clearly. She is smiling shyly as the baby sleeps in her arms. She's holding the baby up on her shoulder, with one hand under the baby's bottom and the other holding the baby against her in a pose that seems a little awkward, as if she's not used to holding something so small. But the baby is firmly held. The baby is wearing a green onesie, with its diaper peeking through the edges of the leg holes. The baby's legs are chubby, feet bare. The baby looks two months old at most but has a head full of black curly hair, with a few bald spots. The baby's skin is brown and clear. Her eyes are closed. It appears that the woman may be jiggling the baby. The woman's eyes are sleepy but content.

This photo is the first one of Cece and me in a public space. The Medici, a dusky pizza place near the University of Chicago—was one of my all-time favorite places. In high school, I hung out with friends there. We'd eat endless baskets of the shoestring fries, telling each other our stories of yearning, carving our names in the wooden backs of the seats, not quite believing that we'd ever be loved.

I was so proud of this baby in my arms. I think you can see my pride in my shy smile and in the way I hold the baby a little more tightly than necessary. We had gone through so much to have her here with us. I almost didn't quite believe that she was ours. For the first time, I was experiencing that feeling of "mine-ness"—a possession so different from anything else I'd felt, different from my possessiveness of my parents or my sister or my partner. Maybe it came closest to my experience of the possessiveness that I felt about my own time and privacy. But already, without even consciously thinking about it, I had surrendered my sense of privacy and self and time. I was ready to be remade and reinvented.

The air was cold, strong air-conditioning contrasting with the muggy August air, and the noise of the restaurant lulled a bit from when we first got there. That brand-new feeling of being a minor celebrity that you feel when you walk in with a baby, that glow, was still with us, and Annie was able to capture that somehow on camera. But Annie was also documenting that, yes, even as new mothers, we were also able to go on with the business of eating, fueling ourselves, socializing, and connecting to each other. While the baby was sleeping, Annie and I had managed to sneak in a conversation about a book we had heard about on NPR. So, in my smile in that picture, you can see, too, that we were going to be okay. Annie and I would find our rhythm again, a way to squeeze in our companionship, even with this little person who needed so much attention and love. We would adjust. We would grow with this moment and all of the moments that would come after it.

Cece was a solid girl and felt so good in my arms. Chubby fat and muscle. She'd already grown so much in the weeks that we'd had her, doubled in size, it seemed, from the day we brought her home. I loved her fat thighs, a sign of her prosperity, perhaps, and her long, luxurious, and kinky hair, which I vowed to teach her how to treasure. She was this great bundle of possibility, but she was also tiny and dear, ears pointed like an elf's. I was hungry when Annie took this photograph because Cece started crying before I had the chance to finish my food. I was also exhausted from lack of sleep and the reality that my relationship to everything familiar—eating, getting dressed, sitting down to read a book—had changed, as had my place in this familiar restaurant. Still, I was content. I understood the meaning of grace.

Maiya Sinclair Shackelford, Black feminist filmmaker and one of my former students who also happens to be my cousin, has described grace as "a gift of favor that is given to you regardless of your personal efforts or your shortcomings. It is a gift that you could never earn." Maiya writes that particularly for Black mothers and daughters, grace is important as a part of the generosity and care, the space for one another that we can provide in our family connections as a balm from the outside world. In the face of others' underestimations, microaggressions, and dismissals, Black mothers and daughters see one another, recognize one another's efforts as well as our failures, like no one else can. This is at the heart of the fierce love that I felt (and feel) for Cece and that I've experienced from her already, even after just a month of being a mother: a steady love back.

12

MOM, SINCE I SAW YOU LAST
Fall 2012

I PEEK INTO CECE'S ROOM and find Annie snoring softly in the hastily assembled rocking chair. Cece is nestled against her, not quite asleep. In my hands is a bottle made from formula mix with a white baby on the packaging. The attic room is the warmest in the house, and I fight the urge to curl up in the chair with them. Instead, I pull Cece from Annie's drowsy grip and walk the baby around her room, whispering softly what I see as we move from wall to wall: the birth announcement that my sister, Becky, embroidered for her, with her birth weight and height, a day we did not witness, and a black-and-white photo of my mother on her high school graduation day, smiling so wide that she showed the chipped front tooth that she usually hid. She is together with her mother and her mother's mother. I call this photo "The Mamas," and I whisper to Cece, "These are your mamas, too." We pass welcoming messages from friends from all over the country that we've framed and displayed on the walls; a blurred photo of her birth mother K., too, the only one we have. It seems important to include her, to keep her in our thoughts, and in Cece's.

When we first moved in, we took down the Barbie wallpaper that belonged to the little girl who lived there before. We painted the walls spring green to cut down on the over determination of pink and blue and began a mural of the garden that we hoped to grow in the backyard. With Cece's arrival, our loved ones came over, adding their own touches to the mural: a bright yellow-and-orange mariposa from Daisy, Cece's first babysitter; a little brown bear from her cousin Connie; a bold rainbow from her cousin Allie; and colorful sturdy tulips from Meechie. On Cece's bookshelf, we loaded books that feature brave brown and Black children and searches for families that echo ours: *A Snowy Day*, *Lola at the Library*, *I Like Myself*, *Last Stop on Market Street*, and *Heather Has Two Mommies*. Each managed to capture at least one truth of our lives, but we kept searching without finding ones that would give the full picture. Sometimes a simple trip to the bookstore became an exercise in frustration. We loved the *Frog and Toad* books because of their cross-species, same-sex friendship and *The Runaway Bunny* for its message of persistent mother love. We made a secret corner in the linen closet where we stashed books and gifts that we couldn't live with but didn't have the heart to throw away: a fairy-tale book featuring golden-haired princesses, ruffled pink socks, and a lamp with a menacing white clown at its base. Some books that I loved as a child brought unexpected pain: the little bird's search for what we now see as his birth mother in *Are You My Mother?*; Curious George's misadventures with his strangely undemonstrative white guardian, the Man with the Yellow Hat; Bambi's early loss of his mother and Dumbo's forced removal from his.

Becoming a mother has made me miss mine. It has made me think differently about my relationships to members of my chosen family, who love me in a mothering way, too. There is Laila who checks the glycemic index of the muffins she's baked for us, or Julie whose quiet encouraging hand rests on my shoulder after we've weathered a rough committee meeting. In many ways, Annie especially has given me the kind of care that for so long only my mother gave me—her ability to see past my cheery, high-functioning public self when I need support but don't know how to ask for it. But becoming a mother has also made me think about the ways that I've absorbed my mother's presence and how it's fortified me.

I remember our own times of grace and fierce love together—my mother could be tough, like when she fussed at me for moping over a breakup when we were traveling in Europe in my early twenties. My mother's brisk, "Come on. It's time to get over it!" interrupted a teary, long (and expensive) late-night overseas phone call with my ex, our on-again, off-again Silly Putty relationship stretching overseas, and shook me from my doldrums, saving what turned out to be the trip of a lifetime. As a young adult, I was lucky to have my mother's frank friendship and companionship, and I'd come home to Chicago from grad school or my first job several times a year just to hang out with her. I remember late-night tea and snacks and *Star Trek: The Next Generation* marathons, and going to yet another production of *A Christmas Carol* and leaving because we were giggling at the sheer absurdity of having seen it so many times before.

It's been ten years since my mother's death, but since Cece's come home, it's like my mother is sitting at my elbow, offering advice on how to get Cece comfortable in her bath, guiding my hands as I do Cece's hair. At quiet times, like when Cece is napping, I have conversations with her.

MOM, SINCE YOU'VE SEEN ME last, my face has been remapped by freckles, tags of brown and black dotting the bridge of my nose, my cheeks, between the folds of my neck. A new one appears every day I bother to notice—a link to redbone grandmothers (yours and mine), to you. The dragonfly tattoo that you praised me for getting, its inked blue-green wing spanning the brown curve from shoulder to collar bone, has faded a little, my totem of flight and transition. I see you now in the rounding space between my chin and neck, the crooked curve of my fingers, my frown lines as I peer over the newspaper. My breasts sit lower now on my ribs like yours did, though I have not fed two children with them. When I hold my breasts, their heft still warms my hands. I want to move like you did, bold and shirtless from shower to hallway to bedroom, powdering yourself as you went. You made up a song for your breasts as you walked, merrily shocking your teenage daughters: "Do your tits swing low? Do they waggle to and fro?" I am the age now that you were when we first became friends, mother and daughter. I miss your medicine of laughter and spare, well-timed cursing.

I'm a mother now, and I know that you know because you had everything to do with it. From the time we were waiting to find out if we were chosen to finally being chosen, while visiting Cece in the nursery and falling in love with her, I knew that you were there, shaping things from afar. I believed that you were watching—not some rarified spirit, but the insightful, funny, sometimes control freak you that you were in life, a force for good in my life every day. And those hard weeks, when Cece's birth mother decided that she needed more time, I wondered if this was a second lesson in loss that you were trying to teach us, in accepting, however gracefully we could, the gradual growing away of your children. Except that this was sped up, as was falling in love with Cece. That first lesson, of course, was losing you.

In my months at home with Cece—the accidental timing of an academic sabbatical giving me the maternity leave that my university didn't yet offer for adoptions—and after Annie has had to return to teaching, we create a routine of feeding and then playing and then napping and then feeding again. At these times, I think about you and me, Mom, when I was in preschool and got to spend the whole day with you. How I loved how time stretched between breakfast and afternoon, when Becky would come home from school, and I'd have to share you again. I loved taking a nap right next to you on the couch, the TV a soft hum in the background, the tastes of fried egg and milk and that irony vitamin still on the back of my tongue. I loved to follow you from room to room. Now with Cece, time feels elastic again. For the first time in years, I can sit still in a chair, looking out the window or watching her sleep. I set things up in the kitchen to catch Cece's eye, magnets and measuring cups and wooden spoons to bang, and when she wakes, we work together, she and I, creating a new rhythm of morning.

How did you do it? You used to brag that you never had a babysitter, keeping the best and the worst work of mothering all to yourself.

I am learning that there is a delicious selfishness in holding so closely the ones that you love. I am learning the paradox of loving with all my heart and then helping that love grow so that they can leave me. Already I feel the anticipation of pain and the speeding of time—all made more poignant because I am coming late to motherhood, almost twice the age that you were when you had me. Long days, short years. Writer Cherríe Moraga captures this lesson so movingly in the final lines of her memoir of queer motherhood, *Waiting in the Wings*:

> How can I describe the lesson—that each day there is a birth and a dying of this time in our lives together . . . my sometimes quiet sadness at the deepest moments of joy with my child has to do with this complete knowledge of impermanence. In the face of that knowledge, I visit my aging parents, bring my woman coffee in bed, and stroke the silk of my son's hair.
>
> This too shall pass.

I appreciate the ways that Moraga conjures up the simultaneous feelings of presence and loss that come from motherhood. She understands the ways that each intimately felt detail of mothering reminds us of our mortality while also raising memories of love and nurturing from our parents. These memories are from a time when our relationships with them were less complicated by the adult challenges of shifting loyalties, expectations, and disappointments. On the most fundamental and spiritual level, her memoir acknowledges the coexistence of birth and death.

When you died, I learned it from a phone call. When I had talked to you a few days before, your voice sounded so far away. However, I chalked it up to long distance, since you were halfway across the world in Bahia, Brazil, for a music conference. You were so excited because this was an essential part of your dream to travel to all of the key posts of the African diaspora. But I knew somehow, even before you left, that change was coming. We spent time the night before you left looking through your different travel photos. I had just moved back to Chicago a few months earlier, and I had not caught up on all your trips. We made tea and ate cookies, like we used to do. I felt so close to you, but there was also this sense of change, hovering. A whisper of dread that I didn't want to listen to. A few weeks before, Annie's mother had died of a heart attack. Afterward, when Annie found random loose aspirins in her coat pockets, she realized that her mother was self-medicating for her symptoms and knew more than she let on. For me, I recalled that time a few weeks before you left for Bahia, going from antiques shop to antiques shop to have appraised some of the objects that Cillie had left you, including candlesticks and an old clock from her longtime employers, the Silvers. You moved with a kind of urgency through the streets, despite the fall chill. And when the appraisers told you that the pieces were worth only a few hundred dollars, you took it personally. I saw your eyes tear up, but I told myself that it was the wind.

I remember riding in the limousine from your funeral service to the burial site with Allie, who was then six. I had given her a pad and pencil to play with, and I watched her drawing a face: two x's for eyes, a crumpled line of a mouth. I knew that Allie was troubled by the same thing that troubled me—you didn't look like yourself in your casket. Your face looked shrunken, even mean. I understood Allie's thinking: this body, this face, even more familiar than our own faces, wasn't yours or ours anymore. It belonged to an experience that was beyond both of us. Funeral rites are intended to help you go along with these changes, to work through it all in an hour or two. But we all have own rate of processing the transformation of body to spirit. Later, it occurred to me that one of the reasons why you looked so strange was that you didn't have your teeth in, something you'd never allow if you were alive.

You spent your last day in Bahia doing what you love most: walking, visiting markets, taking photographs, probably talking to new people, listening to music, and picking up stones as mementos. We found these in your suitcase. Since Becky and I left home, you'd been on a mission to see all of the key spots of the transatlantic slave trade. You'd been to Africa, to the slave castles of Ghana, Senegal, and Sierra Leone. You'd been to Portugal and Spain and England and France. And now, Bahia. At the end of that day in Bahia, you returned to your hotel room and flopped down on your bed. Your roommate, Marsha, whom I had never met but who worked sometimes with you at the Cultural Center downtown, said that your last words were, "This has been the best day." Then you closed your eyes and laid your head down like you were taking a nap, but you never got up. The doctors said that your heart gave out. But maybe it was just too full.

I am so glad that this was the way you died, peacefully after declaring the beauty of the day. One of your greatest fears was to die a slow death, languishing away in a hospital. You feared being a burden on your children and losing control of your body.

It took two weeks to get your body returned to the States. In those weeks, Becky and I kept busy by making phone calls to the doctors and the hotel, writing letters to the state department, and contacting family and friends, the funeral home, and the printer. We were in our own sped-up rhythm, the timing of the rest of the world irrelevant. We spoke with doctors we had never met, government authorities, hotel managers, and folks with the airline. With the help of the funeral director here, we arranged your flight home on a plane with enough room in the cargo section for a coffin. I went into high-efficiency mode, dodging my own sadness when I could. What I've said out loud to others, but only half believed, was that once I saw you in your casket, I'd accept that it wasn't a mistake, that you hadn't just missed your flight or were in a hospital somewhere in Brazil. I'd know that you weren't coming back, at least not in the way that I knew you, and that somehow I'd have to learn how to mother myself.

And for over a decade after your burial, I didn't return to your gravesite. I'm ashamed of that. I guess I was angry at you for dying so far away from me. Really, I just plain didn't want you to die. But if you had to die, I wanted to be the one with you in your last hours. I wish I could keep you with me, Mom. I wish that you were small enough to hold in my hand or to put in a jar on the windowsill by my bed so that you could still watch me while I go to sleep. I wish I could warm you in the palm of my hand each morning, reshape you like God shaped Adam, until, in my own time, and through the changing texture of the clay, I finally understand that you're gone.

I went to your funeral, of course, and oversaw your burial, along with Becky, Annie, nieces, Gramps, uncles and aunts, and so many of your friends. I did what they did: dropped soil on the casket and took one of the wisps of wheat from the bouquet that went down with the casket.

But I never quite let go of you. I kept you around me, feeling you in the Chicago places that had meaning for you rather than in a crowded, jumbled cemetery on the edge of a highway. I felt you whenever I passed the Chicago Cultural Center, where you worked for more than thirty years. I imagined you jamming to reggae at the Wild Hare, or zipping along in a fast car driven by your daughters on Lake Shore Drive. Or I saw you shimmering in the lake itself, the gold on top of the water on certain lucky days. You are awakened when we think of you, when we tell your stories, or when we use your favorite turns of phrase. When we talk to you, like right now.

The ritual of burial has sustained others around the world for millennia, even if it hasn't worked for me. Iraq's Shanidar Cave has evidence of flowers left for a dead loved one some twenty thousand to seventy-five thousand years ago. Some say that those very first cemeteries were unintentional, that Neanderthal hunters who were sick or weak with hunger lay in the caves and were accidentally buried there. But those same Neanderthals were found surrounded by personal effects that would seem to have been left by someone who needed to remember them.

A few months after your burial, Becky and I decided to take a considerable slice from your pension to take the nieces to Disney World. It was the kind of gesture that you would appreciate, always preferring travel and immediate joy to stocks or bonds or real estate. Becky and I had never been to Disney World or Disneyland, but like most kids under the age of seven, Allie and Meechie were fluent in the language of Disney: the classics of Mickey, Donald, Snow White, and Bambi, as well as the films that were created in their lifetimes: *The Lion King, Pocahontas,* and *Mulan.* Since this was only the first year in the new millennium, they had yet to enjoy the first African American princess, Tiana from *The Princess and the Frog*. Meechie and Allie were two and six years of age, old enough to remember watching *Mulan* with you on the VCR and to miss you but also young enough to thoroughly enjoy going to Disney World so soon after the funeral. The girls lived with you for most of their lives, after Becky split from her husband—in the same way that you lived with Cillie, when your parents divorced. You doted on them, and since you passed, they seemed starved for joy and a little extra attention. You can see this in the photographs that we took on the first day: Allie waiting expectantly for Goofy's autograph, Meechie wolfing down an ice cream sandwich, melted chocolate cookie smudged on her chin, both looking expectantly at the camera, prepared to have the experience of a lifetime that they had heard about on TV.

Watching the girls' faces light up to see Buzz Lightyear strolling by or to have breakfast with Goofy didn't end my grief, but it interrupted it. At first I resisted, a Disney cynic. I remember sitting in the bathroom of the hotel room that I shared with Becky and the girls, sharing snarky details on the phone to Annie while everyone was asleep, detailing all of the unbelievable things about the park: the cleanliness—you couldn't even chew gum there—the creepy "It's a Small World" music that greeted you at the entrance and seemed to haunt you wherever you were, the Donny-and-Marie-style stage show, featuring precisely choreographed patriotic songs with a country twang. But I got sucked in, too.

I was still in the free-fall stage of mourning, that unsettled place of disbelief. The funeral over, I still thought that someone would call—a government official or the priest or you yourself— to explain that there had been a terrible mistake. Disney gave me the invitation to let myself become further undone from reality. And I embraced that unmooring of place that came from Disney's appropriation of cultures: moving from huge baobab tree of *The Lion King*'s Africa, to Polynesian luau complete with pupu platter (snicker), to the *Song of the South*'s American South. It gave me the chance to postpone that adult process of putting myself together again. *Let us forget for a while and laugh with the others, and when we return, let the world become more predictable, more gentle again.*

Allie was the first to notice the owl, perched in a large palm tree that lined the road on the way to the park. It seemed to turn its head as we rode past, and to nod. We would see that owl again, on our way home, as if she were waiting to see how our trip went.

Or did we? Truth be told, when I asked her about it later, Allie didn't remember the owl. But in *my* memory, the owl was majestic and white, with yellow, piercing eyes set deep in her oversized head, craning to watch us from above. She followed our tour bus and we all saw her: Becky, Allie, even Meechie, who couldn't talk yet, a collective spiritual vision. In my memory, we shared an unsaid thought: that the owl was you, Mom. You came to watch us on our journey and make sure that we did this work of our mourning, this work of continuing to live and play without you.

But as I write this, I wonder if I've made it up, or even if the owl was a fake, one of Disney's creations, an animatron made to somehow anticipate our desires. I check in with my sister, Becky, leaving a long message on her work number to make sure that she calls me back. "Remember that owl that we saw when we went to Disney World? The one that seemed to be watching us, and we all saw it? What do you remember about it? Give me a call back." She called me as soon as she returned to her office. Becky remembers the owl very vividly, but hers was a much more modest beast: a small brown owl, grungy, with missing feathers, shielding two babies, she said. The owl was perched on a low bush, deep in the leaves, close enough for us to see her. In Becky's memory, we were walking on foot from the hotel to the park because we were scrimping, trying to keep the costs of the trip low. The air, she remembers, was humid and almost unbearably hot. We came across the owl by accident.

Becky's version of the owl story might reflect her own journey, of surviving the unsettling experience of your death with her own children in tow and of her vulnerability and struggle, too, as she was recently divorced. Becky's owl was more realistic, and, I had to admit, more believable. But I can't give up on my owl, larger than life, all knowing, fantastic. I see her in my mind's eye, nodding, approving of our decisions. Maybe that owl is also my hope for myself, no longer weighed down by grief but soaring.

Many who write about mourning experience a sighting of a loved one as an animal, a visitor who comes to initiate and perhaps even oversee the process of mourning, a reminder that one is not alone. In Cheryl Strayed's memoir, *Wild,* her narrative of a three-month hike of the Pacific Crest Trail to mourn her mother, a fox appears on a desolate section of the path at a moment when Cheryl is the loneliest. She yells out first "Fox" and then "Mom! Mom! Mom!" and the fox disappears, it's meaning still open-ended to her.

Owls apparently also haunted Walt Disney himself. In a taped interview with writer Pete Martin for a series of articles for the *Saturday Evening Post* that were later published as *The Story of Walt Disney,* Walt tells this story about owls. Walt is about seven years old. Left alone to play in an orchard when visiting a family farm, he spies a small brown owl on a limb. He gets excited and tries to catch it, but the owl claws and scratches him.

I could see that darn owl in my dreams, you know? But I was just so excited. I didn't want him. I didn't want to kill him. But when he began to claw and everything else, I got so excited I threw him to the ground and stomped on him, you know? And I killed him. I didn't want to kill him. I didn't have it in my mind at all. And I don't know yet why I wanted to have that owl. It was just . . . I could catch him, you know?

What does telling this story do for Disney, I wonder? It brings to mind for me all those stories of rough comings-of-age that he tells through animals' deaths: Bambi's loss of his mother, Simba's loss of his father in *The Lion King*. But in those stories, death is a catalyst, as individual pain yields itself to the larger cycle—the circle of life. In this story, though, it's Disney himself who has blood on his hands. The story captures truths as jolting and sharp as owls' claws: the owl's scramble to keep alive, as well as Disney's own desire to exercise power over its life. The urge to hold on to something mysterious and clawed and wild.

Disney forges a career with animals, watching them, making them talk and sing, versions of ourselves. Creating fantasies, even new worlds out of animals and one's own vision: Mickey, Donald, Pluto, Bambi. And all of the documentaries on real animals brought to our living rooms on Sunday nights via *The Wonderful World of Disney*.

After that trip, I collected owls for a while. Annie's sister Laura found a piece of bark shaped like an owl, and later sent me a photograph of a small, homely brown one, something like the one that Becky remembers. I sought out postcards, journals, mugs, T-shirts, jewelry, all things to bring the owl presence to my here and now, my everyday life. Some way to feel connected, grounded, but even more I wanted to be haunted—to have some access to a presence not yet knowable. After my sighting in Disney World, the owls seemed to find me—a sign, I thought, that somehow you were trying to communicate with me, though its message is unclear.

In my recurring dream about you, Mom, I am able to call you

on the phone, but each time there's something wrong with the technology that makes the connection difficult, fleeting, ultimately disappointing. The line breaks up so that I can only hear every other word. It seems like every friend I have who has lost a parent has had this dream. In the dream, the keys of the touchtone phone stick, or I can't remember the correct sequence of numbers, even though your number has been the same for at least a decade and I called it almost every day.

What is the technology of mourning for those of us who are churchless? What is the means of connection? What helps our worlds cohere again? Going through that long first year, I had no idea what this experience would make of me. I felt I was being reshaped, and I was afraid of that reshaping. Who would make sure that I came out on the other side? In the absence of God, that had always been your role, Mom. You were the person who knew me best. No matter where my life took me, what changes in identity or circumstance, I knew that you would recognize the me in me.

NOW A MOTHER, GROUNDED TO the world by Cece and Annie, I feel ready to go back to the cemetery to visit your grave. It still feels lonely. Lincoln Cemetery is located outside of the Chicago limits, and all you can see for miles around is highway and other cemeteries. The tombstones are mostly on the ground or below waist high, and somehow that makes the sky seem too big.

We live not far from the Bohemian National Cemetery, a lovely cemetery with willow trees and imposing, often intricately carved statues. Some people go there for the fun of it, to walk their dogs, ride their bikes, or view the more famous inhabitants. I envy this cemetery and the people who have such a casual relationship to it, like I envy the lovely brownstones on the Gold Coast, their leaded windows and gargoyles, with a kind of grumpy admiration. Lincoln Cemetery isn't as lovely, but at least you've got good company: Nee Nee and Cillie and also some famous Black Chicagoans, including Gwendolyn Brooks, Bessie Coleman, and Lillian Armstrong, wife of Louis and a jazz musician in her own right. You are just nine miles and a leap across the Little Calumet River from Blue Island, the community where Cece was born.

In 2009, stories came out about the scandal of Emmett Till's body, which was returned from Money, Mississippi, to Chicago after his infamously brutal death and buried by his mother at the Burr Oak Cemetery. Then, unbeknownst to his family, his body was removed from its plot and dumped into a mass grave so that the plot could be resold. These revelations made me nervous about the state of your body. Burr Oak is just a few blocks from Lincoln Cemetery. In fact, the two nearly run into each other. I thought I should return to make sure that you were okay.

But what if I discover the sewer pipe of my own grief pumping beneath my skin, and I accidently pierce it, letting out fumes that I don't know how to control? I plan my trip the day before Halloween, a few days before All Soul's Day and the Day of the Dead. Beforehand, I make myself a big bowl of pasta, as if preparing for a marathon, although the cemetery is only forty minutes away, with traffic. I don't take any other adults with me, but I take Cece, who was seven months old. I want her to meet you and to be part of this memory.

I think I should bring something—flowers? I settle for a bag of Original Sliders from White Castle, your first employer. You worked there as a teenager, back when they had waitresses, for just one day, walking out in exhaustion at day's end. But that didn't spoil your love of those burgers. Even as you grew older and the burgers tampered with your gut, you considered them a guilty pleasure.

Waiting at the White Castle drive-through, I text Annie to tell her what I am doing. She calls back immediately. "Are you going to be okay out there by yourself?" she asks. I tell her that I'm taking

Cece with me for moral support. "Good," she tells me. "Carry me in your pocket, too."

The day is cold and unusually windy, a holdover from Hurricane Sandy's ravaging of the East Coast, the hurricane that bears your name. The weather and Cece's lively conversation from the back seat keep me anchored to the present. I zoom down the Tuskegee Airmen Memorial Highway, a section of Highway 57, on my way to the cemetery, and I let myself think of all of the things you missed since your death: the tragedies of September 11, which was also your birthday; the election of the first Black president (and his reelection for a second term!); the graduations of your granddaughters, Allie and Meechie, from high school; the blossoming of my relationship with Annie, whom you were just getting to know when you died; our buying a house together and our civil union; and maybe most of all, our adoption of Cece.

As I pull off the highway, I see a series of modest Georgian-style homes and strip malls, and then the land opens up to a series of cemeteries, all linked together: Beverly Cemetery, Burr Oak, and then Lincoln. We pull into the driveway, and I ask the woman working at the desk to help me find your gravesite. She pulls out an ancient-looking card catalog tray, army green with yellowing cards, and finds your name on a complicated looking map: number 407. I roll Cece around the graves in her stroller, trying not to disrespect the folks who are buried there. I talk to Cece out of nervousness and also to keep her in a good humor. She looks about cheerfully and occasionally squeals out "Yia Yia! Yia Yia!"—your nickname, and also one of three sounds she makes.

I am relieved to find the cemetery less barren than I remembered it, with a few tall evergreens, as well as shorter trees that had lost their leaves and scrubby bushes spaced every few rows. The grass is neatly clipped and garbage cans sit jauntily every fifty feet or so. In the spring, it will be quite lovely. But we can't find number 407. It is getting cold in the wind. I park the stroller under a spindly tree closest to the place I think you might be and pull out a Slider. "Here's to you, Mom. I love you very much!" I say out loud. I am not quite sure who else is listening, so I add, "And to all of you folks out here. Cheers!" Cece can't eat burgers yet, so I give her an oniony kiss. As I look into the distance to the outer edge of the cemetery, I watch a thatch of trees and gently sloping wheat that provide a cushion from the highway bending in the wind. I leave feeling relieved. I am glad that we have this official place to remember you, even if it is missing your style, your energy, and your humor.

On the car ride home, Cece and I sing along to Jackie Wilson, "Your love keeps lifting me higher."

13
WE'RE GETTING MARRIED
June 2014

THERE IS A LARGE GROUP *filing their way through the Thompson Center, Chicago's one-stop shop for all things legal. They are chatting excitedly, laughing, touching each other lightly, posing and snapping pictures from their iPhones. Three teenagers, two adult women, a little girl. The guards are watching them closely. A few shades of white. A few shades of brown. Definitely some Black. No one matches. A lot of different people pass through their gates, and they're used to odd groupings. Tough-looking teens with baggy pants, off to juvenile, accompanied by mothers who fuss after them with sharp voices and eyes soft with worry. Grumpy old men who've been sent to retake their driver's exams after years of dodging, afraid they'll fail now. Snappy young women on their lunch hour, off to get their nails done at the place near the food court. They look way too good to be stuck in any office, the guards think, and the women may flirt a little with the guards, linger before moving on. The day is hot, humid, and the air conditioner is working like a beast, so once inside, just about everyone shivers a little as they take off their jackets to go through security, but this group, the one with the mismatched children, doesn't seem to notice. They don't complain as they're asked to take out their water bottles or to put their keys in the holders. This group seems to be here for happier business.*

It irritates the guards a little, the fun they seem to be having. And they have odd haircuts. One boy, about twelve or thirteen, has long, floppy bangs he's constantly flipping out of his dark-lashed eyes. The other boy is a little older, almost a man. His hair is cut close—curly choirboy hair. He is slim and neat. Shirt tucked in. The teenage girl who is carrying the baby looks like she's just coming into her womanhood, fourteen or fifteen. Her hair is braided, with some lavender and blue-green, some kind of mermaid. Watching everyone with shining eyes are two women who look like boys at first look. They both wear converse high tops and T-shirts and messy jeans. One is olive skinned, Italian, maybe, the other a Redbone, with not-so-neat dreadlocks, brown with gray at the temples. They stand close to each other so their shoulders are touching. They are holding a little gingersnap girl who is bright-eyed and smiling. Her skin doesn't match anyone else's. She's three at the most, and she smiles at all the strangers, unafraid. Goes right up to them and crows, "We're getting married."

We're getting married! Vincenzo Castaneda, Francesca Royster, Ann Russo, Demitra Pates, Cecelia Royster-Russo, and Nick Russo, Thompson Center, Chicago, Illinois, 2014. Photographer unknown.

14

CECE'S BODY

Fall into Winter, 2014

THE YEAR WE GOT MARRIED, Cece went to daycare for the first time. It was hard to let her go and have others contribute to her upbringing. We didn't want to face the so many hours in a day without her. But, this new daycare experience was an important first step in Cece's learning to be in the world and find her place in it. Still, sometimes it felt as if other people's values and agendas were seeping into the quiet queer homelife that Annie and I had created.

I AM STARING AT A photograph of what might be my daughter's nose. We parents are huddled together, surveying the isolated body parts posted on the wall: eyes and brows, noses and lips. This is only a holiday party game—to break the ice, to bring us together while our children eat cookies, sing carols, and play in another room. I'd rather be with the kids. Because I am starting to sweat. Hard.

One of the mothers jokes, "I bet the fathers will be the ones to get it wrong."

As the only two-mom family in Cece's class, I feel our queerness. I don't think anyone thought of the possibility of adoption when they came up with this game. I choose a smile that is winning, and with the right number of teeth. Miss Erika, Cece's favorite teacher, gayly announces to everyone that no, I am wrong, along with a few sheepish dads. She points to a different photo, one with a pouty, full-lipped mouth, swoonably adorable. Miss Erika says, "I'd know that mouth anywhere." Now it seems obvious that this is my own darling girl, the one I wake up to and feed every morning. I feel like I have failed.

FOR THE FIRST YEARS AFTER we brought Cece home, whenever we're in a crowd, I'd look out for people who might be her relatives. I'd think: that man has Cece's eyes, dark and serious and conversational. That woman dragging along two daughters has Cece's cheekbones.

But more and more with each passing week, Cece in personality and spirit and even body was our child. I could already see reflected in her laugh and gestures those of us who are around her the most: my way of holding my chin when I'm thinking, Annie's nose-crinkling smile, Meechie's willingness to bust a move at a moment's notice.

As a queer mother, I was unlearning the old language of belonging, beyond blood and flesh and family resemblance.

As the Black mother of a little Black girl, I was learning that I do not own her. Cece is our child, but she belongs to all of us, and yet she belongs to no one but herself.

I IMAGINE THAT MY THINKING about Cece's body is shaped by being her adoptive mother. But maybe nonadoptive parents struggle with this, too: how do we really *see* our children? Not as chips off the old block or apples that have fallen not far from the tree, but really grappling with their own personhood? Perhaps to see our children we have to look beyond the body as a mirror. In addition to thinking about genetics, we need to recognize

130

personal idiosyncrasy and style, the influence of family, blood and chosen, and the importance of gender, race, sexuality, culture, economics, and time. In a video project that I think about often now that I'm a mother, Frans Hofmeester, a photographer from the Netherlands, crafted a kind of visual time machine for his daughter. Using time-lapse photography, he chronicled his daughter Lotte's physical and social changes, big and minute, moving through twelve years of her life in a swift two minutes and forty-five seconds.

In Hofmeester's video, we see but don't hear Lotte's sounds and gestures, then words, then conversation. We watch her round face become more angular, her eyes sharpen their focus. At around eleven (eleven already!), Lotte moves with sophisticated, witty gestures. She laughs and slips her hair behind her ear, and yes, she might be batting her eyelashes. We see the child in the adult and the adult in the child. As we watch her changes, and what seems to be a growing self-consciousness, I feel protective of her. I find myself turning to this video as a kind of talisman against the loss that I feel already as Cece ages. It's valuable as a document of a child's shifting physical and psychic presence. Maybe Hofmeester's video attempts to be an antidote for the problem of parental blindness that I share. Maybe that artist filmed his child in order to see and hear her in a way that's impossible because he's otherwise so close. And maybe in order to see the beauty that might otherwise be difficult to bear.

Does Cece have her birth mother's sweeping brow and sweet smile? Did she get her smooth brown skin, her grace and athleticism, her strong feet from her birth father? Is her determination and focus something she got from her birth parents, from us, or is this something that is her very own? We may never know the answer to those questions. But as every day unfolds, these traits have become the language of loveliness for me.

Watching Cece grow has been a source of amazement for me. By the age of two, Cece had begun losing her toddler's tummy and grew long and lean. She could actually perform all of those playground shenanigans that I was both too uncoordinated and too chicken to do: flipping on the bars, making her way back and forth on the monkey bars without stopping for a rest, leaping and twirling. Sometimes she'd get the attention of older kids and their parents. This gave her a kind of confidence in her body that I never had. And it showed as she navigated the space of the playground. If there were big boys lounging on the slide, chatting and taking up space in a way that prevented her from going down, she'd ask them to move. She'd wait with her arms crossed until bigger girls cleared the swing or the one-person merry-go-round, which she'd do like a member of Cirque du Soleil, complete with arms outstretched. She'd enter a group of kids, siblings, or friends that she's never met and join in their tag games. Though she'd grow more self-conscious as she aged, at two and then three she knew how to work her way in and join in their laughter, until they'd notice and include her.

This is so different from my own days of sitting on the sidelines of the playground, last picked to play (unless it was a four-square day—I loved four square!). Even though I wasn't a girlie-girl growing up, I hung out with the clusters of girls who liked to gather below the slides to talk about television and boys and makeup in elementary school, chatting by the one tree that had shade on the playground with the precocious bad boy who snuck cigarettes at age nine, just to avoid the running and ball games. I remember standing in the outfield gazing up at the sky, thinking about the moon and space travel and getting bonked right on the head by a softball, just like Charlie Brown. Maybe my own awkwardness in things sporty has contributed to my own skill set, which includes a comfort in making small talk, a weakness for celebrity gossip, and a soft spot for the bad boys and girls—at least the sweet kind of bad—in my classes.

I hoped that by having us as parents, Cece was getting a training in empathy for those who are not so swift and mobile, from her aging, klutzy, but still pretty energetic mothers. Every day after school and playground, while one parent made dinner, the other parent played, and Cece's regimen was rigorous: games of tag up and down the stairs; leaping under blankets to hide from invisible monsters; dance contests and impromptu parades. But sometimes I was plagued by on-again off-again back pain that made it hard to play. Some weeks I had to sit on the sidelines and couldn't move from standing to sitting without wincing.

Cece, Annie, and I had chats about our ages and growing infirmities. Annie suffered from tinnitus and so our system of calling each other from across the room or upstairs had to adapt, especially in the mornings before Annie puts in her hearing aids. Cece got used to the fact that my back was not always reliable for piggyback rides. Sometimes her desire to be carried won out over her empathy, especially after long, sleepy car rides. But at least she was made aware of our differences. I think this helped her develop empathy in an embodied way; to think outside of the frames of reference that her own younger, able body provided. She learned to see not only how someone else might feel, but to feel it, to understand difference kinetically. And, therefore, to understand herself as separate from us but also caringly connected.

These were moments of realization for me, too—ones that will probably increase as I age—and I'd feel a glimmer of shame. But why did I feel ashamed about getting older? It's the one element I had absolutely no control over. I could do more yoga, and swim more and eat less, but I couldn't really help that I was older and that I lived before Cece came. Most of the time, I thought that Annie and I brought more strengths than weaknesses as older parents. We had a strong relationship and a community that took time to build. We were more financially stable, for sure. We knew and understood ourselves enough to laugh more at our weaknesses.

Sometimes Cece teased us that when we get really old, she'll drive us around in our blue Honda, but with us in the baby seats this time. She seemed excited to imagine this future revenge. Sometimes she got into a small worry loop about dying, and about our dying. But we could usually massage her out of it, by bringing her back to the present, to the importance of all of us being together right there, right then. But more than once, I agreed with her, told her that most of us really don't want to die, and that the knowledge that we will die someday connects us. We don't know what's going to happen when we die. It's one of those mysteries that we all have to figure out for ourselves. When I made those speeches, I wondered if they'd come back to haunt me in some teenage tantrum or therapy session in the future. But it seemed important to be truthful to her about those very basic questions. To share what I don't know with her, as well as what I have faith in, which is the importance of our lives together and our connections with other people.

I wondered if all children must discover in some way that their parents' bodies and selves are separate from their own. I worried sometimes that facing these limits of our own humanity might lead Cece to feel loss and to fear our inevitable abandonment. I wanted to know how to help bridge that experience to independence, empathy, connection, and even faith. Does a child who is adopted necessarily have to learn that lesson with different paths? An adopted child, if he or she is lucky enough to be told at least some of the facts of the adoption early enough, must learn that the person who gave birth to them couldn't take care of them. They may also learn that their adoptive parents, the people entrusted to take care of them, couldn't give birth to them because of some kind of physical difference (infertility, age, or lack of sperm or egg). They must also learn the need to trust in love that does not follow the most likely path of physical proximity. I am loved because I was sought out. My parents searched for and found me. Maybe some children fear the *what ifs* of roads not taken and inevitable change. And, perhaps, for some children, there's also that knowledge of the in-between, a time where there were no parents, no single official person in charge: time in foster care or in orphanages, for example. Cece had nurses and huggers, a staff of people to care for her. She also had a birth mother who couldn't decide if she could live with giving her up. And two women who met her within a few weeks after her birth who were waiting to become her mothers. Her first bonds were both interrupted and then perhaps also multiplied.

15

SISTER-COUSINS
Summer into Fall, 2015

WHEN CECE WAS A LITTLE older than three and just learning how to tell a story, she and her cousin Meechie had a ritual. At the breakfast table, after we'd all had our fill, they'd tell the story about how they spent their time together waiting to be born. They said that they were there, up above the clouds, Cece watching Annie and me, Meechie watching her mom. They were playing Uno, eating Cheez-Its, and telling jokes, until it was time. And then one and then the other swooped down to earth. Cousins, connected before they were born, connected even before the legal act of signing papers that made them cousins, and before that, the waiting and training. This was a creation story that Cece seemed to crave in addition to the one that we told her. Ours was about being chosen by her birth mother, about meeting Cece at the Cradle, and about falling in love with her, and about her adoption. Maybe this other creation story was so powerful because *she* was the one who chose *us*. And maybe because it was less lonely. Instead of waiting at the Cradle in limbo, disconnected from her birth mother and not yet adopted by us, in her fantasy she was waiting with her cousin, family already made.

In African American culture, a cousin is someone with whom you are intimately bonded but not always related to by blood.

There is nothing quite like a cousin. If you're lucky, a cousin can be a friend, a sister from another mother. You can be a "cuz" or "play cousin" or "kissing cousin" with your favorite next-door neighbor, the one you grew up with, or with your best friend, or your first crush. I see this special status of cousins as a reflection of the ways that family boundaries can be extended by need, compatibility, circumstance, geography, and will, similar to the ways that some women take it upon themselves to mother their whole neighborhood as everyone's Grandmama, Big Mama, or Ma'dear.

Meechie's role as a special sister-cousin has been clear from Cece's very first days as part of our family. Our photographs and videos from those first days at home feature Meechie at age fourteen, already prominently involved: holding Cece on her lap; playing with her, together with her sister, Allie; participating in our first trips to restaurants and parks. In one video taken by Meechie of Cece asleep on the red couch her very first night home, Meechie watches Cece as she sleeps. The lens is in extreme close-up, so that you can see the oily folds of Cece's eyelids, the sweet bubble-gum nose taking up a large part of the frame. You hear Cece's quiet breaths, then Meechie exclaiming in wonder and delight, "She's snoring!"

Meechie was Cece's first best friend, even given their more-than-thirteen-year age difference. Sometimes cousins, sometimes mother and daughter, sometimes siblings, their relationship included bickering, snuggling, dance lessons, conversation. They could spend hours on a Saturday evening if Meechie wasn't working or hanging out with her friends sprawled on Meechie's bed, coloring or watching cartoons on an iPad.

Even before we became mothers, Meechie and her sister, Allie, frequently spent time with us on the weekends. Then, the year after we became mothers, my sister decided to change careers and move to Georgia to jump-start her life in a less expensive setting. Becky has been a social worker all her adult life—maybe one of the world's oldest professions and, certainly, one of the least appreciated. Meechie decided that she wanted to stay here in the Chicago area. So, during the week, she lived with my father in St. Charles, Illinois, a nearby suburb to the west of us; most weekends, she lived with us in Annie's study, getting her city fix. As aunts, those weekends with Meechie taught us how to build a home where young people felt cared for and how to balance nurturing and space, flexibility and firmness. Sometimes we made mistakes. We learned how to admit them, how to redraw the boundaries that were too tenuous, how to set a curfew or follow up on a chore. We learned how important it was to think out loud together, to problem solve in ways that included her. Through Meechie, we learned that proximity also means relationship; it can be messy but also full of joy. And much of that joy came from sharing with Meechie our process of becoming mothers to Cece.

Our times together, out at the park, or at the playground, or on weekend trips to waterparks or a rented cabin in Saugatuck, Michigan, were precious. At sixteen, Meechie was able to sustain the level of high-energy activity that Cece craved during her terrible twos and threes. We tried to keep up but sometimes simply ran out of steam. We also had a chance to enjoy Meechie's own beautiful humor and insight. And, it gave us a chance to get snippets of time to ourselves. It gave Cece a younger person to love and play with. Sometimes we ran into wrinkles. We'd assume that Meechie was free to babysit when she had her own plans. Sometimes Meechie needed our undivided attention, and sometimes Cece did, and we'd have to learn how and when to give both. But those tensions are part of making family. Meechie had incredible insights about babies and children that she shared with us. She knew how to talk to Cece, how to dive deep into games of the imagination without self-consciousness, how to lovingly scoop her up and divert her attention, fending off a tantrum. And she seemed to know intuitively when we aunties needed her support.

In public, we found that many people didn't quite know how to read our family, all of us connected and loving but our roles not necessarily clear. Many onlookers faced with the puzzle of two middle-aged women, one Black, one white, a Black teenager and a Black baby, assumed that Meechie was Cece's mother. Meechie told us that this projected image as a teenage mother made her uncomfortable at times, one of the ways that she felt stereotyped. To be put in the role of grandparent reminded me of my age. For those onlookers who had more imagination, Meechie and Cece were both our daughters. While I enjoyed this image, I felt a pang of guilt, worried that my sister was being erased from the picture. Our house was furnished with photos from our trips and Christmas and birthday photos that featured the four of us. Sharing the joy and some responsibility of taking care of Meechie with my sister took some care and balance.

Sometimes Meechie missed her mom, needing her in ways that we couldn't replace. This was especially true during one of the hardest events that we faced together, Meechie's loss of her best friend, Sara, to cancer, a few months after her mother's move to Georgia. Sara was only seventeen.

Meechie, Cece, Annie, and I were playing down in the basement when the phone rang. After hearing a few quiet words on the other end, Meechie flew into the bathroom and locked the door.

Sara's aunt had called with news of her passing. Sara had spent a long time in remission from the cancer that haunted a good part of her teen years. She had spent much of that time with Meechie, styling each other's hair, baking amazing cakes, going to thrift stores and amusement parks, exploring the Hyde Park neighborhood together and the potential of college life at the University of Chicago. But then, just as the summer weather began to turn, a series of difficult flus wore Sara down.

We could hear Meechie's wails from the other side of the door. The sound of her raw anguish chilled me. I asked her to open the door and let me comfort her, which she did. I found this strong girl sitting on the floor, felled by adult-sized shock and pain. I had no advice, no way to fix it. To hold her and rock her was all that I knew how to do.

Meechie went to the funeral by herself, by request, and I waited in a nearby Starbucks so that I could pick her up and take her home. I felt completely out of my depth, none of these challenging months of mothering having prepared me for this. As we drove home, Meechie was closed in on herself, silent, so I didn't talk, either. I did hum a little from time to time.

The next few weekends, Meechie would often stay alone in her room listening to music or quietly sketching. Annie and I would knock softly, trying to bring her out, getting her to come to the table to eat, trying to get her to talk to us and accept our hugs, making sure she didn't sleep too much.

Cece was the only one in the house who seemed to know how to bring Meechie out of her grief, even if briefly. She knew how to make her smile, presenting Meechie with her favorite stuffed animals to hold or making funny faces. She let herself into Meechie's room, flinging herself on her body as she slept, or would bring in a puzzle or a doll and play right there beside her on her bed. Sometimes Meechie tried to explain why she was sad and would cry, and Cece would comfort her.

Sometimes we were worried that Meechie's sadness would be overwhelming to Cece or that Cece's high energy was hard for Meechie. When Meechie seemed especially down, we'd take Cece out of the house to the park or to play outside. Sometimes Cece's bluntness made us flinch. She'd ask Meechie, "Are you sad because of your friend who died? Are you sad because she's not coming back?" Or during Meechie's more cheerful times, Cece would ask her, "You're not going to cry anymore, are you?" We worried that naming this loss would send Meechie to an even more difficult place, but Cece's directness made Meechie smile. It took her out of her own pain to try to make it real to this little person who cared so deeply about her. But sometimes even the care of her young cousin wasn't enough, and Meechie would call her mother. Often in the middle of the night, I could hear my sister's soft, reassuring

Sister-cousins! Demitria Pates and Cecelia Royster-Russo, St. Charles, Illinois, 2015. Photograph by Francesca Royster.

murmur, reading aloud from *Harry Potter* like she did when Meechie was younger. Meechie would put her on speakerphone to help her fall asleep.

Our growth as mothers was simultaneous with Meechie's move from childhood to adulthood, shaped both by the loss of her friend and by her relationship with Cece. We would not have known our own capacities as mothers—when to be playful, how to listen and be open—without our relationship with Meechie. We learned by watching her care for Cece. And, during that difficult time, Cece helped us create a more whole loving picture. We learned, through Cece and Meechie, the power of a cousin to expand our conception of nurturing across age.

For Cece, Meechie gave her someone to lean on, learn from, and trust. But their relationship also gave her a first opportunity to care for someone else in need, to see the impact of loss, and to understand the power of what family members can do for each other—to comfort, to calm, and to witness.

16
RESETTING THE TABLE
August 2015

WE HAD FINISHED HEAPING PLATES of fried chicken, spaghetti, and salad; had eaten from the two birthday cakes, one for the children and one for the adults—two slices for me—and the children were running off the sugar high, pausing to be gathered up onto the laps of their parents before running off to chase, tease, and tickle. It was Jacob's birthday, my seven-year-old cousin, tall and bright-eyed and smart. Jacob and his sister, Brooke, were being raised by their mother, father, grandmother, and aunt in this Bronzeville, Chicago, three-flat apartment that my aunt Carolyn had wisely purchased while the property in this once-famous Black metropolis was still cheap.

Cece, age three, chatted with Jacob about the pros and cons of Spider-Man as Jacob scrambled over the lap of his father. I heard him ask my daughter about her father.

"I don't have one," Cece said, looking toward Annie and me, as if to check her answer.

"Everyone has a dad," Jacob said.

"I don't. I have two moms," she said.

"They can't both be your moms," Jacob said. "Maybe a step-mom. They can't both have made you."

Cece looked like she might cry.

The other adults in the room—until this time immersed in their own stories—became quiet, pausing to listen. Cece seemed all alone then, the space between the children and the adults, just a few feet away, impossible to bridge. The overhead light suddenly seemed so bright in that room, and the rooms around it, on the periphery, dim. The television left on during the meal in the front room cast a blue glow in the dark.

It was the innocent question we knew would be coming when we started our family, yet it had me reeling as if I were drunk. Here we were, two women, Black and white, driving down from our mostly white North Side neighborhood to this mostly Black one, with the Black child we adopted together, crossing lines of race and neighborhood and class. Now Annie, Cece, and I sat closely together at one end of the table.

I stood up.

"We're married," I said out loud to no one in particular, my voice shaking. It was as if Jacob and Cece were in a play, and the adults were in the audience, and I'd violated the rules by speaking to one of the actors. "Did you know that? Annie and I are both Cece's parents and we're married."

The women in the back kitchen were doing the work of scraping and washing the dishes, listening and not listening. They looked small from here, like miniatures. I feared that this interaction had created a breach. A moment of not belonging. A break.

Chicago had seen an epidemic of gunfire that summer of 2015, some of it happening in this community, the evil offspring of gentrification and neglect. But my aunt Carolyn had made her home a place of refuge. The windows had been replaced by translucent cubes of safety glass, but there were plants everywhere despite the dimmed light, along with posters of jazz greats, African statues that she'd unearthed at yard sales, and paintings by friends. I thought of what work it takes to create a space where you can come and go safely in this city. What it takes to create a space where you can be both recognized and seen. And how we also sometimes close ourselves off to create comfort and familiarity.

And then the elders, Aunt Carolyn and the others, moved into the room. They dried their soapy hands on the impromptu aprons they made from dishcloths. Their bodies carried the smells from the meal we've just eaten. They made a circle around us.

PART III

———

GIRL MEETS WORLD

SUMMER 2016

17

WE ALSO BELONG
TO THE WORLD
Summer 2016

I have known from the very first day of each of your lives that I cannot guarantee your safety. That is the thing that the voyeurs really want to drink in. That is why they make me so mad, really. Because the truth is it *is* frightening. But the fear is not the heart of the thing. The fear is what comes because your preciousness collides with the ways of the world.

—Imani Perry, *Breathe: A Letter to My Sons*

IT WAS BECOMING INCREASINGLY CLEAR that our family belonged to the world. This became clearer still in the momentous summer of 2016, as we were rocked by the news of the Orlando Pulse killings, the murders of Freddie Gray, Philando Castile, Alton Sterling, and others. We were already holding in our hearts the unjust deaths of Chicago's Laquan McDonald, Tamir Rice, Michael Brown, Sandra Bland, and Trayvon Martin, and the ways that justice seemed elusive for them. We were on the eve of a contentious election that would further divide the nation, bringing on more violence, more hate. In many ways, belonging to the world was an awareness that Annie and I sought—to expand the nuclear model of a family, rather than to replicate it, in order to open up its boundaries to connect to a larger community. But connecting to the world also meant that we had to grapple with the ways that our lives were shaped by the outside violence in the world. We were learning how to navigate those forces, how to protect Cece while also helping her to understand violence in order to not internalize it, the balance that Black queer poet, scholar, father, and friend Jeffrey Q. McCune, Jr. writes in his poem "For Escobar":

> Know ugly, love pretty.
> You must plant language.
> You mind the matter,
> You sharecrop.
> You help sweep,
> Pray . . .

McCune writes this poem in reflection about raising a Black boy in this current moment, and he evokes the importance of past survival for now. But raising a Black girl also requires instilling this combination of tenderness and knowing. It, too, is a labor of love that must both nurture while being insurgent. In the same way that we had to contend with history, the present was a challenge that unfolded before us. Cece was only four years old, but already some of the most difficult lessons of our motherhood were upon us.

18

STORIES WE TELL AFTER ORLANDO

June 2016

WE WERE IN LAILA'S BACKYARD for a Sunday barbecue, a cool and windy Chicago June day that immediately followed one of the hottest days so far that year. Annie and I brought Cece and her best friend, Gilda, to the barbecue, and they had dressed themselves in layers, with leggings and hoodies and sequined dresses, disco wear for four-year-olds. Gilda and Cece, both only children, loved make-believe and swinging together on the same swing, Gilda's pale chubby arm wrapped around Cece's darker, slender one. We were at the end of a daylong play date, and we'd already survived two playgrounds and several tearful standoffs, the ups and downs that come with best friends so young. So Annie and I came hungry for some time with our adult friends.

The closely packed, brick three-flat apartment buildings on either side of Laila's yard provided us with some protection from the wind for a good part of the afternoon. But as the sun went down and the light dimmed, we piled on more jackets and scarves over our T-shirts and shorts. Gusts of wind randomly fanned the flames until they were visible over the lid of the grill as Laila cooked. I looked out for Laila at the grill while Annie played catch with the little girls. But I had to do so in stealth, because Laila is as stubborn as she is glamorous. She had insisted on wearing a jacket with green flowing sleeves as she tended the fire, and while she put her long, graying blonde hair up in a chopsticked bun, she also pulled out long wispy strands to achieve high femme style. They flew around her face in the wind, flirting with the flames.

We were all getting together because later that week Laila would be boarding a plane for the twelve-hour flight home to spend the summer with her aging mother and father. Her home was Lebanon, and we had already experienced losing her for several months in 2006. During that visit home, Israel and Lebanon's tensions grew into a violent series of bombings that came very close to Laila's Beirut apartment. At the worst of that time, Laila sent her friends here frantic group letters conveying her worry and sometimes her despair. She flashed back to her earlier experiences as a child in wartime Beirut in the 1970s, and again during the war there in 1982. For a few agonizing weeks, her letters stopped coming altogether.

The afternoon of our barbecue was the same day as the early-morning shootings in Orlando, Florida, where forty-nine people were killed and at least fifty others wounded. They were killed while practicing a rite that we all considered as sacred and necessary as going to church might be for some. They were dancing the night away in a gay nightclub called Pulse. That morning, we woke up to this news, blinking still without our glasses. The magnitude of the news headline was hard to fathom as it flashed across the screens of our phones.

It felt wrong that mass shootings were part of the everyday fabric of our lives, and, most likely, for Cece and Gilda, their future. The story felt both shocking and sadly familiar: the apparently easy availability of weapons and that pattern of anger taken to the next outrageous step. And then there's the gay part. Even when I first heard that the shooting took place at a gay bar, I wondered if the killer, Omar Mateen, might be gay himself. Why Orlando, I thought? Why a mostly unknown dance club? I thought of the messy, red-hot fury of hate and desire when they get mixed together. As Annie and I talked about the shooting in hushed voices on the playground that morning, we thought of Matthew Shepard. We thought of the recent theory that Shepard most likely knew his killers.

Some have written that the narrative that Mateen is gay only confirms the idea that gay people are dysfunctional, self-hating, and perverse. But I'd argue that bringing to light that Mateen may have been gay or feared that he was gay confirms that even in this era of marriage equality legislation and positive and authentic-feeling television shows about LGBTQ experiences, such as *Modern Family* and *Grace and Frankie*, homophobia still exists and sometimes turns inward. For both gay and straight people alike, homophobia can dwarf our sense of humanity. When combined with a culture of guns, militarism, and sexism, homophobia—not homosexuality—can kill.

According to some reports, the shooter was a frequenter of gay bars and gay online dating sites. A witness at Pulse said that he remembered seeing Mateen nursing drinks in the back, not dancing, watching others, both yearning and seething in anger. His ex-wife told reporters that his anger turned violent and that he beat her frequently. His ex-wife also said that Mateen shared with her the secret desires that he hated in himself. Omar Mateen's father told reporters that it was ridiculous to think that his son was gay.

In our neighborhood, we sometimes felt conspicuous, as a queer and interracial family, an African American and white mother and an African American child. Would we be the next targets in this moment where all public space felt so tense, we wondered? The news cycle moved on, unfortunately, to more shootings: Philando Castile in Minnesota, Alton Sterling in Baton Rouge, the five police officers in Dallas, mass shootings at the Harvest Music Festival in Las Vegas and at Marjory Stoneman Douglas High School in Parkland, Florida. Even with so much gun violence just about every day here in Chicago, Mateen's has continued to shake us.

And so that afternoon our precarious position was very much on our minds. We could feel it in the care that Laila had taken to pour the chips we brought into little, brightly colored bowls scattered around the yard. In the tender acts of public affection that Laila's partner, Martina, showed her that afternoon, an arm hovering over her waist as they stood at the table, taking stock of condiments. They are both tall, but Martina is thin and wiry, while Laila is more full. Martina made sure that we all knew that Laila had specially grilled the onions and that there was enough for all. Annie and I were sure to remind the two little girls to play with the plastic bowling set that Laila and Martina borrowed from a neighbor especially for them. From the selection of chairs assembled to pull up to the table, I chose the love seat so that Annie and I could sit together. We all wanted to sit close to one another. No one was drinking anything harder than iced tea that day.

We sat down with our grilled hotdogs, chicken, Italian sausages, ballpark plumpers, and tofu (just to keep the bases covered). It was then that Cece asked us to tell a story of when each of us hurt ourselves, and when we got better. That had become one of her favorite topics of conversation. She started being interested in these "hurt-and-sick" stories, I suspect, after witnessing Annie seriously ill from a twenty-four-hour stomach virus. It might be the first time that Cece had seen one of us ill. Annie, usually a stoic, couldn't even move to shut the door to the bathroom. She was on the floor, moaning loudly. As I ran to help her, Cece bounced from chair to couch and back again in a kind of manic despair, her eyes feverishly bright in her velvet-dark skin. Luckily, Meechie felt for her and took her out of the house to a family baby shower for the day. By the time they returned, Annie was sleeping peacefully, and the next day, she seemed pretty much herself, able to sit up in bed and play with Cece. After that day, Cece started collecting stories of accidents and sickness, best with the details of blood and puke included, but always with the ending that things got better.

When Cece asked us for our stories, we paused. How to choose just the right story? How to choose the story that captures just the right amount of real-life pain? Collectively, we had experienced war, interpersonal violence, car accidents, cancer, the death of a parent. I could see in Cece's eyes that she was waiting for *that* story, the one where I climbed up on a closet shelf and fell, cutting off half of my littlest toe along the way.

"I was about four, your age," I say, "and Granddad had been watching me while working on his dissertation, typing away in his study while I played close by. There was all this blood. I had never seen so much blood! And Granddad wrapped my foot in a towel and threw me in the front seat. He forgot about the car seat! He drove me to the hospital, honking at the other cars all the way."

I saw my father then, tenderly wrapping my foot with a small Holiday Inn hand towel, his hands shaking. Even while I felt the strength of his arms as he carried me to the car, I could feel him shaking.

Then it was Laila's turn. She told of being hit by a car as a little girl in Beirut, and then being picked up by a neighbor, dusted off, and carried upstairs to her mother. Martina told of the time that she was bumped into by "a big white lady" on the streets of Bogota, where she grew up. She told Cece that her mother took care of her and helped her feel better. But she didn't mention whether the big white lady ever apologized. Annie described riding her bike in our neighborhood with her friend Lourdes and falling off as boys threw firecrackers at her, skinning both of her knees. As I listened, I pictured my sturdy girlfriend, vulnerable on her wobbling bike as she made her way home. Even though I'd heard this story many times, I found myself wondering if Annie was targeted by the boys because she was a lesbian, or a woman, or a white person in a mostly Black and brown neighborhood, or just that she happened to ride by at the wrong time. Annie reached over to Cece and pulled her to her lap. Cece touched the network of white squiggly scars on Annie's knee with her long fingers as she listened.

This process of carefully and tenderly choosing which stories to tell this young person, a person we all loved, helped soothe the jitteriness of the day. As her mother, I wondered if Cece somehow gleaned this connection between storytelling and healing. Our gratitude for the occasion was heard in our laughter at the end of each story, which might have been a little louder than usual.

None of us brought up what had happened in Orlando, though it was on all of our minds.

Joy, who prefers the pronoun "they," offered to go next. They were one of Annie's former students, and this was Cece's first time meeting them, so Cece was a little shy at first. But Joy has a wide boyish grin and kind green eyes, and Cece quickly warmed up to them. Cece started calling Joy "Joey," to their delight. Even though they are very serious-minded in their work around international rights, they laugh easily and often.

Joy told us of being on a bus in Syria in 2009 or 2010, before the revolution, when they heard a man standing just outside the steps to the bus let out a yelp. He had just sliced the top of his head on a jagged piece of metal, a part of the aging body of the bus. At first, an Iraqi man who was also on the bus tried to help, but the injured man, a Korean tourist, spoke English but not Arabic, and so Joy stepped in to help. The three, an American-born transgender person, an Iraqi refugee, and a Korean tourist, nervously made their way to the hospital. Joy looked at each of us for recognition as they shared the fear of going to the Syrian police, or of giving the hospital their names. All three were outsiders, each vulnerable.

At Joy's precise description of the injury, their hand chopping the air to show the angle of the slice of metal into skin, Cece ran into Laila's arms and hid her head in her chest. Cece asked hesitantly how much blood there was, but Joy was somewhere else, back perhaps at the busy road, hot and maybe dusty, too. The harsh afternoon sun made waves of heat rise from the tar, and there were the fumes from the buses and cars. Maybe Joy was carrying the injured man on their shoulders, even though the man was considerably taller, trying to get him to walk. Maybe they had to pass a checkpoint, or maybe the police were interspersed in the crowd, guns strapped to their uniformed chests or in holsters, and Joy had no choice but to look them each in the eye, searching for the right face to ask for help.

Cece turned away to give Laila a raspberry on her sunburned neck. Then Cece and Laila went back and forth, exchanging raspberries and squealing with laughter. They grew louder and louder and then Laila stood up and swung Cece in her arms, higher than her mothers would, and Cece kicked her legs out behind her with excitement. She seemed to hover there, impossibly swimming the air. Her friend Gilda held up her arms to be swung, too. Then we passed the girls between us, swinging them high, dipping them low, giggling in defiance of their full stomachs. We danced together in a circle without music. Cece jumped and skipped, her small dreadlocks bobbing. Gilda twirled. Annie and I started a boogaloo. We never learned if Joy and the injured man made it to the hospital.

I HAD NEVER BEEN TO Pulse. I had only been to Orlando for vacation destinations, such as a trip to Disney World and sailing from nearby Cape Canaveral for a cruise to the Bahamas with my mother. But when I heard the news reports, Pulse seemed very familiar to me. I had been to many lesbian and gay clubs. In Milwaukee, Annie and I walked into the quietest gay club we'd ever seen. Just seven or eight men, nursing their drinks and not looking or speaking to one another. No one looked up when we entered, and we walked out almost as fast as we came in. But the place itself was beautiful: art deco mirrors, a green-and-pink neon jukebox. *Someone* cared or once cared about that place.

At Star Gaze, one of Chicago's few lesbian bars, now defunct, I had been part of a crowd of dancing women so joyful and so overheated that when the owner cranked up the massive fan, we let our shirts and skirts fly up with the breeze to show our underwear, giving a collective "whoop!" More than once, I have gotten so lost in the bass of the music, dancing by myself, that I became oblivious to those around me. One night, I sat with a group of friends for hours at an "Alternative Lifestyles Night" in State College, Pennsylvania, drinking but mostly talking about the future for hours, until our waitress sat down with us, the club ready to close, the ice in our glasses long melted.

I didn't know what the DJ had chosen for Latin Night at Pulse in Orlando on Saturday, June 11, 2016. Maybe salsa, maybe house, maybe oldies that parents and grandparents once enjoyed. Folks might have been dancing in couples or by themselves. There might have been regulars and newbies, maybe even people who just wandered in, a break from traveling with their families. From the news, I learned that the crowd was predominantly brown and Black like me and my friends, and so young. Actually, Omar Mateen was only twenty-nine years old. I imagined myself, my younger self, there in that crowd.

I didn't know if Omar Mateen had a lover who was at Pulse that night. The reports denied that rumor. But I imagined that his hate for himself, and for the reflections of himself that he saw in the others, overwhelmed any feelings of love. I didn't know if he wanted to kill himself, or if was he was trying to save himself somehow. But I wondered what was the definitive moment of despair for him that night? What was the tipping point when he felt that the joy that the others were expressing around him seemed impossible to enter? Their collective whoop of joy? When did despair turn to rage?

Even having felt moments of despair myself, I couldn't wrap my head around what Omar did, its violence, its desire to upend, to punish, to erase. I forced myself to read the stories of the survivors. When I read them, I was there. I flashed on an image of myself trapped in a bathroom stall with fifteen or twenty others. What would I have done? In my mind's eye, I looked everywhere else, at the rose tattoo on the back of someone else's neck, at someone's worn Doc Martens, at my hands that have calmed Cece during her worst tantrums, at my silver spiral wedding ring, but I couldn't make myself raise my head. I was afraid but it seemed important to me to somehow imagine looking Omar Mateen in the eye. To see him in all of his humanity, even in the face of my destruction.

Thinking of this, I reached out to hold my daughter a little tighter on my lap.

19
TO MY LOVE
July 2016

ANNIE, IF YOU COME DOWN *Arthur Avenue on an early summer evening, you'll see the red clouds, with blue and gray and even green behind the railroad tracks. You'll see the seafoam green of the Electric Company, the orange lights come on, and the colors start to fade. But not quite yet. As your eyes adjust to the dusky light, you'll be able to make out the children on bicycles and the people still lingering on their porches, having a smoke or a beer. The street is narrow enough that you can talk across it, and someone will hear you. You don't even have to yell, just a loud "outside" voice is enough. You'll hear the last of the rush hour trains and occasional cars, but it's quiet for Chicago, because the linden trees seem to protect the little street from the busy ones around it, the sound of buses and city busyness down Clark Street. Only when it's the middle of the night and you've left your window open to let in the smell of the linden trees and to cool down the air, might you hear the floating sound of the Red Line, which is a whole five blocks away, and it might sound like it's right there. Bing, Bong! Loyola. Or firecrackers, you hope they're firecrackers, the Fourth of July was weeks ago but they could be firecrackers, you tell yourself. Pop! Pop! Pop! Pop! And the silence, no sound again. No screams, that may have come from an alley or the kid's park a few blocks away. But that's later, after you've fallen asleep, arms around your pillow or around the child who is sleeping on our chest or your arm or your tummy, or who has worked her way all the way upside down, so that it's her feet, running in her sleep and her hard, strong toes gripping onto your leg, but you try not to cry out or hold any resentment, because she took so long to go to sleep. And when you hear the firecrackers (firecrackers? says your heart), I watch you reach and pat the back of the child, and you reach over the child to pat me, your sweetheart, and it reassures you and you can fall back to sleep.*

I see you. Now it's early evening again, another day is done so soon, so soon, and you have just made your way upstairs, at last, to your bed, and I see you. The little girl who seems to never want to sleep is in her room, playing Legos instead of putting on her pajamas like she's supposed to, and you can see her from your bed down the long hallway. I am making up Cece's bed, setting up the pillows and blankets and huge white bear that you and I bought the day after Valentine's Day, when we were supposed to be on a date. Cece loved it, but she still never actually sleeps in her own bed. It's a twin, a big girl bed, we reassure her, but it doesn't stick. And so we put on our pajamas, and we set the bed up for the nighttime ritual that might just take two hours, or more. You set up her snacks, the yogurt and the milk and the water, just a centimeter in each glass, to prevent bedwetting. I plug in my phone, the alarm set for an alarming time of 4:45. I see you. My bookcase has a huge pile of books that I haven't read yet. (Why is it that all of my favorite authors have written books this summer, when I have just about no reading time?) My bookcase has a shell, a little painting of a flower, a photo of our little one at age two, blurry because it is capturing the movement of a toddler, and an old framed photo of you when you were only fourteen and on the bowling team. Your team was called "The Regulars." The bookcase has sex positive books that have not been cracked in a while, and they are dusty. We'll have to probably put them away soon, since Cece is five and fast learning how to read.

This is our life. We are the regulars. And even though we don't have enough time alone right now, I want you to know that I see you. I love our life, and I see you.

20
BLACK LIVES MATTER AT HOME
August 2016

You stayed up till 11 pm that night, waiting for the announcement of an indictment. When, instead, it was announced that there was none, you said, "I've got to go." You went into your room, and I heard you crying. I came in five minutes after. I didn't hug you, and I didn't comfort you. I did not tell you that it would be OK, because I have never believed it would be okay. What I told you is what your grandparents tried to tell me: that this is your country, that this is your world, that this is your body, and that you must find some way to live within the all of it. I tell you now that the question of how one should live within a Black body, within a country lost in a Dream, is the question of my life, and the pursuit of this question, I have found, ultimately answers itself.

—Ta-Nehisi Coates, *Between the World and Me*

OURS WAS PROBABLY THE FRIENDLIEST neighborhood I've ever lived in, with neighbors who were in our business, but in a good way. We were in a book club with four women whom I admire greatly: Stacy, a university administrator; Pat, a child psychologist; Emily, a labor organizer; and Nancy, an ex-schoolteacher and artist. Before she passed, our neighbor who lived next door for fifty years, knew the names, ages, and ethnicities of every household on the block. Many of our neighbors bought their houses generations ago and held on to them through difficult times, passing them along to their children, thereby inadvertently keeping outsiders out. These first families on our street mirrored the layered and difficult history of immigration in Chicago: Irish and Jewish and Swedish immigrants who lived here in houses first built after World War I; then, as the city's racial boundaries expanded, Latinx and Asian and African and African American families have moved in. Annie and I are among three other LGBTQ households, though we are the first interracial one and the first raising a child.

For the most part, our neighbors have embraced Annie and me as we created our new home. They've celebrated Cece's adoption with us, stopped by and partied along with our blood and chosen families when Annie and I celebrated first our civil union and then, when the laws changed, our marriage. Cece could ride her bike and scooter outside in all weather, draw on our neighbors' sidewalks with her sidewalk chalk, and make snow angels in their front yards. We've felt safe as a queer multiracial family.

For the most part.

As things heated up in the city in the summer of 2016, I noticed a Black Lives Matter banner in the neighborhood, a simple one made with a white sheet and a black Sharpie. Someone had hung it on the fence along the tracks at Ravenswood Avenue, the quiet one-way street intersecting ours, where block clubs labored to make gardens of sunflowers and redbud trees in spite of the weeds. The banner lasted only a few days before it was taken down. In its place were blue ribbons that looked like they were made up of the torn plastic recycling bags circulated by the city. The ribbons were everywhere. Blue Lives Matter. These stayed up. I could feel the neighborhood hunkering down, bracing itself against the violence it perceives elsewhere in the city. There were 762 homicides in Chicago in 2016. When we opened our bedroom windows at night, we could sometimes hear gunshots. Maybe we all wanted to imagine that those gunshots were happening somewhere else, blocks, miles, neighborhoods away from us.

Later that summer, Annie and Cece were on their way to the park after school. They pass the courtyard of the police station around the corner along the way. A scruffy older white man asked Cece, who was riding her bike on the sidewalk a little ahead of Annie, "What are you doing riding on this sidewalk? Where is your mother?" He was putting up the blue ribbons as he did this. Annie said, "I *am* her mother," and the man was taken aback. He seemed not to know what to say at first. Then he said to Cece, "Well, you should listen to your mother." Cece, who often talked to strangers, asked him why he's putting up the ribbons and he said, "To help with peace." He managed to compliment Cece on her dress.

I wondered and feared what Cece was learning about her Black body and how others saw it, how she was learning to occupy space. I wondered and feared what would have happened if she were alone and a little bit older. I wondered what would have happened if I had been the mother who was walking with Cece past the police station, two Black people with no white buffer. I thought about our experiences in restaurants and stores, how people sometimes treated us differently when Annie was with us versus when Cece and I were alone, the increased chill in the atmosphere, the mood of impatience as we'd decide on our order.

After one of these experiences in a café in our neighborhood, Annie and I confronted the owners, describing the tension there when Cece and I were alone. The owners, a white couple, shook their heads. They said our experience was "impossible."

"We're sorry if you felt that way. But we serve every kind of people here. We even have transgender people here. We are more liberal than liberal," they told us. The couple prided themselves on their international savvy, you could tell. In fact, the café made international travel its theme, and the couple often dressed the part. That day, one of them was wearing a Batik print shirt and a battered straw fedora, as if just arriving from vacation. The other's thin wrists and arms were lined with bangles made of silver and bone. They jangled as she put her blonde hair behind her ears. "We hope you don't let this incident end a really good business relationship," she said, smiling as if to say, "We're all good, right?" The exchange ended with one of the co-owners asking me if I'd email the server to explain, because she was so upset that she'd been accused of being a racist. "You're a teacher. Maybe you can talk her through it." Even in my anger, I accepted the torn piece of paper with her email, the reflex of politeness deep in my muscle memory.

I thought of my own experience of racism growing up in Chicago and then in Nashville, Tennessee, as a young girl, and about the precise lessons that I learned about the relative value of my skin, darker than sand, lighter than a paper bag, as I came of age. How even I learned to compare my skin with that of the other Black girls around me, to decide who would be understood as smarter, more crush-worthy, nicer, safer. I tried to remember when I learned to round my shoulders to make myself less visible, so that I can unlearn it now; when I learned to smile and nod at whatever anyone asked me. I wondered about my good manners and "proper" voice, the ways that it opened many doors. Sometimes my voice wasn't enough, though. I remembered looking for my first apartment as a new graduate student in liberal Berkeley, California, in the late 1980s. I spoke first on the phone to my prospective landlord. She loved that I was going to be a graduate student in English, that I would study Shakespeare. She told me that I sounded "very bright" and invited me to come check out the apartment on the spot. But when I arrived on her doorstep and held out my hand to shake hers, she only shook her head. "No, not you. There must be some sort of mistake," she said.

We put a Black Lives Matter sign in our window and, as I discovered at our next book club, it was the subject of conversation on our street. One of our neighbors told us that her son was upset about the sign. He told his mother that he didn't understand why it had to be here, in this neighborhood. I wasn't sure if her son was upset because he felt that the sign wasn't needed or because he felt it was. His own skin is racially ambiguous and could be read as Latinx or multiracial or Italian or Greek. Like many teenagers in Chicago, he wore loose-fitting hip-hop-inspired clothing. I'd seen him strolling down the sidewalk with clusters of his friends, or sitting with a girlfriend in a parked car listening to music. I wondered what his own experience in our neighborhood had been, if he had ever been stopped by the police. Later that afternoon, I watched him as he slammed a tennis ball against the wall of his house. He didn't look up when Cece and I walked past. He just continued throwing the ball. *Wham. Wham.* The ball always hit the same spot, just below his porch window. Precise. Thinking about his intensity, I wondered, what was he learning about his body, and ours, that summer? What was he learning about our neighborhood?

It was clear that a second civil rights movement was happening all around us. Black Lives Matter was growing into a powerful national movement, with expanded agendas to address all kinds of matters of structural racism, from housing to education inequities to gun violence. That summer in our city, protesters occupied Homan Square, a secretive police detention facility, demanding attention to brutality there. Black Lives protestors marched down Michigan Avenue, Chicago's number one shopping district, shutting the area down for three days. In July 2016, Natalie Braye, Sophia Byrd, Eva Lewis, and Maxine Wint, four Black teenage girls, organized a successful peaceful silent sit-in with more than one thousand attendees at Millennium Park downtown. They protested gun violence and police brutality in Chicago and strove to bring together divided communities of youth. I tried my best to keep up with the protests, and I reposted stories and art on Black Lives Matter on Facebook, talked about it with friends and family and at our breakfast table. But I wouldn't go to the protests myself. I told myself it was because I was busy as a working mother, which was true, and that I was too old. But the truth was, I was afraid. At least once every day, I thought about dying and about not being there for Cece. What would happen to her if we weren't there? Would she become part of the system that we've always feared? I knew friends who had gone to jail in the recent wave of protests leading up to the election and had limbs broken. One of my students watched her friend get punched in the face at a protest on our campus that past spring. I had protested before, during the Gulf War, during the many invasions of Central America, in support of women's rights over their bodies, but I always avoided jail—when it was time to move up in line to be taken away, I always opted out. I had things to get done, I told myself. I was in school. I was "uplifting the race" my way. I told myself I was afraid of disappointing my family. But the truth was, I was afraid for my body. And then, I was afraid for Cece's body, too. What I was learning that summer was just how expendable we were.

My fear for Cece's body, as well as my own, was powerfully captured in a graphic, "The Invisible Load of Motherhood: Mothering Black Children," created by Chasity Holcomb, a Black mother of two girls and a licensed counselor in Texas, and Erica Djossa, a white mother of three biracial children and a licensed psychotherapist. The graphic includes the hidden labor of explaining police violence, worrying that their child will be perceived as a threat, and protecting their innocence. For our family, queerness as it works together with race adds another layer of difference. But queerness also gives us a lens of reinvention to dream beyond the present.

ANNIE AND I THOUGHT ABOUT our home as a place of protection, our own queer world. Our favorite thing was our dining room table, a modest wooden table that was meant to seat six but where we sometimes crammed in as many as eighteen people, pushing together folding chairs. Queers, especially queers of color, have always been making their homes where we can, at community centers, encounter groups, night clubs and bars, rent parties, back porches, overflowing living rooms. We are never just individuals. We have never been just individuals. We need home, but our homes are always part of something else, a larger project of survival that is connected to others' projects of survival, even when it appears that we are hunkering down, going underground, tending our yards and our window boxes.

Sometimes, Annie and I questioned our choice to live in our North Side neighborhood, farther away from much of Chicago's Black community on the South Side. I knew that if we had to leave this home, we would make home somewhere else. But we continued to build and nest. We put images of up strong Black women for Cece on the walls: Audre and Lorraine and June and Octavia. A needlepoint of Ida B. Wells. An Alvin Ailey dancer, leaping through the air. Multiple Doc McStuffins squeeze toys lined the bathtub. At the breakfast table, I sneaked Cece videos of Michael Jackson moonwalking, Ella Fitzgerald scatting and swinging to "Mack the Knife." I wanted everything in this space to confirm her Blackness and her beauty. I wanted our home to give her a sense of possibility, to nurture and protect her. But I knew outside comes inside, too. Something—history, my own experience—told me that Cece's future depended not so much on these walls but on her ability to build a home of her own making, her own vision, and to connect that vision to that of others. I was looking forward to someday pulling up a chair at her table.

PART IV

CECE'S JOURNEY

DREAMING THE FUTURE

21
TIME LINE: AGE FIVE
Summer 2017

IT IS A TIME WHEN *Mary Janes are everything, along with head-bands and unicorns and anything featuring rainbows, including paint chips. When it's still okay to sing made-up songs in front of your moms and to kiss the dog on the lips. Right now, matching your clothes with your friends is important, as is the ability to type your name and recognize a list of sight words.*

You like your adult friends and can hold a conversation with them. You are comfortable asking a question at a public art opening: "Why did you choose the color blue?" But sometimes, long political talks at the dinner table make you restless, and you try to get us to play "Little Red School House" instead (a contest where you see who can be the quietest). Or you move over to the couch to watch a show, listening in case anyone mentions your name.

You and I like to go into the garden before camp to watch the flowers grow, and you like to have your shoes and socks off with the sun on your toes. And you still remember that our visit to Puerto Rico two years ago was one of your favorite plane trips. Sometimes you tell people that's where you're from.

Auntie Becky gives you summer knitting lessons, and when you're done, you use the yarn to cocoon your dining room chair, so that you always have the pastel beauty and softness with you.

You make up rhymes with hidden "bad words" in them (fart, booty) to trip up your mother, who might be dazzled by your word play.

You like spending hours in the bathtub, pouring bottles of cold water over your head and practicing flips. You are proud that you've mastered putting your whole head underwater and opening your eyes without your goggles, even though it makes your eyes red. You do it over and over, practicing the hard things until you master them. That's something that you've always done since you were a baby.

You want a little sister really bad.

You're a great friend. I am so proud of that part of you, that loyal openheartedness and empathy, even though I worry about you and want to protect your feelings.

Your temper tantrums are lively and sometimes acrobatic, taking up lots of space. You told me during one of them, "Never laugh at a kid." I will never forget that.

I love sitting in the back seat with you, in the middle seat where the belt mostly works, and where you and I watch my phone. Sometimes you lean your head on my shoulder or take my arm as we watch and ride, and I feel a selfish love then. I hope Annie, stuck in the driver's seat, doesn't feel too left out at those times.

This week, all in one week, you lose your first tooth, and the tooth fairy leaves you sugarless bubble gum, a necklace, and earrings. This week we take you to meet the kids that will be in your class in a new school this fall, and after playing alone and with us for a few minutes, we watch you form a cluster with new girls to dig and pull leaves off of bushes. We watch you both lead and follow. This week, you tell us that a boy from camp has shown you his penis as you walk with your camp group to the Park. You can't remember the word "penis" at first. "It's that funny word," you say. When I say it, I try to keep my voice calm. This week, too, you meet a neighbor boy who invites you to play and then changes the rules as you win the race. I flinch as I overhear him say, "Get me a bottle of water. Get me some ice cream." I can't hear what you say, but a few minutes later, you come in to get two popsicles. We find the white plastic wrapper and the reddened stick on the ground. That will be the last time you play together.

This week there is an eclipse, and it's also the week that you begin kindergarten. I am beset by a fog of mourning about the lightness of time that lifts only after I watch the shadow of the moon cover the sun, and then return us to light four times on the NASA broadcast, moving west to east, from Oregon to Idaho to Missouri to South Carolina.

You have your own thoughts, your own conclusions, and your own theories, which you sometimes voice very clearly and sometimes with a salty look. I try to pay close attention. Sometimes I fail to understand you because we share a healthy faith in our own rightness of things.

Some of the things that you have been right about lately: that you can hold the leash when we walk our new dog, Ruthie, around our block, even when she pulls hard; that plums are good to buy, even when they are not on the grocery list; that rolling down the windows is better than air-conditioning; that it's good to give away the things that you make rather than keep them in a storage box; that you can tell for yourself if the bath water's too hot. You know how to ride your bike on our sidewalk, stopping at the alley, and how to be safe on your scooter, even when doing tricks. Minnie Mouse really is kind of cool and peaches taste better without their skin.

22
A TOY STORY
September 2017

"SORRY, BUT NO *BARBIE AND Friends*." I was peering over Cece's shoulder as she manipulated the Netflix menu. At five years old, she was already very comfortable with my iPhone, clicking and swiping at will. She remembered our passwords better than we did, and one weekend she downloaded two new video games, informing us only after the fact. Cece had heard the Barbie rule so many times before, whether when looking for a TV show or at Target, perusing the toy aisle. "Anything but Barbie. She's too . . . old for you."

Maybe Cece already sensed that this is a ruse, that there would be no Barbie for her at any age, and that we were just stalling while we worked up a good and age-appropriate feminist and anti–white supremacy critique of the doll to tell her. Cece hadn't commented on the fact that her blonde Elsa doll seemed to find herself lost so much of the time, often relegated to the bottom of the toy box or found under a couch cushion or under the bed, where she had been "accidentally" kicked to back among the shadows and gnarliest dust bunnies. Cece might have noticed that when Annie and I played dolls with her, I always made Elsa a whiny villain, bad at backflips and the other stunts that Addy, the American Girl doll who escaped slavery, and Dora the Explorer could do with ease.

Annie refused to handle Elsa at all, preferring instead the little brown baby doll with painted-on brown curls and soft humanely proportioned toddler body, and who smelled inexplicably of chocolate. Cece didn't comment on these things, but I think she was learning.

Like some, but not all, African Americans, when I was Cece's age I wasn't allowed to have Barbie, either. I was told by my parents that they "didn't believe in Barbies," and so that put her somewhere in my mind with toy soldiers (bad) and with Nixon (very bad). I had seen a cartoon of Nixon in my sister's *Mad Magazine*, his jowly, nightmarishly two-toned white and blue-tinged face bursting from the page, holding up his fingers in two peace signs, one tooth colored in. I knew that this was our president, and I got that he was not to be trusted. (Unfortunately, among these lessons, I may have picked up the message that having bad teeth and an unshaved face might also make you untrustworthy, things I have since unlearned.) Nixon and the U.S. military were among the bad things that made my parents and their friends cranky, although sometimes I got in trouble if I said their critiques out loud to my friends or my teachers or out in public. Sure, they liked it when my sister and I stuck our fists out of the window of our moving car, shouting "Black Is Beautiful" and "Power to the People," but I got in trouble when I asked out loud in front of a police officer, "Mom, is that a Pig?"

Anyway, I had a Diahann-Carroll-as-Julia doll, named after the first television show starring a Black actress. It was a birthday gift from my next-door neighbor Monty, one of my first crushes. Julia was ridiculously skinny like Barbie, with hard, knobby breasts and stiff fingers that I had to chew in order to create more pliable gestures. Her shiny bouffant hair was too short to practice cornrowing on, but she had a familiar shade of brown skin, a few shades darker than mine, and she wore a cool nurse's uniform, with a hat and a black velvet cape that I thought made her look like a spy.

Cece knew that Barbie was against our rules. We just hadn't said out loud why she was against our rules, and I was beginning to realize we owed that to her. It was her unrealistic body, of course, and her blankly white, blue-eyed, blonde-haired formulaic beauty. But our distaste for her also had to do with her lack of depth. She had no story to her. Yes, there have been multiple story*lines* written for her, but she never seemed to grow or change. (This might be where she differed from Elsa, who was also blue-eyed and blonde but who did have magical ice powers and, over the course of *Frozen*, managed to work through some pretty serious psychological baggage. And she could sing.) Barbie seemed to exist only in order for one to buy clothing for her, or to apply makeup, or to add a braid. Her camper, her dream house, even her teacher's desk, seemed engineered to put her in poses, rather than in adventures. Poses that required further, perhaps infinite, accessorizing.

At best, in Barbie's world, Cece would see herself as a sidekick. At worst, we feared, she'd see herself as another accessory.

But maybe I was underestimating the power of the imagination. Meechie created a whole lush world for her Barbies, teaching them to fly and to time travel. And many of my queer friends, when they were little, shaved their Barbies' heads, sewed cool, gender-bending clothes for them, created orgies for them, or did other subversive things to make them better represent themselves and their desires.

But I felt like Barbie had an unfair advantage. The mainstream popular kid culture that streamed into our living room still centered on white images and white experiences, even after *Fat Albert and the Cosby Kids*, even after the *Wee Pals* and *Magic School Bus* of my youth. Sure, Doc McStuffins was a godsend, a smart Black girl with imagination and the drive to heal, but did she have to be so selfless? There was Moana and Elena of Avalor, commanding and charismatic brown sheroes, but ones relegated to a mythical past. There were the Trolls in their first movie, with stiff sweeps of bright hair, pastel skin, squat bodies, and comically fat feet. Their embrace of joy and disco in the recent film and television show gave them a definite queer-of-color edge, even if the biggest roles are voiced by white actors and artists—aside from Ron Funches's Cooper. On every kid's channel, you could hear the influences of hip-hop, disco, jazz, and funk, from StoryBots to Nickelodeon to the Disney Channel, but it was rare to see Black kids or adults playing that music. Barbie and those of her ilk—Elsa and Anna and Rapunzel; Wonder Woman and Zena and Mighty Isis; Polly Pocket and Holly Hobbie and even Strawberry Shortcake—all centered on whiteness. Angelina Ballerina, with her upturned nose and posh accent, reads as white, even if she was a mouse. And this still mattered, especially in our historic moment, when our nation remained hopelessly segregated and roiling in racial tension.

The continuation of white-centered kid culture was especially significant in our family. After all, our family looked nothing like any Cece was seeing on television or in the movies. It had been a little more than a year since Cece had looked at her lighter-skinned cousins and said out loud that she wished she could erase her own skin and start over. Just over a year since we'd had talks with teachers, confronted them with a stack of children's books about race and queer families for their woefully lightweight libraries. (This, at a school that has been praised as one of the best public schools in the city.) That year, we tried to look beyond our own painful memories of racism that her comments brought up for us, to really listen to her. We swallowed our shame and the feeling that, as teachers ourselves, we should know better. We organized a Black girls' group to create community with other girls facing similar struggles. We bought Black art for our walls. We gave Cece the chance to pick her own clothes, to develop her own quirky, colorful style, to do her own hair and put lotion on her own skin. Every day, we remembered to tell her that we love her hair, her skin, her ideas, that she's our treasure, and that she's smart and funny and strong and kind.

We reached out to our friends and family for advice, and I sought out one of my best friends from graduate school, Betsy. Over the course of Betsy's own queer motherhood, she has negotiated issues that accompany multiracial identity, disability, and the shifting terrains of gender, as both her partner and one of her children have transitioned. I have been inspired by her gentle, quirky, and clear-eyed children as they've grown to become teenagers and then young adults, making their own way through the world with confidence. Betsy's advice was to try to name, as much as we could, injustice when we saw it, in front of Cece. To model and engage her in analysis of why we think things in our world are unfair. And to dream together of the world that we want to create for ourselves and for others.

Which was why it was important to tell Cece what we truly thought about Barbie. That it wasn't just a doll or just a show. Afterward, we turned off the computer and the iPhone and plopped down with Cece and a stack of drawing paper and colored pencils. We dug out a huge cardboard box and some paints to see what could happen. And we read to her. And we went outside to play and feel the wind and our muscles and our skin browning in the hot September sun, loving ourselves all the more for it.

23
MAKE IT FUNKY, MOM
November 2017

I love myself when I am laughing and
also when I'm looking mean and impressive.

—Zora Neale Hurston

DEAR CECE, I LOVE MYSELF and you too in our Blackness when we are dancing and singing at the top of our lungs. We love show tunes the best, the ones with a little bit of soul: Dreamgirls, Hamilton, Moana. *I watch in your dancing all the styles that you see in our house, Annie's spirited bop, Meechie's muscular leaps, and my loose, goofy boogie. I watch your growing awareness of your own body as you move and love that you are interpreting all of us, as well as the music, and adding to all these moves your own style. I love your willingness to go for broke, as you throw your head back or as you skid like a Lindy Hop dancer between our legs. You have somehow picked up on the moves of vogueing, that imitation of every day giving face, as you spin on the floor and then land on your belly with your head in your hands. The power of extreme juxtaposition and the ephebism—your willingness to do what you do as well as you can, even in an after-homework dining room dance party, your powers of appropriation, branding with your own style—link you to the best African dancers, even as you are making it up as you go along. I marvel in your speed and ability to break, shift, from spot to spot. Unlike shy me, you never seem to hesitate at the start of a Soul Train Line, thinking self-consciously what to do while biting your lip. You jump on in, bring on your favorite moves. I hope you never lose that! You sing, sometimes making up words but hearing and remembering the sounds of the words and the rhythms after one first listen. When I dance with you, I laugh merrily, releasing the stresses of the day, working up a sweat, remembering to move through the room, taking in the beauty of the room as we've made it together, the paintings and the photographs, the warm saffron and mango that we've painted it, the sense of light despite the dimness of the winter sun. You make me take it all in and become a part of the room and also move me from my post behind my camera, constantly snapping pictures in fear of losing the moment, to living in the moment, taking stock of the space instead with my arms and legs and hips and movement. Enjoying the surprise of you, little girl, as you make it up as you go along. If we let you, you could put your favorite songs on repeat: "Step into the Bad Side," "Shiny," Michael Jackson always, miscellaneous dance songs from the Gipsy Kings, and you could dance all night, maybe never actually sleeping. "Make it a funky one, Mom!" you shout.*

24
THE BABY STORE
January 2018

ONE SUNDAY EVENING, CECE, ANNIE, and I were getting ready for bed, winding down by talking about our days. Cece had spent the previous night at her friend Mia's house, and she was telling us how Mia gets ready for bed. Mia and her mother, Sonia, did many of the same rituals that we did: reading books together, brushing teeth, listening to music, or doing yoga to calm down. Unlike us, Sonia had the girls clean the bedroom before settling down to sleep, and we made note of it. We have long admired Sonia's neat whiteboard of chores and affirmations and her intricate system of storage bins for Mia's toys, though we had doubts that we could duplicate it.

"And then Sonia told us about the Baby Store," Cece said casually.

"The Baby Store? What's that?" I asked.

"You know, it's the place where you get babies. Like where you and Annie got me. Sonia said that since we like each other so much, maybe she'll return Mia so that you and Annie can buy her at the Baby Store and we can be sisters."

Cece and Mia became fast friends in kindergarten. They were the only children with the same yearning for a sibling. They bonded over being two of a small number of Black girls at their school and of being raised in mother-led households. Sonia, Annie, and I have bonded over the pressure we've sometimes felt on the playground to be the perfect mom. As a single mother who is also one of the few Black mothers, Sonia has said that she often feels invisible compared with the other mothers. We've felt that, too, while our experiences as adoptive lesbian mothers may have been different. We've shared a similar commitment to uplifting our daughters in a culture that often overlooks them.

Cece told us about the Baby Store with glee, half-believing, it seemed, that Sonia had come up with a solution to their daily separation. As I listened, I reviewed all of the conversations that we've had with Cece about her adoption, and my heart moved from frustration to sadness to empathy. We've told Cece that her birth mother, K., carried her in her belly, loved her, and took care of her while she was there, but couldn't take care of her after she was born. And that K. found Annie and me in a photobook at the Cradle and brought Cece there after she was born. Key to Cece's adoption story is the idea of her birth mother's adoption plan as a lasting act of love for her. We've told Cece this story every time she's asked about it, showing her the photos that convinced her birth mother. There have been stretches of time when it's come up more often than others: near her birthday and Christmastime; watching another mother breastfeeding; on the anniversary of her Coming Home day; or when she's had a particularly bad day at school. As we've told Cece the story of her adoption, we've tried to keep it as light as we could while keeping it truthful. But sometimes, Cece has seemed frustrated with our positivity. "Why does that picture of K. have to be so big," she asked once, pointing to a collage of photos of family that we made for Cece's bedroom wall. Sometimes Cece wanted to know why K. didn't just take her along with her, whatever her struggles. "Why didn't she want me?" This last question has the power to take the air right out of my lungs, like a blow to the kidneys. "She did, she did want you," I told her, talking quickly. "She loved you so much. But she wanted you to thrive, and she thought that we would be the right family to help you grow." Annie and I would then hold her hard, hoping that our bodies could say how much we love her, how lucky we feel to have her, that somehow this would anchor her when our words don't seem like enough. I didn't blame Cece for having questions about this woman who gave her life, who has been so absent but so unavoidably present. I've often wondered how Cece holds on to these truths. It's felt so complex and layered for both Annie and me, let alone a five-year-old girl. Maybe it's no wonder that some days, a simpler story is easier. Like the Baby Store.

A few weeks after the first mention of the Baby Store, Mia was over at our house and the two were playing rambunctiously in Cece's bedroom, as usual, spinning and turning cartwheels, while we folded laundry in our bedroom across the hall. Cece knocked over a glass of milk, and we overheard Mia joke, "Oh-oh. Your moms are going to take you back to the Baby Store and get a new one!" We both walked into the room, and Annie said quietly to Mia, "We don't say things like that here." Annie's voice shook with emotion. I could feel my blood pounding in my ears. Mia seemed both puzzled and chastened. "Okay, okay," she said, giggling, but also looking at Cece for backup. Cece was silent, sensing the tension in our responses. Later, we brought up the conversations with Sonia, and she seemed embarrassed. She asked if we'd be willing to talk about adoption with her and Mia sometime soon. "My kid has questions that I don't really know how to answer." We agreed. "Yes. Join the club."

In my own generation, adoption was often a secret, or even an insult. "You must be adopted," a bratty sibling might say in the midst of a fight. Or "I must be adopted," a dreamer might wonder, imagining a family somewhere else that fits better. There was less room to talk about it as an everyday reality.

We didn't want to ignore the sweet part of the Baby Store idea, that it stemmed from the girls wanting to be connected, that Cece and Mia already felt like family. But that idea of buying and maybe returning Cece was so deeply disturbing.

As a Black woman raising a Black girl in this still white supremacist society, the idea of the Baby Store had a sinister resonance. Who wants to think of themselves as participating in a trade in bodies, given our shared history of enslavement? It also hits close to home in terms of some African Americans' suspicion of adoption as the selling of Black children, depleting the community. A common myth about adoption in some working-class African American communities is that wealthier parents, often imagined as white, use their power to remove children through adoption, an extension of the already feared system of social workers and police. According to Azzizi Powell, writing for PACT, a not-for-profit in Northern California dedicated to the rights of adopted children of color, African American birth mothers are often shamed within their communities for giving up "blood" to outsiders. For some African Americans, to put your child up for adoption is an act of betrayal. In this view, African American adoptive parents are invisible.

The suspicions of adoption for some working-class folks in the Black community might have some justification. African American children are put into foster care in far greater numbers than other groups, including white and Latino children. Sociologist Dorothy Roberts, who has written extensively on the racial politics of the child welfare system in the United States, says that here in Illinois, in a 1995 study, Black children made up nearly half of the foster care system, while they make up only 19 percent of the state population. Black families are watched more closely, Roberts argues, and often are treated more harshly than white families on the margins, which might contribute to the loss of custody of the children at a higher rate than white families. And according to the organization Kids Count, while the rate of Black children in foster care has gotten smaller since the 1990s, as of a 2018 study, Black children still make up 23 percent of all of the children in the foster system, the biggest group, while they only make up 14 percent of the population. These statistics bear out in the ways that Black mothers and Black families are stereotyped as negligent and even criminal, the same ideas that were used to justify slavery and that continue to shape our everyday experiences in this country. Intellectually, I understand the pervasiveness of stereotypes of bad Black mothers as a scholar of Black culture (thinking, for example about the Welfare Queen who has haunted both popular culture and political speeches); and I *feel* it as a mother whenever I've sent Cece back upstairs to change her pants because they have grass stains or torn knees, anticipating judgment; when our morning ritual of having a popsicle on the way to school is noticed and commented upon by another (white) parent; whenever I've carried Cece out of a store kicking and screaming in the middle of a tantrum.

While Annie and I chose not to adopt through a foster program, we've come to recognize that our lives, and Cece's life, are shaped by these systems. The broken state of the child welfare system shapes the perception of what it means to be an adopted child held by others, particularly if you are an African American, which is one reason that the Sayer's Program at the Cradle was so important to us.

On every form at school or at camp we've faced the question, "Is there anything else you'd like for us to know about your child?" We've taken that opportunity to say that Cece is adopted and that she has two moms. With this disclosure is a plea: "We're sharing something private about Cece's story. So please use this information thoughtfully." It has been important for teachers, school administrators, and camp counselors to know that Cece is adopted in order to think intentionally about how they talk about family. At the same time, we've worried about how that information will shape the assumptions about her. What if they respond to her, consciously or unconsciously, as a child who was unwanted, as one who has been thoughtlessly given away?

BACK WHEN CECE WAS IN preschool, at a bouncy house birthday party for one of her classmates, I stood with the circle of parents who were trying to look casual as our children leapt toward one another with abandon. Lynn, the only other African American parent in the group, stood next to me. Our daughters were in the same class, and we often ended up making friendly small talk together at these parties. Annie and I invited her daughter to Cece's birthday party, but the invitation hadn't been reciprocated. I figured that it was because they were busy with their growing family, but truthfully, there did seem to be a boundary between us, an unspoken but palpable tension that kept us from getting to know each other better. Lynn was Southern, from small-town Texas, and had a gentle, traditionally feminine way about her; her husband was a charismatic entrepreneur from Lagos, who would sweep into any room with jokes and a winning smile. They were a beautiful couple. I realized I didn't know much about them and what they believed and valued, but I knew that we shared the experience of being the only Black people at many of these gatherings, and that seemed to bring us together, if only briefly.

Lynn stroked her pregnant belly absently as she watched her child.

"I'm so excited for you all," I said over the din of children's laughter, nodding in the direction of her tummy.

"Oh, yes," said Lynn, smiling serenely. "So are we. Now don't you want to have another one, too? I bet Cece would love to have a little sister or brother."

I smiled and laughed. "She would love that, but it is not happening. We are way too old now. Once we adopted Cece, we decided we would put all of our energy into raising her right. And besides, she has lots of cousins and fam to hang out with."

Lynn gave me a look of concern, and then said: "What? Do you mean to tell me someone gave away that beautiful girl? Who would do such a thing?"

I sighed. If I told Lynn that we're glad that Cece's birth mother chose adoption, because Cece has made our lives infinitely better, I would feel like I was talking about her as a commodity, a beautiful girl bought and sold. And I didn't want to erase how difficult the choice was for her birth mother, and the deep possibility that it may not have felt like much of a choice for her. But I also wanted to agree and confirm Cece's value, in terms that Lynn would hear. I don't ever want Cece to feel like someone who was "just" given away, or for people to treat her that way. So I responded, "Yes, Cece is so precious to us. It couldn't have been an easy decision for her birth mother."

"Well," Lynn responded, "she is lucky to have you," a frown still creasing her forehead.

"Oh, no," I said. "*We* are the lucky ones."

ADOPTED OR NOT, BLACK CHILDREN are sometimes seen as lesser in our society, especially as they grow into teenagers, and that's reflected in limited access to innovative schools; negligent, and sometimes hostile, policing; and more tenuous access to health care. The everyday papercuts of microaggressions are felt by Black children, who face lowered expectations about their intelligence from their teachers and the stealing and then belittling of their style and culture from their classmates. Sometimes this hostility takes the form of humor and entertainment. (For example, on a 2016 Black lesbian parenting vlog, "Parenting Black Children," a troubled couple shared this "joke" told to their fifteen-year-old girl by her white friends: "Q: How long does it take a Black woman to take out the trash? A: Nine months.")

I wonder what will happen when Cece grows older, more vocal, maybe more rebellious. What will happen to her sense of herself as beautiful, valued, and adored, as she moves in the world? While Black children—particularly Black girls—are sometimes seen as cute by some white folks, being precocious or outspoken or just unwilling to smile in public is seen as suspicious by many white people, even those who claim to be liberal. Black girls' hair, style, dances, and bodies are often treated as spectacle, even as Black girl culture is appropriated and commodified into memes or TikTok dances. Black girls and Black boys are sexualized and criminalized, especially as they grow into teenagers, viewed as "fast," "ratchet," or thugs. In all, as Black children are under surveillance, Black childhood is cut short. How can we give Cece a story about herself that counters these deeply held prejudices? And in the context of being adopted, how do we affirm her so that she never has to feel like she needs to prove her worth to us and to the world?

The idea that Black children, especially Black adoptive children, have to earn their worth is reflected in popular cultural images of adoption. As Colin Kaepernick says about his own struggles with self-image as an adopted mixed race/African American boy raised by white parents in the 2021 Netflix show, *Colin in Black and White*, "I was never anyone's first choice." Kaepernick was chosen by his adoptive parents at the age of four, after their first choice for adoption, a white infant, fell through. The show waits until the final episode to reveal his birth story, but throughout the show, set in the rural California town of Turlock, that feeling of being second best haunts both Kaepernick's successes and his failures, as he struggles with others' judgments of him as a young Black athlete coming of age. Kaepernick's statement is both heartbreaking to me, as an adoptive parent, and revelatory—reminding me both of the ways that being Black and adopted were intertwined for him, and also showing how his adoption story continued to shape his life, from childhood to adulthood.

The very first image that I remember of an adopted Black child on television was that of *Diff'rent Strokes'* Arnold, played by the diminutive Gary Coleman from 1978 to 1986, when I was a child myself. I remember thinking of Arnold as a little smarmy then, always small and cute and ingratiating, but thinking about his character now, I hear an echo of Kaepernick's feeling of always being second best. On the show, a wealthy white widower, do-gooder, and businessman, Philip Drummond (played by Conrad Bain), adopts Arnold and his older brother, Willis (Todd Bridges), the children of his deceased employees. He moves them from "the ghetto" to his Park Avenue penthouse, where they are joined by Drummond's white teenage daughter, Kimberly (played by Dana Plato) and are watched over by his white housekeeper, Mrs. Garrett (played by Charlotte Rae). On each episode, Arnold's wit, his awareness of his own precarious position, and his sass (i.e., his catchphrase, "What you talkin' 'bout, Willis?") had to be tamed and domesticated, never blossoming into true rebellion, so that he could fit into his new life. Over the years, *Diff'rent Strokes* addressed some serious issues, including racism, classism, drug addiction, and child sexual abuse. But, whenever conflicts or misunderstandings got too sticky, it was the always diminutive Arnold who would crack a joke and be scooped up into his father's arms, making everything okay. (Coleman, whose small size was because of a kidney condition, continued to play the child, even as he aged into an adult.) The image of adoption, especially transracial adoption, offered by *Diff'rent Strokes* was one of acceptance of difference (suggested by the title, different strokes for different folks), but underneath the surface, the burden was put on the adopted child to educate his parent and the white people around him by being charming and mediating any fear or discomfort that the white people might be feeling.

In contrast is Nicole Holofcener's 2001 film, *Lovely & Amazing*, where Jane, an older white mother (played by Brenda Blethyn) raises an adopted eight-year-old Black girl, Annie (played by Raven Goodwin), along with two adult white daughters. In this film, the Black adoptive daughter is allowed complexity and an inner life usually denied adopted Black children in mainstream films. Goodwin's character Annie is cute and smart, but she also doesn't always smile or mug for the camera. And though we aren't told the story of her adoption, we get some sense of her complex inner life. She worries about whether her natural, kinky hair is pretty. She worries about her weight. She yearns to have white skin like her adoptive mother and sisters. This complexity in turn yields a series of layered emotional responses in her family, in conflicts that are allowed to remain unresolved. In a scene in the bathtub, Annie tells her white mother that she'd like to remove her skin to be more like her, which is both heartbreaking and familiar. Annie is vulnerable and trusting as she shares this desire with her white mother. And the film rings as truthful when we see Jane's flustered, troubled expression as she whispers, "You *are* beautiful," scrubbing the child's ears vigorously with a washcloth, as if to remove her doubt. These are questions that echo Cece's own, especially as she's navigated mostly white spaces.

As I've become an adoptive mother, I've continued to appreciate *Lovely & Amazing*, the first film that I ever saw that tells a story about transracial adoption that includes a believable portrait from a Black child's point of view. More recently, the television show

This Is Us, which premiered in 2016, follows the life and journey of belonging for Randall, a Black man who was adopted by a white family as an infant and who is a major character on the show. As the show loops and zooms through time in a nonlinear way, we see how adoption shapes in complex ways Randall's relationships throughout his life: with his siblings, his adoptive parents as well as his birth father, his partner and the children they raise together. (Randall is played on the show by Lonnie Chavis as a child, Niles Fitch as a teenager, and Sterling K. Brown as an adult.)

In general, storylines about Black or interracial adoptive *parents* are a rarity, and queer ones are almost never represented on film or in television. The exception to this television rule is *The Fosters*, a powerful and unprecedented dramatic series created by Peter Paige that ran on Freeform (previously ABC Family) from 2013 to 2018 and that featured adoptive moms who are lesbians, one African American (played by Sherri Saum) and one white (Teri Polo). The show portrayed a multiracial family (Black, white, and Latino) and included biological, adopted, and foster children. *The Fosters* thoughtfully portrayed struggles around belonging and connection, sexual, racial, and gender identity, and negotiating difficult adoption stories that include trauma. As Tracy Gilchrist of *The Advocate* notes, the show was ahead of the curve in treating adoption, race, queerness, and their intersections with current events in complex ways:

> Throughout its run, the show explored the importance of marriage equality before it became the law of the land, tackled racism, coming out stories, featured one of television's first transgender characters (played by a trans man), and covered rape, school shootings, immigration and ICE, sex trafficking, breast cancer, and the multitude of issues kids in the foster system face daily.

Despite these stellar moments, the problem with the majority of representations of adoption, especially ones that feature Black children, is that they seem to suggest that these children are only of value when they are of use: to teach a lesson about morality or to foreground another character's journey. They are not usually allowed their own particularity, their own complicated, often conflicted, lives. This is also the problem of the Baby Store, a fantasy that seeks to avoid the very historical and current complications that shape adoption.

But this gives me pause. Am I also guilty of making Cece a vehicle, a way to tell a story that is really, well, about me? In some unavoidable ways this is true. This *is* a story of my own motherhood, tracing the wayward paths of my thinking. As a writer of this memoir, I am trapped, still, in the limits of my own perceptions and memories and the particular bent of my own imagination. My daughter is at the center of this story, but her own experiences blur into mine. I think about that as I imagine her reading this as a teenager, and imagine that I am guilty as charged. She may even write a rebuttal to my version of things. My only hope is to write our story with room for what I don't know, hoping that she'll find in it the invitation to tell her own version of our story.

PART V

RECKONINGS

ALL YOU CHANGE CHANGES YOU

25

WHEN TROUBLE CALLS
February 2018

THE EXPERIENCE OF BECOMING A mother has heightened my experience of time, making it both more full and more precarious. I find myself missing things even as I experience them: Cece's tooth that's gone wiggly; a favorite pair of sneakers that's developed holes in the toes. As I age, life speeds up, weightless and heavy both, capable of stretching and then, just when I take its elasticity for granted, stopping short until—*pop!* It can break like a piece of Silly Putty. I soothe myself with the process of writing down stories. I can slow things down, examine them, skip over parts, and then return. I try to shape the past in ways that make narrative sense, searching for patterns, searching for warnings for the future. Maybe it is a luxury to will your life into a good story. Sometimes writing things down, and then rewriting them, threatens to keep me at a distance when I am most needed. And yet I keep at it.

In February 2018, my father called Annie and me to tell us that the lesion on his tongue might be cancer. Dad had been nursing a cough and was having trouble swallowing. When he went to his doctor, they found a lump at the very back where his tongue meets his throat, near his tonsils. My dad's father, Maurice, also had this kind of cancer, and although he didn't die of it, it knocked him flat. I remember visiting him, bringing him new cassettes of classical music because the jazz that he loved felt too raucous. My grandfather eventually died of colon cancer a few years after his tongue cancer was diagnosed. As we were talking, my dad revealed that he was regularly screened for colon cancer, occasionally with procedures to remove polyps over the years. It made me realize that there were parts of his life that he didn't share with me. But his health was his business and mine, too, wasn't it?

A week later, we visited Cece's eye doctor and found out that her vision had become considerably worse since her last visit. Already, her severe nearsightedness had meant thick eyeglasses and special annual trips to a major children's hospital in the area. That hospital was among the few places with instruments strong enough to measure her off-the-charts prescription. But since both Annie and I also had dismal eyesight, we had minimized the problems with Cece's eyes, cheering ourselves up with the most colorful, stylish kids' glasses we could find. This time, though, her eye doctor noticed that the lenses of her eyes seemed to be slipping upward. He warned us that this might mean that she would need surgery in some time. He added that the slipping lenses might also be linked to a bigger problem, such as Marfan syndrome, a serious, lifelong genetic connective tissue disease that can affect the health of the eyes, lungs, bones, and heart.

Cece's doctor, Dr. M., had a kind, Muppet-like face, yet he had almost no bedside manner. While we were convinced that he knew his stuff, he had the habit of testing out worst-case scenarios out loud, seemingly unaware of their effect of putting us all in a panic. Dr. M. thrust a poorly Xeroxed information sheet on Marfan syndrome into our hands. Stunned, we scanned the images, unable yet to process the text. We saw close-ups of a child's elongated arms and legs, the face cut off by the camera. A single eye stared back at us, lids forced open by some sort of metal instrument, to illustrate what lenses that have slipped look like. We saw a shadowy graphic of a heart, surrounded by a scary forest of fibrous walls. "Don't read that part. Just look at the section about the eyes," he said, taking the sheet away, refolding it, and giving it back to us. Impossible.

As we struggled to process this news over the next few days, I felt pressure to postpone my own feelings to get through school and meals, conversations, and errands. I didn't tell my dad or Phyliss what was happening, knowing that they were already struggling under the weight of my dad's cancer diagnosis. As I wrote in my journal, I searched for the right language to express how I felt. Sometimes in writing, I was able to say to myself what I feared articulating out loud. I was sad and worried for Cece and for my dad, and I was worried that they were worried. I felt raw, each moment heavy with significance. Some part of me felt guilty, too. Maybe this was my fault for being a little too happy, for not foreseeing, somehow, the bumps in the road. And for silencing or at least quieting my fear of unexpected loss that my sister's late-night phone call about my mother's death instilled in me. But I know deep in my heart of hearts that we are put on this earth to love one another, and also to die. It's that ache of awareness that sharpens each photograph that I take marking Cece's growth, from first day of school to Christmas to a day with a friend at the beach, each season passing.

This past year, I found out that two friends from my past had died without my knowing. Both were old sweethearts with whom I had fallen out of touch. But I had loved them both once. Both were my age, give or take a year or two. I found out about one of the exes while casually looking him up on Wikipedia. He was a relatively well-known poet, and from time to time I got a kick out of checking up on him online to see his latest books and accolades. But I this time, I noticed that his Wikipedia entry was written in the past tense. I clicked on his Facebook page, which had been converted into an ongoing memorial, a cultural phenomenon that I find eerie if efficient. There I saw photos from a wake that had already happened months ago, loved ones packed shoulder to shoulder in his tiny Alaska cabin. I found a stream of grieving messages: poems, songs, photographs, and other posts. I sighed and added mine.

I found out about the loss of another old friend, a geographer, when I noticed that a special panel was being organized about his work at an academic conference that we both frequently attend. I was excited that he had finally made the Big Time, the impact of his scholarship on the Great Migration recognized by his peers. I was already penning in my head a congratulatory email. But then I read the fine print: "A panel to honor the legacy of . . ."

For most of us, to live past fifty means to possibly have lost a parent, to watch a child get ill, to help a friend die. It likely means facing one's own health worries: a chronic illness that requires tending, special diets and regular doctor's check-ins, cancer scares, accidents. Trouble had already come to call. So I told myself that this news about Cece and my father was good information to have. That it's better to know what might be coming down the road than not to know. But it was hard not to know what would happen next.

Winter dragged on, and Annie and I had been trying to absorb the news about Cece and my dad for a few weeks. We met up in the kitchen after a sleepless night, getting our lunches ready for the day. Annie told me, "I just try to remember that we're strong, and we'll get through it."

"That's great advice," I said, adding Cheetos to Cece's lunchbox. I was so grateful for Annie, for her solid, everyday good sense, her kindness.

"It's what you told me last week," she said, smiling.

Most of the time, we took turns being upset about Cece and my dad, one stepping in to keep the other one up. We had in common that we're both much better at coping with other people's problems than our own. Annie is great at listening to her students work through the most extreme traumas, an important skill for a women's studies professor. Her experience growing up in a tense family household meant that she'd learned how to defuse emotions. I am a diehard optimist, almost always able to spin a difficult situation to see the bright side. That works for other people's problems the best. For myself, though, if I can't spin the problem to the bright side, I get quiet. An "undersharer," Annie calls me. Or I sail away to the clouds, daydream, with the plan to return only when the coast is clear.

So some days we pretended that only one of us was suffering, temporarily bracketing ourselves. And that worked most of the time.

Cece wasn't sleeping much, either. She'd sometimes wake up rubbing her eyes, telling us that she was worried about her vision, that she'd have to get an operation soon. She was there in the doctor's office when Dr. M. was telling us about his concerns, including the possibility of an operation down the road. We were frustrated that he didn't wait until we were alone to tell us, but maybe it was better for her to know. We tried our best to translate, but we were also struggling to understand ourselves. When Dr. M. spoke that day, Cece grew quiet, watching his face closely. Would she become an undersharer like me?

MY DAD, IT TURNED OUT, did need chemotherapy and radiation. I accidentally called him while he was at the doctor's office, just processing the news, and his voice was raw, shaken. Even though I'd rehearsed this possibility with myself, the news hit like a punch. When I got off the phone, a panicked child's voice deep within me whispered, "But I don't want to be an orphan." But I soon translated my panic into efficiency, a former department chair's trick, writing lists, looking for the smallest pieces of the puzzle to solve.

I started researching his condition on the internet, taking notes on my phone. I began a calling campaign, checking up on my father each morning in the days leading up to his treatment.

Once he began his treatments, I worried about calling and interrupting him. In my imagination, my superefficient dad became childlike, and I forgot that he would very likely just turn off the phone. So I tried random texts, figuring he can read them any time. I asked him about his treatments, or I picked up a thread of a past conversation. Sometimes I sent him links to music that reminded me of him. Or I'd send a photo of Cece doing something fun. I still didn't tell him of our worries about Cece.

In my texts, I approached the subject of my father's health gingerly. I told myself I was doing that because I was being protective of his pride. I reminded myself how defensive my father got if I tried to hold the door for him, his cheery "I've got it, thanks!" edged with impatience. Dad had always been very health-conscious, proud of his success in taking care of his body. A nonsmoker (except for that pot phase in the 1970s), he'd been a vegetarian since he turned thirty. Even after turning seventy-five that year, he glowed with good health, his walks around his neighborhood still jaunty and energetic, and his frequent laughter punctuated by his own gleaming teeth. I thought of the treadmill that he kept in his office, the Soloflex weight machine with its gleaming angles that he'd kept in fine working condition for the past thirty years. He was the only one I knew who actually used his home exercise machines, instead of letting them gather dust in a basement or closet.

But I began to question whether it was my protection of my dad's pride that made me shy to ask about his health. My father had never been traditionally macho. He'd always been very expressive of his feelings, crying openly as he taught me how to first ride a bike, calling all of my undergrad professors when I got into grad school to thank and bless them. My father was a poet who had learned the lessons of feminism well. He always let us know exactly how he was feeling as he felt it, wearing his heart on his sleeve just below the shoulder where he carries his man bag. So when I finally got the strength to call him a few weeks into his treatment, and I heard the weariness that he didn't bother to mask in his voice, I realized that I was the one who was afraid.

Each morning that winter before leaving for the office, I did my checking-in ritual, doing all of the things that I dreaded with hopes that it would turn our luck around. I graded my papers, paid my bills. And then sometimes, I'd check in at the Marfan Foundation Facebook page. Cece's doctor warned us not to go on the internet, but what parent could follow that advice? I needed to see what could happen, to try to understand and absorb it, to weave it into my vision of Cece as an adult, to try imagining her still doing the things that she loves.

On the webpage, I found photos of smiling, confident adults, and happy, active-looking kids, most very tall, with long thin limbs and wearing thick glasses, like Cece. The way that Marfan syndrome has come into public knowledge has been in cases of student athletes who are seemingly at the top of health and then drop dead during practice from a heart attack. Marfan produces some of the traits that make for great basketball players, with the height, flexibility, and large hands. Historians say that Abraham Lincoln, our tallest, lankiest president, may have had Marfan syndrome. While there are typical traits that are associated with Marfan's, it can also go undiagnosed, unless your doctor recognizes it. I learned from the site that not only can it affect your heart, lungs, and bones, but it can have accompanying psychological issues, including depression and pain management. Some adults are unable to work because of their health problems.

As I scanned the Facebook page, I paused on an African American woman wearing snazzy rimless glasses and a blue business suit. She looked assertive and successful. She was older than many of the others on the page. She looked to be in her thirties, maybe even her forties. Good.

While we waited to find out more definitive information about Cece's eyes, her doctor warned us to avoid any big jolts or blows to the head. He wasn't very specific, so we considered all of the things that Cece loves the most: bouncy houses, turning cartwheels, racing down the halls with Ruthie, playing with our Jack Russell terrier nipping at her heels. She hadn't yet discovered basketball or baseball, but could bouncy houses bring on a blow to the head? I remembered her last birthday party, which was at The Jump Zone, a crazy-loud warehouse of bouncy houses and games; children's bodies flying everywhere, parents huddled together in watchful clumps around them. Cece would have to take a break from these parties, even though they were a frequent choice for the kids her age. We encouraged Cece to engage in milder activities to unwind at the end of the day, like coloring, dancing, and yoga. She tried. We did them with her, realizing that we needed to wind down at the end of the day, too.

I found myself lingering more often over Cece's photographs as I passed them on the bookcase by my bed. I looked at her face as it's changed from last year's preschool picture to this one, noting the ways that her cheekbones and forehead have grown stronger, older, to me more beautiful and burnished under the skin. I tried to imagine this line of development shifting, the bones of her face moving outward, her joints extending, the lines of her body lengthening more than normal. I wanted to twist away from that word, but it caught me. Normal. "Please be normal," I whispered to the photograph. Where in the hell did that come from? When did normal become my measure of beauty, of strength? Wasn't that what I'd always avoided for myself?

I remembered my father's fear when I told him that I was queer. His fear, he told me, was not because he didn't love me but because he was worried that I'd have to face a lack of acceptance, or even violence. "People out there aren't as good as you think they are. I worry about you getting hurt. People get killed for less." Maybe it makes sense that my father, a survivor of violence himself, would think of this worst-case scenario when I came out to him, instead of the sexual freedom or increased self-knowledge that it meant for me. And maybe he danced with that word normal, too. Maybe normal was a parent's shorthand for a vision of the world without bumps or bruises. That made me feel more empathetic about my father's earlier worries, and slowly, more empathetic toward my own. Of course I wanted Cece to be happy, self-knowing, engaged with the world. I wanted her to be loving and loved. It's what all parents want. I wanted her to live. I wanted more than anything for Cece to thrive. But "normal" had crept its way into my vision, too.

CECE'S FIRST ECHOCARDIOGRAM WAS ON a Tuesday early afternoon a few days after Valentine's Day. We'd taken her out of school and stopped before the appointment for lunch in the hospital cafeteria. Annie and I tried to make the lunch as festive as we could, choosing all of Cece's favorites: pizza and fruit and chips. We each got a freshly baked chocolate chip cookie and promised Cece that she could pick something out at the gift shop before we left for the day. The hospital was still decorated with pink and red paper hearts.

At the hospital, the children themselves reflected the full racial and cultural makeup of Chicago: all kinds of colors and languages happening around us. That made us feel more at home. The mostly Black and brown support staff that we saw working at the hospital as orderlies and security guards or in the lunchroom also offered an extra serving of comfort. We saw a sprinkling of Black and brown doctors, nurses, and technicians.

When we got to the examination room, I could tell that Cece was feeling nervous from the quiet way she held her body. The young technician in bright patterned scrubs and a blonde messy bun instructed her to lie down on the exam table on her side, and we noticed that Cece held her stomach in, keeping it as far away from the technician's hands as possible. Noticing this, I moved closer to the table and took Cece's hand and asked her how she was feeling, my voice sounding a little too loud. "I'm scared," she whispered. I looked into her eyes, and I told her that everything was going to be all right. They were just going to take some pictures of her heart while she watched a movie. Was Cece thinking, like I was, that this could be one of many heart exams in her future? Or was she just focused on the unknown of the moment? I breathed deeply, trying to model calmness.

Annie often got queasy in doctors' offices and usually avoided any procedure for Cece that involved shots or blood. But she was hanging in there. Before the exam began, Annie asked the technician to walk us through the process while she took notes. Then she sat quietly in one of the adult chairs, staring straight ahead, breathing deeply, too.

The technician moved the echocardiogram wand around Cece's chest to look at her heart's chambers, monitoring her heartbeat. I was watching Cece's face, making sure that she was comfortable, and then I turned to watch the screen on the ultrasound. The peaks and valleys of her heartbeat looked beautiful on the screen, silver on black, like a skyline of some unknown city, reflected in a large body of water. I had no idea how to read these things. Since we didn't meet Cece and prepare for her adoption until a few days after she was born, we didn't get to see an ultrasound of Cece when she was in utero, but if we did, I would have struggled to make sense of it, too. I am always astounded that anyone is able to tell if there are twins or anything useful from those things. I just go along with it, and say, "Wow. How beautiful." Which it was. I was full of wonder, even if I didn't know what I was seeing. The technician asked Cece to bend her head back on a pillow, so that she could scan the main arteries of her neck, which I was sure wasn't comfortable. But Cece did it without complaining. I worried that she couldn't swallow that way, but she managed to hold her head in that position for the full five minutes. I watched on the screen the coursing rhythm of Cece's heart, flashing, sometimes with red and blue lightning on the screen. All I saw was evidence of life, energy, the wonder of her.

The technician had given the choice of a film for Cece to watch, and she chose *The Princess and the Frog*, the only of Disney's major films with an African American heroine, and Annie and I caught one another's eye, smiling with pride for her choice. *The Princess and the Frog* might have a Black princess, but it's far from soothing: there's a scatting Cab Calloway voodoo priest conjuring demons, a swamp chase of the Frog Princess and Prince by a team of hungry 'gators. The Frog Prince and Princess get tangled up with each other's long tongues with the hectic pace of it all. I worried that the film would make Cece's heart race and somehow skew the test. But the technician, I had to hope, had already thought of this.

I turned my attention back to the echocardiogram screen and tried to breathe. I let my eyes narrow and unfocus so that the screen and the movie both seemed like part of some postmodern art installation.

Annie and I sat next to each other. Annie whispered to me, "Are you resting?"

"No, I'm just watching," I answered.

"Me, too," she said, and she moved her seat closer to me, so that our shoulders were touching.

A FEW WEEKS INTO MARCH, Phyliss called to tell us that my father was in the hospital. His chemo and radiation were done, but he'd developed a blood clot, something that might have been triggered by the treatments. Annie and Cece and I immediately abandoned our Saturday plans and hopped in the car to drive the hour and a half to St. Charles, the suburban town where they lived. We brought Cece with us, both because we thought my dad would be glad to see her and hopefully to help with Cece's own growing anxiety about doctors and hospitals. At first Cece hadn't wanted to come and pulled away as we entered each automatically opening doorway. A worker at the front desk noticed her nervousness and offered her a soft plushy to hold, an eyeless rabbit sewn from purple calico.

I had to admit I was excited by this hospital's luxury. Cece's own hospital was well-supplied and efficient, and I was confident that we were receiving great care. But the lines sometimes felt long, the elevators crowded. This hospital's ability to seemingly anticipate everything, even a child-visitor's nervousness, was reassuring and felt to me the result of its moneyed zip code. Phyliss, who was trained as a nurse specializing in geriatric care, told me that their county, DuPage, is one of the best-funded counties in the United States, and I believed her. The hospital had a quiet that suggested enough doctors, enough nurses, enough people to clean, a staff of chipper candy stripers—I thought they only had candy stripers on *General Hospital*. It actually smelled good in there, without the electric funk of panic. The waiting room had warm natural lighting. Tastefully modern photographs of flowers lead to the elevator. I was glad to see that my father had his own room, and I took a moment to appreciate the PhD and lifetime of hard work that earned him that luxury.

When we entered his room, the lights were dimmed to a gray because Phyliss was sleeping on the couch nearby. We spoke in whispers. She'd stayed up the whole night while they worked on him, my dad told us, and I was reminded that they were both vulnerable at ages seventy-one and seventy-five, weathering such a serious illness together.

This was the first time I'd seen my father in person since he began his treatments, and I was relieved to see that he still looked like himself, except without the beard and mustache I had known since my childhood. He was wearing the stylish white cotton shirt and pants he used to do his yoga in. His relaxed feet turned in a little pigeon-toed under the blankets, like mine. He made jokes, accepted Cece's big hug without wincing. She'd brought him a plastic strawberry ice cream soda from her doll's house, which he happily accepted. (Cece expected to get it back at the end of the visit, but I talked her out of asking for it back.) "Maybe he's okay," I thought to myself. Maybe this whole process hadn't been as hard on him as I feared.

After a half-hour or so of chatting, I noticed that Dad was drifting off to sleep. But even then he seemed in control. He told us that the doctor was coming in soon to show him how to give himself a shot if he got another blood clot, and so he'd better be sure to get some rest. His eyes were already closing, but his words were still cogent. Always the teacher.

But just as he fell asleep, he murmured, "This radiation stuff reminds me of what the slaves must have felt, the ones in Mississippi, the terrible pain they had to endure."

I was not quite sure what to say, how to witness the intensity of his pain. "I'm so sorry, Dad," I whispered. Annie let out a little sob.

Later in the car, Annie, who is hard of hearing, asked me to repeat what he said. I did, and she was shocked, saying, "I didn't hear what he said, just the tone, and I knew it was bad." I nodded, completely understanding. I could only take in the situation bit by bit. During the visit, I drifted in and out, only half listening for what I needed. Toward the end, when he was talking about the slaves, I floated somewhere above, still listening, but just taking a little break with the trees outside. My mind hovered between these two places, not quite ready to return.

As Annie started the engine of the car and we got ready to head home, I realized that I was still disoriented and had no idea where my purse was. I must have left it in the hospital room after my father dozed off. I ran back to the room. Dad and Phyliss were both sleeping in the dimmed daylight, so I moved stealthily, hoping that the keys didn't jangle. When I left their room, I somehow got turned around and I took the wrong elevator down again. I was completely lost, panicking that I'd never find the car. I'd ended up at the back of the hospital complex, several buildings away from the lot where we parked. I passed the emergency room building, which was strangely quiet except for an orderly finishing a cigarette outside. "Were there no emergencies in St. Charles on Saturday afternoons?" I thought. The March wind was cold, and it blew my dreadlocks into my eyes, but there was a damp, loamy promise in the wind that the green things might soon return. Rather than give in to my panic, I embraced this small break from the seriousness of things. The bite of the wind helped me come back.

THAT SAME WEEK, DR. M. called to let us know that Cece's echocardiogram was normal. "So that's good news." He added tersely, "I see that you have an appointment with the geneticist. I think you should go ahead with it. We'll see how it all adds up (click)." So was the coast clear? We decided to consult with Cece's pediatrician, who'd been treating her since she was just a few weeks old. She helped translate the results. She encouraged us to focus on the moment of each diagnosis. Cece's heart was heathy. It didn't rule out development of heart problems down the road, or the other symptoms of Marfan's developing, but for right now, everything was okay. We tried to focus on the good news that Cece's heart was healthy but knew that we needed as much information as possible.

As March ended, a few days before Cece's birthday, we returned to the hospital to visit with the genetic specialist and her nurse. Their manner was kind, and they both talked to Cece and us with respect. But as the nurse posed Cece to take photographs of her in profile, turning her head this way and that, I couldn't help thinking of mug shots. When she took out a tape measure to measure Cece's arm span and then the circumference of her head, I recoiled further. I remembered the books I'd read about early-twentieth-century eugenics movements, the charts comparing the head sizes of the races, the categories of intelligence based on the shape of a nose, based on skin. I knew that this wasn't what was actually happening, that the doctors were here to help us, that we were in the twenty-first century and that we had ordered this exam ourselves, hopefully covered by our health insurance, but I was still taken back to those charts. The test required a lot of touching and posing, photographs and notes scribbled in a file. I tried not to let my suspicion show, but as the nurse pivoted Cece this way and that, I moved closer to my girl, stroking her arm in between positions. They took vials of Cece's blood that would sit in a refrigerator while they waited for insurance to approve the expensive genetic tests. They jotted things down in their notebooks, murmuring together. I knew that all of these measurements were probably relevant to their diagnosis, but I got the feeling that they were not telling us everything. Even as a well-educated middle-class African American woman, I still felt a distrust of doctors and hospitals. I imagined the photographs of Cece in the geneticist's file, pictured them with the eyes blocked out with black bars. I imagined others pouring over the photos, pointing, debating, sizing up our daughter.

Later that night in the kitchen, after Cece had fallen asleep, Annie and I admitted to each other that we both felt uncomfortable during the genetic testing. We were both stunned at watching those measuring tapes and rulers, the white strangers' hands pressing against Cece's flesh and what that reminded us of (teeth counting, checking for lice and scars, the auction block). We've both studied the histories of scientific racism, the sad stories of Sarah Baartman and Henrietta Lacks, both Black women whose bodies were exploited by scientists to further knowledge, without consideration of the lived quality of their lives. We talked about the photographs that the nurse laughingly said were "Just so that I can remember Cece later," and admitted that it made us feel suspicious. Why couldn't the nurse just tell us that they were part of the study? We were doctors too, after all (not that a doctorate in philosophy helped much in this case. In fact, our studies of race and gender may have made us even more suspicious). I shared with Annie my irrational protectiveness of those vials of Cece's blood still sitting in the hospital's refrigerator. Would the insurance company approve the tests? And if not, what would happen to them? Would the blood really be used for what they've told us? It felt like a part of Cece had been left there in that hospital. It was another way that we felt out of control. Annie and I let those fears out in whispers, and they swirled around us in our green kitchen, ghosts that we hoped to exorcise by saying them out loud.

Easter weekend came and my dad was home from the hospital. Phyliss called to invite us for dinner, her voice quiet but buoyant, relieved that we were back to our calendar of family get-togethers.

But I knew as soon as my stepsister Tara opened the door that I shouldn't let go of my worry yet. She looked at me with sympathy and concern on her face. Tara lived with Phyliss and my dad, and while she lived a very busy life as a social worker, she'd had the time to note the changes in my dad's body in a way that I hadn't.

One of the things that struck me: Dad looked more like his own dad. The radiation had darkened his skin, browning it like his father's, and his beard was still missing, though he was able to keep his mustache. My grandfather sported a full white mustache, of which he was very proud and which he treated daily with wax so that it would curl at the ends. My father has also been very proud of his facial hair, and I assumed at first that this change was only cosmetic. Actually, without his beard, my father looked dapper, from a different era. It suited him. It made his bright round eyes even more noticeable, and it returned to view the cleft in his chin, the one that my sister and I also share. When I complimented him on it, he let me know that the decision to wear only the mustache was in response to losing the hair of his beard. It came out in patches after the treatment, so he decided to shave it.

When my father discussed the cancer, he treated it with respect and a sense of endurance, like the eight-hundred-page biography of Phyliss's father that he'd been writing for the past decade. He's always up for a challenge, he told us. "But this is definitely the hardest part. Not getting to enjoy that great food along with you." He eyed the full vegetarian feast before us: black-eyed peas and rice, corn bread, greens, potato salad, green salad, green beans with garlic and onions and red peppers. He had a full cup of some kind of protein shake, which he sipped gingerly from time to time through a straw. He attempted a chuckle, but it sounded more like a cough.

The conversation covered the usual range of familiar subjects, checking in on relatives, then movies, then politics. After about an hour or so, Dad dismissed himself to go up to bed. We all took turns giving him gentle hugs before he went, and I tried to take it all in: the new narrowness of his back and shoulders, the way I could feel even more his heart against mine, the surprising strength of his arms as he held me tight.

This was a journey that I'd never made with my mother. I'd watched her cope with her diabetes. But I wasn't there when she got her diagnosis, when it may have felt like some door to her life had suddenly closed. Because she had been diabetic since she was a teen, the only mother I knew was one who had already absorbed this information, who had already learned how to live with her illness. Becky, Annie, and I had all planned on helping my mother as she aged, which would probably have meant multiple hospital stays, her heart and circulatory system worn out in the end by its lifelong stresses. However, her sudden death took us all by surprise and changed the script. I'd never watched the process of taking on a life-threatening illness from scratch. I was learning from Dad's process of facing his possible death and learning how to live again.

All that summer, Dad went to weekly physical therapy sessions to regain full use of his body, including his tongue and throat. By September, he was declared cancer free. He wore the aura of gratitude of someone who's seen the bottom but who is also aware that it could have been worse. At family gatherings, he has become a little more quiet than usual, happy to eat and listen attentively.

That fall, too, Cece's genetic testing was approved and we learned that she does indeed carry the genetic code for Marfan syndrome. We learned that Cece's troubles with her eyes, the lenses that have threatened to detach, are most likely a symptom of this genetic code, which targets the connective tissue. But knowledge is still inclusive. The geneticist told us that her current eye trouble could be her only symptom. For many children and adults with this Marfan's code, one isolated symptom is all that they develop. For others, there are a series of symptoms, most frightening of which is the development of a malformed chamber to the heart. So as we listened to this information, given to us over the phone and jotted down on a motley set of sticky notes, Annie and I dried our tears and committed to the regimen of annual echocardiograms for Cece. We committed to teaching ourselves the most we could about Marfan's and to find out about communities of others diagnosed with it. We pledged to get more medical opinions, to share the news with our family, and to rely on their wisdom and support. Quietly, too, we mourned this result and the possibility that Cece would face struggles with her health later down the line. The mantra that got us through her adoption, that we "don't know," would still be ours. Maybe this was the mantra all parents have to rely on.

It's unavoidable not to think about Cece's adoption as we've faced this possible illness. We only had a skeleton of a medical history for Cece's birth mother, and none for her father. Sometimes when we've told doctors that we don't know, there was tension and a whiff of judgment, as if passing along genetic material was something that anyone could control. Cece's first pediatrician, when he read our note that she was adopted, assumed that meant that she was also neglected by her birth mother, even though K. took good care of herself during her pregnancy. (We fired him.) One of our friends, when she found out that Cece had other birth siblings who had also been adopted, exclaimed, "Doesn't anyone know anything about birth control anymore?" We'd been told by friends, teachers, even complete strangers, how lucky Cece was to be adopted by us. We didn't ever want Cece to feel grateful to us in that way.

I realized that I'd created a kind of body blindness about Cece, sort of like well-meaning white folks who claim that they are colorblind. Instead of thinking that Cece may have inherited a flawed body (like the rest of us), I'd given her a kind of superhuman body to combat the shame that might follow her. The stories that I guess about her birth parents are stories of struggle, of making do, of loss, but somehow I'd twisted that struggle into a kind of Wakanda-like power.

Maybe in the face of the unknown, I projected onto Cece's body all of the strengths that I wished I had. In my mind, Cece was like me, but better, stronger. It's true that she had no allergies, while I woke up every fall and winter morning with pink, crusted eyes, my inhaler part of my daily wake-up routine. Cece learned to run and jump almost as soon as she could walk. She was graceful, where I was clumsy and slow growing up, and even more so as I aged. Maybe it was only a matter of time that these visions were forced to be more complicated.

As I worried about Cece's future, I might also have been mourning that vision of Cece as my own Wonder Girl. I was a little ashamed that I'd projected my own fantasies of invincibility upon her. My work ahead was to face our own shared mortality. Even if I did still think that she was a wonder.

26
TRACING TIME: SEVEN TATTOOS
Summer 2018

THE FIRST TATTOO ISN'T REALLY a tattoo; it's a birthmark.

Cece's finger traced the small greenish splotch on my back, near the curve of my hips. "What is that, Mom?" she asked. The mark, a birthmark, looked something like an amoeba, or maybe a penny after it's been elongated by turning a crank at one of those souvenir machines at the aquarium and the zoo, the ones that transform your penny into a replica of a building for only a dollar.

Cece and I were having one of our just-out-of-the-shower conversations, a ritual formed in no small degree by the fact that the lock on our bathroom door has never worked. On any given day, Cece came in and out of the bathroom freely while Annie or I were showering, to tell us something that she wanted us to know, to use the bathroom herself because she was afraid of the one in the basement, or just to have a look at us. At six, she was curious about our bodies, as well as hers, remarking on our flab and folds and moles, our similarities and our differences; where we had hair where she didn't yet, how our upper arms jiggled while hers were firm. She monitored us both with curiosity and a bit of possessiveness, tracking Annie's sunburns and my ever-stubborn chin hair.

In those moments of interruption, whether Cece tapped softly on the door or just barged right in, I thought about my connection to my own mother's body—my wonder that it produced my life from hers. I thought about what her body looked like in comparison with my own, the developing fleshiness of my chin and the rounding of my tummy that mimicked hers in her fifties. I thought about how she would let my sister and me watch her own rituals of getting ready for the world, as she chose her clothing and styled her hair. How, when I was a toddler, she'd let me trace the line of the caesarian scar on her belly as we watched TV.

I was quickly squirming into my underwear as I told her the story, balancing on one leg and then the other, while my daughter watched.

"I got it on the very first day I was born. The doctors took me out of my mother's stomach with these calipers, these tongs. My mother needed help because I was getting bigger and bigger—much bigger than anyone expected, even though I was a month early, and my mother needed help getting me out. And the tongs left a mark on my skin."

"Is it like this?" Cece asked, holding up her left little finger, which had a tiny bump from an extra digit, removed by doctors when she was born. All that was left was a small bump that seemed even smaller as the rest of her hand grew bigger. Sometimes the bump hurt when she knocked it accidentally. Until then, Annie and I had avoided saying explicitly to her that the bump had been an extra finger, afraid that she would feel ashamed of it, or, like a missing twin, the bump would somehow remind her of the loss that accompanies her birth story and of the mother who birthed her and held her for the first time. But then Cece had met other kids who also had these missing fingers, the bumps marking a secret kinship.

"That's the place where you had an extra bone removed on your very first day, at the hospital. When you came home to us, your hand was still all wrapped up in a bandage while it healed," I told her.

"We're lucky that we both have something to remind us of the day we were born. We're alike that way, Mama."

"Yes, *we are* alike," I said. "We are lucky."

My mind traveled, not to the doctor's calipers but to the labor of my mother's body, the work that it took to have me. Since my mother was a diabetic, my birth was a risky one. The doctors had scheduled my birth for more than a month later, on March 5 (coincidentally, Annie's birthday). But my own genetic mix—my mother's mother weighed thirteen pounds at birth!—as well as the effects of my mother's daily injections of insulin, which traveled along through the umbilical cord to me, contributed to my full nine pounds in my eighth month. So to spare my petite mother the work of giving birth to an eleven- or twelve-pound baby, and also to reduce the risks to her life and mine, the doctors rescheduled my birth a month earlier, for a snowy afternoon on January 30 at 1:00 p.m., after lunch and in first hours of what would become a huge blizzard that lasted several days, Chicago's Blizzard of '67.

I've always found it strange that my birth date, so often talked about by astrologers as the outcome of fate or the constellations, was also shaped by calculation and strategy, determined by doctors' medical hunches as well as their lunch schedules and worries about post-blizzard traffic. My birth, often romantically imagined as an instinctual pact between mother and child, had these other intermediaries, worldly in a way that is often invisible in stories about births. That birthmark reminded me that there were people helping get me into the world; people marking and shaping me. The birthmark, in my mind, also connected me to Cece. Her entry into the world was also shaped by people in addition to her birth mother. Not just the doctors, but also the family members who encouraged her mother to follow through with her pregnancy, as well as social workers and counselors. The fact of Cece's safe birth may even have been shaped by us or the idea of us, first when we were just a hypothetical plan, and eventually when we took shape as ourselves in her mother's mind, two enthusiastic adoptive mothers picked from a photobook.

Like a tattoo, my birthmark and Cece's finger bump are the evidence that we are connected to others who have shaped our lives, traced out on our skins.

THE NEXT TWO TATTOOS ARE of dragonflies.

As I think about my body and Cece's and the scars they bear, accidental and purposeful, I think about my tattoos.

My tattoos have helped me rethink my ideas about commitment, consistency, and permanence. Even though they are inked in with the idea of permanence, tattoos are always changing, both physically and in terms of the stories we tell about them. Wherein the first few hours after being tattooed there is only pain and a bandage, our skin begins to transform, dead skin peeling to reveal something bright and clear beneath.

Permanence, the yearning for it, the navigation of its certainty, has everything to do with adoption, both for children and adults. In our training, we learned to call ourselves "forever families," moving the focus from the loss of the birth mother to the stability of the family that we're forming. And while I've found myself pulled by that language of forever, I also know that change is the state of the world and that change creates possibility as well as loss. While we've pledged to be Cece's forever family, our goal has been to teach Cece how to embrace change without fear, even if it's a lesson that we're also still learning.

An awareness of the inevitability of change can be painful and hard to face as a parent. Annie has said that she sometimes hates looking at photos of Cece as a toddler, knowing she will never again be that little person. And yet, that awareness also heightens our appreciation of the past and the present, knowing that it, too, is fleeting. The fact of change is also what helps us survive trauma and loss. Change, but also a sense of continuity and connection. "We are our ancestor's wildest dreams."

Even at age six, Cece also had to face change and the foiled desire for permanence. Change might be the element of her birth story that she knows best. Her birth mother changed the course of their own bond and Cece's life by seeking us out. With that change came the loss of not knowing her, at least for now, and not knowing Cece's birth siblings and other family. The loss that comes from change, especially that first change, might be the feeling that returns every time she faces a new school or a new set of friends.

The first tattoo I ever got, twenty years ago, came out of desperately wanting to change my life. I set out to get an ouroboros, a snake swallowing itself, a sign of infinite life, and for me, a claim to badasshood. I was knee-deep in research about Cleopatra for my first book, a figure of great powers of reinvention for me. I wanted to claim some of her powers of rejuvenation and infinite variety after feeling pigeonholed in my academic life and stalled in my personal life. So I gathered my posse, my two friends Amy and Elizabeth, and headed down to the tattoo parlor. It was located down a bit on Highway 322, a few minutes outside of State College city limits, where the cute university town drops out into rural space. The tattoo artist blasted his heavy metal even before we began, and he had the dirty-blond, curly shoulder-length hair of someone who either was a musician or admired musicians. I remember him without a shirt, but that may just have been my imagination. I told him what I was thinking about, an ouroboros, a symbol of rejuvenation and possibility and fierceness. What he drew was a big bulging snake with fangs. Clearly his idea of fierceness was different from mine. But I knew I needed the tattoo. I needed to act on my desire for change in order to expedite the other changes that I needed to take place: to find a new job, to stop settling and find a true life partner, to boldly claim public space and the queer woman I felt inside. This tattoo was part of my coming out, part my desire to reclaim my skin and challenge those whose approval silenced me—at this point, the university and the town. The phallic snake that the artist drew didn't quite capture my sense of my own queerness, so I switched to the prettiest tattoo I saw on the wall: a dragonfly, an image that suggested to me lightness, movement, and grace. The artist turned the music up higher, gave us all cherry lollipops to suck, and got to work. In the fugue of excitement and pain, I grew to trust those hands that were reworking the skin over my left shoulder. I even grew to appreciate the music, just the right amount of fury to focus my pain and enough chord changes to keep me entertained. And even though it was just a dragonfly from a pre-drawn flash sheet, I grew to love that dragonfly, to think of it as mine and as unique. I thought of that dragonfly as my companion, my pledge both to change and to longevity. (As my friend Rich told me after, the dragonfly is one of the most resilient of creatures, having survived the throes of evolution—a primitive survivor.)

The story that I told about that first tattoo grew richer with time. The dragonfly was my companion, perched on my shoulder, just below the fabric of my blazer (eavesdropping during department meetings). It became my totem for survival and my impetus for change, my inspiration to fly. The dragonfly fueled my energy to redream my life, to move from stasis to find a new job in the city (Chicago, finally calling to me), to come out to my family, to tell my friends who I loved that I needed a change. Later, after Annie and I found each other, we came up with a slogan for the little dragonfly: "So long, suckers!"

Over time, meeting Annie, adopting Cece, deepening my sense of community and chosen family in Chicago shifted the feeling of having to flee to something else: a grounding sense of home. I felt like I needed another tattoo to mark that change in myself, the opening up of my heart. I wanted company for my lonely dragonfly.

Googling "feminist tattoos," I found Dawn, a tattoo artist located in a hip neighborhood to the west of me. Dawn's style draws from traditions all over the world: Celtic, Persian, Indian, and Indigenous American. Yet there was also a sense of Chicago grit in her aesthetic. I consulted with her to help me think of a design that would connect and expand the first tattoo. I told her about a hike we took as a family to a forest preserve in Gary, Indiana. Right in the middle of the vacant lots, abandoned buildings, and steel mills was this oasis, a trail with rusted train tracks on one side and a pond with lotus flowers and hovering dragonflies on the other. I wanted the tattoo to feel both abstract and specific and to capture a feeling of being centered and part of a community. I worried a little that the lotus flower would feel like an orientalist cliché, but Dawn reassured me that she would draw a "very Midwestern pond," with cattails.

THE NEXT TATTOOS AREN'T EVEN mine.

One of my favorite poets, Mark Doty, has written several poems about his tattoos. He writes about them not only as totems of his own queer desire, his yearning for change and surprise, but as totems of his survival, including the loss of his partner Wally to AIDS in 1994. In his 2001 poem, "To the Engraver of My Skin," the act of tattooing marks his commitment to being always vulnerable and open, even when paradoxically marking himself permanently:

"I'm here / For revision, discoloration, here to fade / And last, ineradicable, blue. Write me! / This ink lasts longer than I do." His command, "Write me!" cements a pact between his tattoo artist and himself to revise his body and, in the process, to keep retelling its story. His story, through the tattoo and through the poem about the tattoo, reopens and renews every time we read it. I can read that poem now, almost twenty years later, and it is still new, the engraver's pen hovering over his flesh.

Our bodies, the poem suggests, are never permanent but are always changing and shifting. Tattoos tell stories about our bodies—they remind us of our histories, and they present them to others visually. Our understanding of these stories changes too, even as the bodies that support them—our skin, our sight—might diminish over time. Tattoos are evidence of the fact that others change us, too, and change the stories that we tell about ourselves, our passions, and what makes our time on earth meaningful.

A young David Bowie, the ultimate shape-changer, sings in his 1971 song "Changes," "Time may change me. But I can't trace time." But I have to respectfully disagree with him. Isn't singing and telling a story the attempt to trace time, to give shape to it, to create a narrative to then go back upon, not to master in understanding time, or to stop it, but to see its shapes, flows, and circles? Looking back at his career now, there is something still elusive about David Bowie; as we shift our gaze from one eye green and the other eye blue, we never quite grasp what he's thinking. But we can still see the twirls, the swirls, the repetitions as his self moves through space. The shape of those changes sometimes follows the major shifts in the culture and sometimes actually shapes them: from blue-eyed soul to psychedelia to glam to the Thin White Duke to *Aladdin Sane* and onward. Through the shape of his music, we might trace the emotional shape of his times, as well as the overall spirit of contrariness and utopianism that he still offers us through his music and image, even after his death.

Maybe as he got older, Bowie sensed this idea of the importance of tracing time and of allowing oneself to be traced and marked by time. In the last decades of his life, he got a tattoo on his left calf: a slender, naked, gender nonbinary person riding a dolphin, below which sits part of The Serenity Prayer, written in kanji: "Help me know the things I can't change." Bowie designed the artwork himself, together with a Japanese tattoo artist, who inked it for him in 1991, "as a confirmation of the love I feel for my wife, and my knowledge of the power of life itself," he said. I sense in the combination of these images a dance between permanence and change, movement and commitment, singularity and connection.

THE SIXTH TATTOO IS OF three owls in a tree and is on my upper right shoulder.

The owls, wide-eyed and whimsical, are based on a design on a pair of Cece's baby pajamas, a pair that I almost couldn't bear to throw away, even after she grew too tall for them, even after we cut off the feet so that she could continue wearing them. I loved the innocence of their eyes, the lively colors of orange and pink that suggested Cece's own curious spirit. The tree branches where the three owls sit are lit by a moon and by stars, and it's all designed in a dreamlike style, vaguely reminiscent of a henna tattoo, with its curves and scrolls.

As time has passed, this tattoo has changed for me. At first it reminded me most of those early days of taking care of Cece. At times, the owls called on the force of my mother, her protection, reminding me of the owl vision that I had just after her death. And it has grown from a promise to mother to my family, to a reflection of how we can all also mother one another. We are the house of fierce mothers. And each day, the owls have reminded me to hold together the power to protect with the power of flight.

THE SEVENTH TATTOO IS A daydream.

We were on the fourth of a five-day visit to Seattle to see Annie's family. Cece had been inseparable from her Russo cousins, Isabella, Maria, and Eliana. But that morning, everyone seemed to be beset by weariness, maybe from days of too much play and too little sleep, and as we walked to a restaurant for breakfast, the group clustered back to its more familiar households. Annie and I flanked Cece, falling back from the crowd, swinging her hands as we walked. Cece watched hungrily as her older cousin Maria lifted Isabella onto her shoulders in a moment of big-sister-little-sister bonding. Cece still hadn't gotten over that desire to have a sibling in our household, and sometimes it felt like nothing could shake that desire, not our dog Ruthie or sleepovers with Cece's best friend or Annie's and my efforts to be both playmates and parents. Lately, Cece had become very interested in her six biological siblings, whose photographs were on her bedroom walls. She would tell anyone new whom she met about them. And a few times, Cece asked us why some of them got to stay with her biological mother, while some of them didn't. We told her that was a question that we couldn't answer, but that we trusted K.'s decision that this was the best thing for everyone.

We arrived at the restaurant. As we sat down to eat, I noticed that Cece was quieter than usual. I leaned into her and gave her a peck on the top of her head. She looked up at me, annoyed, and muttered, "You are not my mother." I was startled, but I reminded myself that in current kid discourse, this comment doesn't have to mean what it sounded like to me. It could mean, "You're not the boss of me." Or just, "Give me some space." But Cece continued. "You're not my real mother. Neither is Annie. My real mother is

K.—whoever she is." A small-scale tantrum quickly moved into deeper territory. I swallowed my hurt as quickly as I could, and responded, "Yes, we are, Sugar. We are absolutely your real mothers. We are on your team forever." And I gave her a hug for as long as she'd let me, which was a little longer than I expected. I reminded myself that those feelings of loss were ones that we'd always have to work with, part of the terrain of our life together as an adoptive family. And also that travel was always a little discombobulating. I remembered Cece's comment a few days earlier, when we were walking along Seattle's affluent Queen Anne neighborhood where her cousins live: "There aren't many brown people here." And I tried to think about how Cece might have felt walking in public in this mostly white neighborhood as the darkest member of this mostly white group. While I've felt like a racial outsider plenty of times throughout my life, I am also an adult. It occurred to me that, given our distance in age and other differences, maybe I'd never fully understand how she feels. But I am glad, at least, that Cece felt that she could say out loud what she was thinking, that she felt safe enough to utter those taboo words. Cece's funk passed, and she and her cousins cooked up some game involving hiding the silverware. Still, after I told Annie and her brother Mark what Cece had said, and I saw them both wince, I left the table to have a little cry in the bathroom. Mark was worried that his girls had contributed somehow. But I told him that maybe Cece just needed some extra hugs today. So for all the rest of the day, as we moved from breakfast to bookstore to museum, while we didn't mention her words again, Annie and I looked for ways to remind Cece of our connection, to help her feel its strength through touch. Annie played "hot hands" with her. I gave Cece a piggyback ride up the steep Seattle hills. We grabbed her hand to run across the street and we kept our grip on her hands light but steady.

Later that day, as we rode together in the backseat of Mark's SUV, I forgot our campaign a little and started to daydream, gazing out the window at the passing greenery. Cece grabbed my arm and traced the tattoo on my forearm, the words "You can never have too much sky," surrounded by moons and stars. It's a quote from Sandra Cisneros's novel *The House on Mango Street*. The line is from a moment in the novel where a young girl is gazing out of the window in her schoolroom, willing herself somewhere else in her future. I chose it as a nod of empathy to all of my bored students, but also in honor of my younger self, a frequent daydreamer. The passage in the novel continues, "You can fall asleep and wake up drunk on sky, and sky can keep you safe when you are sad." The quote reminds me to honor my imagination as a solution to a struggle that often feels impossible, something that has felt especially urgent to do in these dark political times. That day, thanks to Cece, the tattoo expressed hope in the face of unsteady change, hope even with the reality of sadness.

Even though Cece was still learning how to read, I'd told her many times what the tattoo says and what it means to me. As her fingers traveled up my arm, she pulled me back from my daydream, and I willed those words to steady her as she navigated her own set of losses and struggles that day. Maybe touch itself, the skin itself, warm and familiar, even if it can't erase loss, even as it holds evidence of pain, could also give her a sense of my commitment to her, and the knowledge that however the landscape changes, our love, together with her imagination, will help us survive. Even if I can't give her permanence in all things, I can give her forever.

27

KISSING DOESN'T KILL
And Other Queer Lessons
I Learned from My Mother

MY HISTORY HAS TAUGHT ME that I didn't invent queer/chosen family. Beginning with my mother, and reaching back to each generation before me, my family, especially the women in my family, have survived by reinventing home, family, and desire, creating bonds and pleasures in one another's company. And while I didn't recognize it at the time, my own coming out process was simultaneous with my mother's own creation of queer family. Hers would continue to inspire and shape mine, even after her death.

WHAT I REMEMBER ABOUT THAT poster right off was the two girls. I loved them because they were both brown. They looked the most alike, freckles on cheeks, curly-kinky hair swept up in gel as my sister and I used to do with our hair in the bathtub, playing with the shampoo. They wear the sides of their heads shaved down to the scalp. They could have been Black; they could have been brown; they could be either or both. It didn't seem to matter as much in the worlds I associated them with:

the Bronx, or London, or maybe Oakland, where I was. One girl, a little shorter than the other, teases the other with a long finger on her chin. She has the attitude of the actor Rosie Perez, or maybe Salt-N-Pepa. Flirty. The other girl's eyes are squeezed tight in anticipation, as she is drawn into the other's kiss. I imagined her as the quieter one, a little shy like me, until she gets going. Each of the pairings offered to me the possibility of something else, a new life. It wasn't just the fact that the girls were kissing, but also their attitude, their hair, their clothes. The style of the poster—bright colors, the right-now street style, the bold and direct sloganing—was designed by the activist artists' co-op Gran Fury; it was intended to borrow the provocateur style of Benetton ads. But this was better than any Benetton ad I had seen because they were selling sex, resistance, fun, freedom, and political consciousness, without sweaters as the price for the ticket. "Kissing Doesn't Kill," the poster's copy says, "Corporate Greed, Government Inaction, and Public Indifference make AIDS a Political Crisis." In other words, we should not have to give up our freedom, our joy in ourselves and our bodies, in order to live. It was a shamelessly beautiful poster.

"Kissing Doesn't Kill: Greed and Indifference Do," Gran Fury, poster and public art on buses of New York City, San Francisco, and Chicago, 1989. Image courtesy of the Gran Fury Collection, Manuscripts and Archives Division, New York Public Library Digital Collections.

The poster was part of my newly queer life as I entered my mid-twenties, when sex and desire still felt uncharted. It seemed to capture the fluidity of my own desires and the way that I seem to have been wired for shape-shifting and queer rebellion, a reflection of the sex-positive spirit of those times. I "borrowed" it from my then boyfriend, Ted, who was brilliant, sexually ambiguous, and politically brave. I kept it when we broke up, when Ted began dating men again, and I began dating women for the first time. Water-stained, crackled with time, ripped and with old tape on the back on it, that poster traveled with me, from bathroom to bathroom in my young adult life, from the run-down house I shared with my dozen or so roommates in Oakland, to my sex-and-the-single-girl loft in State College, Pennsylvania, where I got my first real job, to my apartment when I moved back to Chicago, to when I met Annie and my life started to take its firmer, more adult, and more contented shape.

THE FIRST WAVE OF REAL public awareness of the AIDS epidemic happened when I was in college in the 1980s, and though I was better informed about sex than many, this danger still felt like more an "issue" than something that directly shaped my own life. It was dwarfed by my fear that I would get pregnant and that my plans for graduate school and a life of the mind would be thrown off track. While I seemed to get into many fretful emotional attachments and sexual entanglements, mostly among my circle of friends, actual dates and sex (you know, the kind involving the mutual exchange of fluids) and the trust that was required by me to be fully naked with someone else, were relatively rare. Maybe this was because I was still discovering myself. Still, despite my low (to me) sex rate, I had my own box of condoms and read up on safe-sex practices, including those involving making your own dental dams from Saran Wrap if the occasion ever arose. Still, the liquid danger of AIDs was less a reality than other questions, like whom do I love? How do I desire? How do those desires shape who and how I want to be in the world?

By the 1990s, I had moved from college town drama in Kansas to graduate school in California's East Bay, and suddenly the psychic and literal maps of my sexuality expanded.

Right across the street from my first apartment on Telegraph Avenue was Mama Bears, a feminist bookstore that included a bearded-lady reading group. After classes, we might stop for a pitcher, pool, and nonstop dancing at the White Horse Inn, which happens to be the oldest continually operating gay bar in the United States. The White Horse was charmingly nonexclusive, where everyone danced with everyone, regardless of whom you planned to take home. Across the Bay in San Francisco, I went to hear Susie Bright, author of *Susie Sexpert's Lesbian Sex World*, and squirreled away videos by sex-positive feminist performance artist Annie Sprinkle, suddenly now differently aware of the power of my hands: fingers, nails, long or short, even gentle fists, as sites of pleasure. We listened to Queen Latifah, Arrested Development, Salt-N-Pepa, and this new band of misfit burnouts called Nirvana. Salt-N-Pepa, who after telling us how to shoop and p-push it *real* good, ended my favorite album of theirs with a tragic little playette, "I've Got AIDS," which after the first listen I would fast-forward through. (Even in the brave new world of CDs, I still defiantly listened to cassettes.) Prince, my longtime guide to all things erotic, wrote a song of mourning about the "big disease with a little name," "Sign o' the Times."

My friend Simon, bibliophilic grad school geek by day, sexually liberated gay barfly by night, came to class wearing T-shirts of two men kissing and told us which men's bathrooms on campus were the most active hook-up sites. He told us about the kiss-ins and die-ins that he had been going to in San Francisco and Oakland, and eventually, I went to them, too.

I began to be shaped by the resistant spirit of protest, as well as the re-embrace of freedom and joy in my new environment. There was the melancholy of loss but also the assertiveness that threat forced into me. My roommates and I went together to the free clinic for AIDS tests. And while going and then waiting for the results were terrifying, more than the threat of the war in the Gulf and right up there with West Oakland drive-by shootings and police harassment. Waiting overshadowed the everyday worries of writer's block, bounced rent checks, and the occasional roommate who went AWOL when the bills were due. Still, I felt like I was shaping my own sexual story.

We called our group house "The House of Slow Children." Someone had "liberated" a "Slow: Children at Play" street sign from one of the corners in our Oakland neighborhood. It showed the silhouette of a child, neither boy nor girl, Black angled body in motion. We set it up next to the group cubbies in our kitchen. We felt like it captured the mood of the house, our sense of arrested development.

Some of my housemates accepted temp work after completing college. One was living on the fee from donating her eggs to an infertile couple. My friend Jenny had dropped out of our graduate school program in English to ride the last waves of the dot-com boom and soon moved into the house. Most of us felt a little in between. While economic necessity meant that we couldn't fully embrace the relaxed vibe of the proverbial Gen X "slackers," the jobs of our dreams hadn't fully materialized, either. Although I was also moving slowly, I didn't feel entirely lost. I was writing my dissertation on Shakespeare, though I really wanted to be writing about Grace Jones and The Jackson 5. Maybe I had a little too much time to think. But our house, miles away from campus, was my refuge, a way of mediating the pressures of deadlines and competition and scrutiny. That time for me instilled the inevitability of change and loss of AIDS but also the joy and pleasure in facing change and risk as a collective that has become key to my view of queer family.

WHILE I WAS MAKING UP my newly adult life in the East Bay, little did I realize that in those same years in the 1990s my mother was creating her own new "queer" family back in Chicago. I am calling her queer, even though she wouldn't use that term for herself. After my parents' divorce, my mother continued to date men, but her main emotional sustenance, aside from my sister and me, came from her wide circle of friends: men, women, young, old, straight, and gay.

My mother had renewed her involvement in the Catholic Church after being a "take-what-you-will-and-leave-the-rest" kind of follower, who only attended church on Easter Sundays for most of my childhood. Her church, Our Lady of Mount Carmel Church, was on Belmont, between Broadway and Halsted, in the heart of the rising gay community of Boystown on the North Side of Chicago. The congregation at the time reflected a strong gay and mostly white male presence in the neighborhood, but it also reflected earlier waves of community in that area, including older white people, some who emigrated from Poland and other places in Eastern Europe, and a sprinkling of African Americans and Latinos. Besides being an overwhelmingly beautiful building, Mount Carmel was known for its amazing music, especially for its choir, which was directed with artistry and entrepreneurial verve by Jim Ferris. To walk into that church and feel that organ shooting shock waves of "Ave Maria" right into your chest, buffeted by layers of almost inhuman harmonies of voice, was to risk conversion, even for the most stubborn of agnostics like me. Mount Carmel's choir was so wonderful that they actually sold their own CDs at Christmastime. And in the late 1980s and 1990s, it was known for having one of the most active AIDS ministries in the city.

My awareness of the depth of my mother's involvement in working with people with AIDS came slowly. She had had a strong foundation of gay male friends for decades. But when I'd come home to visit from Oakland, I noticed that her circle of friends now included priests who defined themselves as gay and other church activists involved in AIDS activism. Sometimes they'd all go out together for brunch after mass on Sundays or take week-end trips to the Indiana Dunes. This group was very affectionate. Members would hug frequently and kiss hello on the cheeks and the lips. I remember a snapshot of them all sitting at a sunny café table in a small town somewhere near the Dunes. My mom looked a little incongruous in her cornrows and Peter Tosh T-shirt, arm in

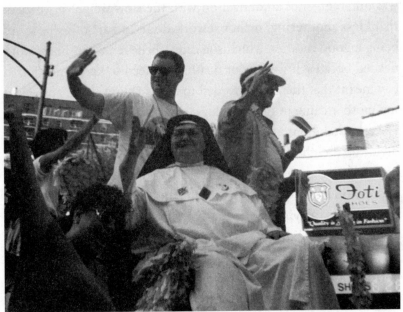

Chicago Pride Parade, Chicago, Illinois, early 1990s. Photograph by Sandra H. Royster.

arm among a circle of smiling, beefy white men. My mother's link to this community seemed to be both social and spiritual. A way of connecting to like-minded people who were liberal, loved the arts, were funny, and were also driven by a strong ethical and spiritual sense of loving Chicago and building community.

Mom worked at the Bonaventure House, an AIDS hospice on the North Side, on a pleasant Ravenswood street surrounded by tall, full trees and neat apartment buildings and single-unit houses. I say worked, even though she volunteered, because it was hard work. She'd come home describing what she did: scrubbing down a kitchen with bleach or washing all of the dishes for the entire crew. Stuff that, I was amused to note, she never did at home. (To be fair, *no one* really scrubbed anything down with bleach at our house. Before we each moved out, my sister and I more often did the dishes, and then eventually, when she could afford to, my mother hired a cleaning lady to come in once a week.) But this was different—not an obligation with the slow weight of years of thankless mothering, or housework done as part of a "pose" of being a good mother, which she didn't believe in, but housework needed because it was life or death. The need to keep infection at bay meant that the house needed to be sparkling clean, and when my mother came in on Saturdays, she'd do whatever was needed. Clean or hang out and play cards with a group, or help someone divide up their best party clothes to give away, or gossip one on one. My mother did a mean manicure. She helped battle the patients' depression and frustration by joking and sometimes praying with the patients, playing them her favorite "dusties" or organizing a ragtag Electric Slide in the sitting room.

And when someone passed, my mother helped the families and friends who remained bury their dead. Or, if there was no circle of kin left, she worked with the director of the house to plan a service and always attended them.

When I came home for the summer after my mother's first year of volunteer work, I had the chance to visit her at Bonaventure House. I began to understand how central this work was to her core. I learned more about the men and, more and more often, the women with whom she worked. There was Jerry, a longtime resident who liked to be referred to as "The Mayor." Jerry was a talkative, funny, sweet man with a steel gray, well-tended handlebar mustache and cheeks and a nose that were permanently rosy.

Bill, whose room smelled like sandalwood. Esperanza, whose daughter always promised to come and visit but didn't. They were people who had already experienced a gamut of illnesses, who had been wiped out and then revived themselves and then were wiped out again. They were there because they had reached a point where they could not take care of themselves independently. Some had lovers or parents or sons or daughters. Many were alone. But they created a circle of kinship among the others in the house, and my mother was included. Sometimes she was mother, sometimes she was sister friend. Sometimes a little bit of it all.

I thought I knew why she began this work. Her best friend, Demitrius—someone whom she loved—had died a few years before from AIDS. When Dem died, my mother grieved deeply. She never took off the jade and silver Greek crucifix that he gave to her. She had traveled to Greece, his birthplace, and when she became a grandmother, she asked to be called Yia Yia, the Greek diminutive for grandmother.

But her creation of this new family through her work at the Bonaventure House seemed to be more than a reaction to one person's death. It seemed to be a part of the spiritual renaissance that she had after Dem's death, a renaissance that blossomed and grew until it became a key source of community for her. It was a part of her political self. She always had the heart of an activist, and this was something very concrete and hands on that she could do. An intervention into something that felt in those days to be unstoppable.

Perhaps it also had to do with my sister's and my shifting need for her, our becoming adults and her own changing role as our mother. My mother's work at the Bonaventure House represented a family that my mother made alongside our nuclear family. A way of thinking about herself separate from mothering us. This didn't take her away from us—she always had time for my sister and me, as well as for her parents, brothers, and sisters. She was not just a doting grandmother, ordering up outrageously expensive children's clothing from French catalogues for my nieces. My mother had another group of intimates, and the role that she had with them might have been as mother, and it might have been something else entirely. My mother had created her own chosen family, a concept that I thought of then, and still think of, as "queer."

As I write about this time with the hindsight of my mother's death, I wonder whether this work was a way for her to cope with her own disease, the one that eventually killed her. The diabetes that she had had since she was thirteen years old was becoming more present, more visible, a source of frustration and grief for her. Maybe her working so closely with people with AIDS, most of whom were "out" about their disease, was a way of reconciling with her own illness. A way of identifying and being more open about something that she had always taught should be her own secret struggle.

I think of the ways that HIV-positive people and people with type 1 diabetes share a cost for being public with their disease. People with AIDS have had to face violence, fear, and neglect, as well as a steady blame for their own disease that is particular and distinct. But with both diseases, there's a sense of stigma, a sense that you are not in control of your body and that you have not been in control of your body. That your appetites, whether for sugar or sex or drugs, is in excess. (I base this on my own experience as a diabetic, too. While my own type 2 diabetes is a different and often less lethal disease, it shares some of the surveillance and shaming of type 1, especially around food and other sites of excess.) As someone caring for people with AIDS, my mother I think would have brought that understanding, and with it, a sense of the importance of self-respect and agency. I think about how often men, especially men who didn't know her well, referred to my mother by diminutive nicknames: Sis, Lil' Bit, Ginger Snap. She *was* tiny, for a good amount of her life—wearing a size zero or two well into her thirties—but these pet names suggested a childlike powerlessness that absolutely did not match her "take-no-prisoners" personality. She was a doer who could very creatively curse out anyone who got in her way: cab drivers who took circuitous routes to stretch their fare; superiors at work who underestimated her savvy; rude salespeople; the elderly white matron downstairs who touched her hair in the elevator; even her daughters, when we got too salty in our new adulthood.

I've remembered my mom's experiences with disease, her own and those she worked with, as I've watched Cece learning how to be strong and vulnerable at the same time. She's a great helper, but I've also worried: does she know how to make her own needs visible? How can I help her to do that—as someone who's struggled with this myself? My mother was on a journey that we both share: discovering how to be a whole, multidimensional person in a world that wants to see you flat, capable of being categorized, and nonthreatening. How to take up space.

Looking at these photos, I search for more clues of this new mother, the one that I didn't always see, to find out all the ways that she was growing and changing. Her death also links us, our family, our mourning, to these other deaths, expanding, and maybe also queering our family, opening its boundaries and bringing in unforeseen lines of caring.

MY MOTHER'S MEMORY IS KEPT by many people, beyond blood. Ultimately, that is a joyful revelation—that queer family has existed in my past, for my mother, and for the generations before it. The lessons that I am learning about flesh and belonging as an adoptive mother might in fact be deeply woven into the fabric of the family and culture that I inherited.

I have thought about the queer lessons that my mother taught me as we've raised Cece, and as I've faced the fact that there are key parts of my mother that I didn't know. She had her own identity, beyond being my mother. And her desires, including her sexual ones, weren't always shared with me. What will Cece know about

We are family! Laila, Farah, Annie, and Cece at the Chicago Dyke March, 2013. Photograph by Francesca Royster.

and not know about Annie and me? Would she recognize her mothers in those rebellious kissing girls on the "Kissing Doesn't Kill" poster? While we try to be transparent with Cece about who we are and who we've been in all of our complexities and contradictions, there will inevitably be things about us that she won't know or fully understand. Some of those unknowns might reflect our different historical times and experiences; some might reflect the necessary boundaries between parent and child.

Cece knows that Mama Annie and Mama Frannie love each other and share a bed. We kiss and hug and hold hands openly in front of her. Cece was present when we got married in 2014, but as a young child she might not be aware of the historical significance of that act.

Cece knows which of our friends are coupled, and who lives alone. She knows that some of our friends are "man ladies" and

Frannie, Annie, and Cece fight for the future. Women's March, Chicago, Illinois, 2017. Photograph by Francesca Royster.

that some her of uncles in our chosen family might prefer to be called aunties. The need to name those truths drives me to write, in part for her to read.

I also know that there might come a day when Cece won't feel as comfortable with this motley group that is our chosen family. She might feel ashamed of her mothers and might avoid naming our relationship. She might try to revise the true stories about us that we've given her. I try to prepare myself for that, with hope that if this day comes it will be temporary, a phase of her learning about and loving herself. And that maybe by living our lives as truly as we can and by writing down our stories of families and sex and love, we can change the world that she inherits.

CODA
STONE SOUP LOVE, WITH ANN RUSSO

WHEN I THINK OF THE phrase "chosen family," I think of an ethical obligation to be responsible to each other that is also sacred. To keep—to both watch and to hold in one's heart. To commit to keep those whom we know—our blood and chosen families, our friends and coworkers, our students, even ourselves—is the hard work of intimacy. It is work that requires the risk of facing our own fears and sometimes, too, the things we hate in ourselves. To keep those whom we don't know means to always approach any other while keeping sight of their humanity, to be open, to be surprised, to lose control.

Each morning, I light a candle and stand in front of the altar that I've built on a cleared bookshelf. On that shelf are several photos of Annie: perching on a rock like a garden elf, at the cabin where we stayed in Vashon Island, Washington, the summer before Cece was born. In another photo, two-year-old Cece is reading a book upside down in her high chair, a smile wide on her face. I have one of my favorite photos of my father wearing a birthday hat and spinning a pinwheel. Next to it is a photo of my sister, Becky, and me, stuck in a photo booth. I'm two, like Cece, and Becky is six. Becky is posed with a scarf tied neatly over her head, while I look like I'm mid-yowl, eyes and 'fro a little wild. My mother is invisible, standing behind us, and I remember her saying at the moment of the flash, "Hold your head up, baby." Sometimes I still listen out for her to say that. "Hold your head up." On the altar I have an Egyptian necklace from my mother, and two signs of my commitment to being a writer: a crystal ink bottle with golden feather, a gift from my father and Phyliss, and a typewriter's "X" that I bought in a thrift store in State College, dreaming up my next steps. There are photos of Stevie Wonder and Eartha Kitt, two of my muses, and a postcard that says "A Big Hello from Rogers Park," a symbol of my commitment to the neighborhood.

I start the day thinking about the people I love, the people I belong to. I breathe in their love for me, breathe out love for them. And then I set about breathing in love for those who are more difficult to love. People who may have crossed, inconvenienced, or hurt me in big ways or small. And then I send love to strangers, to people I don't know. I can't imagine them fully in my head, so I imagine instead a shower of white petals. This is my one spiritual practice, one that doesn't claim a particular god, except for the beauty of each other, and the commitment to the activism of love as a verb.

This extraordinary year has turned out to be a continuation of the last extraordinary year of the COVID-19 pandemic and quarantine. Even after vaccines, the future still looks uncertain. Cece completed the last months of second grade and the entire year of third grade remotely, separated from other kids and from her teachers by her computer screen. For many of those class days, pressure to keep on camera for eight hours a day felt excruciating for her. But at least we had the privilege of all working in the same house together, Annie and I taking turns sitting next to Cece as she slogged through her school day, while we taught our classes on Zoom from our home offices. This time of intense togetherness has had moments of great joy: cooking together, puzzles, and time in the backyard with our pups. We got to watch Cece's learning process and she got the chance to really see what we do for a living, day to day. But we have all also experienced anxiety, frustration, boredom, grief, and loss, and just the foggy-headed feeling of too much togetherness.

We've been lucky. We didn't lose anyone closest to us to COVID, though it traveled through many of our households. We've been able to keep and do our jobs from the safety of our home. But we are still grieving. One of the biggest losses during this time has been the casual gatherings of loved ones at our dining room table, the ability to sit on the red couch and share news and long hugs with our friends. So like the rest of the country, we've improvised with Zoom parties and air hugs and drive-by birthdays. We have all had to be inventive in how we re-create our rituals of love. I think of Jen and Choua, sending us handmade postcards from their apartment three blocks away; Laurie and Erica biking through rain, sleet, and snow to leave home-baked bread on our doorstep while we were in quarantine; Laila donning plastic gloves and masks to bake us her patented Frittata Mumbata; Andrea's steady stream of winsome TikToks to lift our spirits; Brian's heartfelt listening and advice, counseling us through the rough spots of the pandemic on his weekly Sunday-evening Zoom calls. We've all had to be a little queer, as the world has felt less safe, more dangerous, more stingy with its safe places.

When I think of queer love, I think about how much we all need it, how much we hunger for new blueprints for connecting our lives and living out our dreams.

A queer ethos of love to me captures the ways that we might come to each other vulnerable, with all of our soft spots, our oddities right on the surface, to wear our lumpy, fat-coated hearts right on our sleeves, to keep making community, to keep trying. To be queer, here, to me means to be both "odd" or "strange," and to be open, against an ethos of fronting and self-protection.

BACK IN 2012, A FEW months after Cece came home, Annie and I created a welcoming ceremony for her, to bring her into both our blood and chosen families. Our small red velvet couch was crammed with four people instead of its usual two, with two more perched on its arms. Every surface where one can sit or lean was filled, folks filling two rooms and even spilling out of the front door whose doorbell kept on ringing. We were there to welcome this little person, just four months old, who spent her first weeks being cared for by nurses and volunteer huggers at her adoption agency. She already knew what it meant to have an open circle of love. We came to testify our commitment to her: her moms, grandparents, blood and chosen aunties and uncles, cousins, friends. My father looked onto the group, a few of whom he was meeting for the first time, but many he had forged friendships with at our gatherings, along with those he calls family, and cautioned us: "We have to remember that she's not really ours. She belongs to her Creator, whoever you think that might be. We are temporarily in her life, hopefully for as long as possible and we have to remain cognizant and respectful of her autonomy, of her dignity, and of her self-worth. Help her to be who she is meant to be, and not who we think she should be," he said. (Over the years, that lesson has proven to be challenging, because for each of us, Cece is a little bit ours.)

We passed the mic—letting anyone who wanted to give an offering of peace and hope to Cece to share with the group. Meechie sang a heartfelt rendition of The Jackson 5's "I'll Be There," leading us to join in, shifting the "I" to "we." Laila sung a song in Arabic, her own song to her Cece-Beesy (Cece Kitten). Caryn and Beth gave Jewish songs and prayers. Auntie Carolyn handed out scrolls, a pledge for all of us to be one family. Lourdes told Cece how much love she's entered and how much we've already been changed by her: "And I want Frannie and Annie to know that we're committed to help bring up Cece. And we're committed to you, Cece, to help bring up Annie and Frannie. So give us a call if they start getting out of line!" Amina filmed the whole ceremony interspersed with interviews of family/friends talking directly to Cece. There in the room, we had represented aspects of many parts of our lives, as professors, students, friends, allies; as daughters, sisters, nieces, aunties. There were multiple sexualities, genders, ages, races, ethnicities, spiritual practices. We were all there to celebrate this new member of our community, to watch her reflect the mosaic of loving people around her and also to discover her own, shining self.

WHEN I THINK OF CHOSEN family, I think of reaching deep underneath our skins, bringing our strengths, forged from home spaces and past places of safety to share with each other. When I think of chosen family, I think of a stone soup of love.

I came from a family where blood loyalty ran high. The three of us, Becky, my mother, and I, were a tight, tight unit after my parents' divorce. And our bonds were even tighter because my mother was open about her struggles with money, her love life, the pressures of parenthood. For better or for worse, my sister and I shared those struggles with my mother, as best we could, as children. My father, whether living at my house or not, has always been my source of pride, the angel on my shoulder, and as I've grown into adulthood, one of my best friends.

However much I've valued those blood connections, a nuclear family was not the model that Annie and I have chosen to build with Cece. Instead of the tight circle, we want an open table. We want family, chosen and blood together, even with potential clashes of beliefs and ways of doing things. For me it's meant coming up with new rules of family. It's meant sharing struggles, as well as food. It's meant letting down my guard, letting work life and homelife, activist life, and fun mix together. Letting folks drop in, listening to their advice, accepting help. It was challenging at first, to be vulnerable to the people who didn't know me forever, whom I feared might not be around for the long haul. But it has also been incredibly rewarding. Queer family has helped me to heal in the company of others, even when our specificity of loss has been different. We can forge our strengths and rebuild ourselves separately *and* together.

Chicana feminist theorist Aimee Carrillo Rowe, surfing expert and chosen fam, aptly captures what this kind of belonging can feel like:

> We encounter collision ... when our belongings are stripped
> from us. And also when our belongings challenge us to
> rewrite the consciousness of our notions of "self." But even
> such collisions occur in motion, washing over us like waves.
> We, sucked under, gasp for air. We, turn and ride.

I think it's an ethos of queer love that Audre Lorde has in mind, when she writes in the poem "For Each of You":

> Do not let your head deny
> your hands
> any memory of what passes through them
> nor your eyes
> nor your heart

I think Audre means to embrace the words "I don't know" even when also embracing our heart's yearning. I think that she means that as we connect, make community, let others into ourselves, no effort to meet others where they are is a waste. I think she means that memory and story can sustain us, even when we lose the people we love, even when we find ourselves alone or confused or wronged or floating without direction. And by sharing our stories, we are making home.

AUTHOR'S NOTE

THIS BOOK IS BASED ON my own experiences, memories, and analysis, as well as family stories and memories shared with me. Some of the names and identifying details have been changed to protect the privacy of those involved. Conversations included here have been reconstructed from memory, with some support from my imagination. I've done my best to capture the heart of those conversations, but I take responsibility for any mistakes or omissions.

ACKNOWLEDGMENTS

THAT FAMILIAR SAYING ABOUT RAISING a child also applies to finishing a memoir: it takes a village! My editor, Chelsea Cutchens, has been a dream to work with, as has been everyone who helped bring this book to fruition at Abrams Press. And I am so thankful for the support and advocacy of my agent, Claire Anderson-Wheeler at Regal Hoffman and Associates. Thanks to Michele Morano, Miles Harvey, Lauren Cowen, Laura Jones Hunt, Andy White, Maria Finitzo, Gail Siegel, Peter Handler, Gwen Macsai, the late and wonderful Doro Boehme, Nadine Kenney Johnstone, and all of my Story Studio friends for your writerly brilliance; and special thanks to Nancy Wieting for painting the family portrait that graces this cover.

This book is written in memory of my mother, Sandra H. Royster, whose extraordinary mothering shaped me and this book in ways I'm always appreciating anew. I would like to thank my dear chosen and blood family, who've cooked meals, read drafts, shared their care, time, stories, photos, and hugs over these years. Thank you to my parents, Philip and Phyliss Royster; my sisters, Rebecca Royster, Tara Hammonds, Barbara Asare-Bediako, and Kenya Raybon; my nieces Demitria Pates, Alexandra Pates, as well as darling Kaleyah. I am lucky to have gained family in the Russos, including Mark and Becky, Maria, Eliana, and Isabella Russo, Laura Castaneda, Michele and Johnny Carruthers, Rose and Steve Rosedahl, John and Susan Russo, Connie, Artie, Maddie, and

Vincenzo Castaneda, and Nick Russo. And so thankful for Carolyn Royster, Joyce Royster, Jasmine, Brooke and Jacob Reams, Toya Harvey, and Kevin Lewis, Gordon and John McClure, Beth Womack, Laverne, Kevin, Faith and Grace Bartee, and all of my Russo, Harvey, Royster, Hammond, McClure, Reames, Lewis, and Pates fam. Thanks to the following circle of colleagues and loved ones for being in community with me. I am holding you all close as I remember and tell these stories: Carolyn Aguila, Margarita Alario, Juliana Pino Alcaraz, Vidura Jang Badahur, Hope Barrett, Kai Barrett-Bennet, Natalie Bennett, Barrie Jean Borich, Donna Hedberg Burns, Rachael and Maya Cade-Cunningham, Aimee Carrillo Rowe, Caryn Chaden, Amina Chaudhri, Susan Chaudhri, Kristal Moore Clemons, Cathy Cohen, Maxine Craig, Jen Curley, Halee Curtis, Misty DeBerry, Monica Dolan, Rich Doyle, Joy Ellison, Bill Fahrenbach, Jim Fairhall, Laila Farah, Cindy Franklin, Laurie Fuller, Shelly and Nia Gore, Alexis Pauline Gumbs, Nadine Hubbs, Pat Husband, Hugh Ingrasci, E. Patrick Johnson, Bill Johnson-Gonzalez, Lorrie, Edde, and Sienna Jones, Kate Kane, Cricket Keating, Amor Kohli, Phyllis Laughlin, Shirin Lee, Stephen Lewis, Sheena Malhotra Joyce Mariano, Helen Marlborough, Jeffrey Q. McCune, Erica Meiners, Julie Moody-Freeman, Mary Morten, Sanjukta Mukherjee, Jacqueline Shea Murphy, Paige Nichols, Corri, Scott and Gilda Pasko, Lori Peirce, Thomas Pusateri, Andrew and Kevin Quirk, Kenya Raybon, Beth Richie, Emily Rosenberg, Kimberlee Perez, Brian Ragsdale, Manju Rajendran, Elsa Saeta, Qua Sayles, Barry Schuchter, Lance Schwultz, Maiya Sinclair Shackelford, Jordan Shin, Andrea Solomon, Kathryn Sorrells, Kaila Story, Willa Taylor, Erin Tinnon, Lourdes Torres, Irene Pish Tucker, Choua Vue, Stacy Wenzel, Cheryl, Skylyn and Cici West, Betsy Wheeler, Nina Wilson, Sule Greg and Vanessa Wilson, Hanna Wisner, Nijole Yutkowitz, Daisy Zamora, and to the Black

Girls Group (Genesis, Octavia, Zoe, Lily, Maya, Sienna, Nia, Sofia, and Sadie).

I especially want to acknowledge Annie and Cece, who are at the heart of this book, for trusting me to share our lives together in writing. Annie, I wouldn't go on this journey with anyone but you. Thanks for reading and talking through this book in all of its stages and for filling my life with love and light every single day. Never a dull moment!

And Cece, thank you for your laughter, insights, kindness, hugs, and good company. Since I've become your mother, every single day is filled with purpose and joy. This book is for you.

NOTES

PREFACE. LOOKING FOR SIGNS: APRIL 2012

xvi **I am writing this in a time of reckoning**: Elle Moxley, "Protesters Demanded Justice for Nina Pop. A Year After Her Death, What Happened to Everyone Saying Black Trans Lives Matter?," *Time* (May 3, 2021), time .com/6023622/nina-pop-death-anniversary/.

1. EVOCATION: A GATHERING OF MOTHERS

7 **"We bind where law fails . . ."**: Imani Perry, *Breathe: A Letter to My Sons* (Boston: Beacon, 2019), 36.

12 **For me, growing up**: Sandra H. Royster, "A Sentimental Journey," *Chicago* 39, no. 2 (February 1990): 56.

13 **"Who, we might ask, is truly on the outside . . ."**: Cathy J. Cohen, "Punks, Bulldaggers, and Welfare Queens: The Radical Potential of Queer Politics?" in *Black Queer Studies: A Critical Anthology*, ed. E. Patrick Johnson and Mae G. Henderson (Durham, NC: Duke University Press, 2005), 42.

2. QUEER ROOTS: WHEN THE WORLD IS NOT ENOUGH

26 **We have always been here.**: Darnell L. Moore, *No Ashes in the Fire: Coming of Age Black and Free in America* (New York: Bold Type, 2019), 10–11.

4. CHANGING MY MIND: RETHINKING MARRIAGE

51 **I love you more each day.**: Willie Bobo, "Dindi," *Lost and Found*, Concord Records, 2006.

5. THE LITTLE HOUSE: MAKING HOME WITH QUEER JOY

60 In her 1993 photograph **"Self Portrait/Cutting"**: Both Catherine Opie, "Self Portrait/Cutting" (1993) and "Self-Portrait/Nursing" (2003) are printed and discussed in Ariel Levy, ed., "Catherine Opie: All-American Subversive," *New Yorker* (March 5, 2017), www.newyorker.com/magazine/2017/03/13/catherine -opie-all-american-subversive.

61 **Throughout that fall**: Maggie Nelson, *The Argonauts* (Minneapolis, MN: Graywolf, 2015), 10–11.

62 **For far, far too long**: La Marr Jurelle Bruce, "Careful Now: Seven Notes Toward Self Care," *Powerlines: An Interdisciplinary Online Journal of American Studies* 3, no. 1 (2015), amst.umd.edu/powerlines/volume3-issue-1 /digital-roundtable/la-marr-jurelle-bruce-respondent.

6. ADOPTION: AND THE ARITHMETIC OF LOSS AND GAIN

64 **"Scared you good, didn't I?"**: Audre Lorde, *Zami: A New Spelling of My Name; A Biomythography* (Freedom, CA: Crossing, 1982), 207.

65 **"for the majority of people who entered the house scene . . ."**: Quoted in Marlon M. Bailey, *Butch Queens Up in Pumps: Gender, Performance and Ballroom Culture in Detroit* (Ann Arbor: University of Michigan Press, 2013), 77.

65 **Among the tenants in that big old house**: Toni Morrison, *Sula* (New York: Vintage, 2004), 37.

69 **"the right *not to have* children, . . ."**: Sistersong: Women of Color Reproductive Justice Collective, accessed February 8, 2022, www.sistersong.net /reproductive-justice.

72 **South Africa is currently the only**: Samantha Moore, "LGBT Adoptions in the U.S. and South Africa," *Eastern Illinois University Political Science Review* 2, no. 1 (2012): thekeep.eiu.edu/eiupsr/vol2/iss1/2/.

8. DOING THE LIMBO: THE WINTER BEFORE, 2012

90 **for these were my great grandmother's**: C. C. Carter, "The Herstory of My Hips," *Body Language* (Atlanta, GA: Kings Crossing, 2002), 84.

11. SNAPSHOT: SUMMER 2012

109 **grace as "a gift . . .":** Maiya Sinclair Shackelford, "Grace" (unpublished MA thesis, DePaul University Department of Interdisciplinary Studies, December 2021), 1.

12. MOM, SINCE I SAW YOU LAST: FALL 2012

114 **How can I describe the lesson:** Cherrie Moraga, *Waiting in the Wings: Portrait of a Queer Motherhood* (Ann Arbor, MI: Firebrand, 1997), 126–27.

122 **I could see that darn owl in my dreams:** Walt Disney, quoted in Jim Korkis, "Walt Disney and the Owl," *Mouseplanet* (July 27, 2011), www.mouseplanet .com/9697/Walt_Disney_and_the_Owl.

14. CECE'S BODY: FALL INTO WINTER, 2014

131 **In a video project that I think about often:** Frans Hofmeester, "Lotte Time Lapse (Birth to 12 years in two min. and 45 sec. Time Lapse Lotte)," YouTube, accessed February 8, 2022, www.youtube.com/watch?v=RtyqS68ViWk.

17. WE ALSO BELONG TO THE WORLD: SUMMER 2016

149 **I have known from the very first day:** Perry, *Breathe*, 8.

150 **Know ugly, love pretty.:** Jeffrey McCune, "For Escobar" (unpublished poem).

22. A TOY STORY: SEPTEMBER 2017

163 **You stayed up till 11 pm that night:** Ta-Nehisi Coates, *Between the World and Me* (New York: One World, 2015), 11.

168 **My fear for Cece's body:** Chastity Holcomb and Erica Djossa, "The Invisible Load of Motherhood; Mothering Black Children," quoted in Rachel Garlinghouse, "Black Motherhood comes with an invisible weight,

and this graphic perfectly sums it up," *ScaryMommy* (June 18, 2020), www.scarymommy.com/invisible-load-black-motherhood-explained/.

24. THE BABY STORE: JANUARY 2018

186 **According to Azzizi Powell:** Azzizi Powell, "African American Perceptions of Adoption," *PACT's Point of View* (1997), pactadoptcms.pactadopt.org /app/servlet/documentapp.DisplayDocument?DocID=53.

186 **Sociologist Dorothy Roberts:** Dorothy Roberts, *Shattered Bonds: The Color of Child Welfare* (New York: Basic Civitas, 2002), vi.

193 **Throughout its run, the show explored:** Tracy Gilchrist, "10 Ways *The Fosters* changed TV, As remembered by Cast and Creator," *Advocate* (June 6, 2018), www.advocate.com/arts-entertainment/2018/6/06/10-ways-fosters -changed-tv-remembered-cast-and-creator#media-gallery-media-1.

26. TRACING TIME: SEVEN TATTOOS: SUMMER 2018

224 **"I'm here / For revision, . . .":** Mark Doty, "To the Engraver of My Skin," in *Fire to Fire: New and Selected Poems* (New York: HarperCollins, 2008), 244.

225 **Bowie designed the artwork himself:** "Frequently Asked Questions: David Bowie" (n.d.), www.bowiewonderworld.com/faq.htm.

228 **"You can never have too much sky":** Sandra Cisneros, *The House on Mango Street* (New York: Vintage, 1991), 33.

27. KISSING DOESN'T KILL: AND OTHER QUEER LESSONS I LEARNED FROM MY MOTHER

229 **What I remember about that poster:** Gran Fury, "Kissing Doesn't Kill, Greed and Indifference Do," New York, commissioned by Creative Time (1989), ime.org/projects/kissing-doesnt-kill-greed-and-indifference-do/.

CODA. STONE SOUP LOVE, WITH ANN RUSSO

248 **We encounter collision**: Aimee Carillo-Rowe, "Be Longing: Toward a Feminist Politics of Relation," *NWSA Journal* 17, no. 2 (Summer 2005) 17.

248 **Do not let your head deny**: Audre Lorde, "For Each of You," in *Undersong: Chosen Poems Old and New* (New York: W. W. Norton, 1992), 80.

FURTHER READING

Breitbart, Vicki, and Nan Bauer-Maglin. *Tick-Tock: Essays on Becoming a Parent After 40*. New York: Dottir, 2021.

Erdrich, Louise. *The Blue Jay's Dance: A Memoir of Early Motherhood*. New York: Harper, 1995.

Gillespie, Peggy, ed. *Love Makes a Family: Portraits of Lesbian, Gay, Bisexual and Transgender Parents and their Families*. Photographs by Gigi Kaeser. Amherst: University of Massachusetts Press, 1999.

Gumbs, Alexis Pauline, China Martens, and Mai'a Williams, eds. *Revolutionary Mothering: Love on the Front Lines*. Preface by Loretta J. Ross. Toronto, Canada: PM, 2016.

Herman, Gabriela. *The Kids: The Children of LGBTQ Parents in the USA*. New York: New Press, 2017.

Johnson, E. Patrick, and Mae G. Henderson, eds. *Black Queer Studies: A Critical Anthology*. Durham, NC: Duke University Press, 2005.

Jordan, Jamal. *Queer Love in Color*. New York: Ten Speed, 2021.

Katz, Jonathan David, et al. *ArtAIDSAmerica*. Tacoma and Seattle, WA: Tacoma Art Museum in association with the University of Washington Press, 2015.

McClain, Dani. *We Live for the We: The Political Power of Black Motherhood*. New York: Bold Type, 2019.

Moore, Mignon R. *Invisible Families: Gay Identities, Relationships, and Motherhood among Black Women*. Berkeley: University of California Press, 2011.

Nash, Jennifer. *Birthing Black Mothers*. Durham, NC: Duke University Press, 2021.

Of Many Colors: Portraits of Multiracial Families. Photographs by Gigi Kaeser. Interviews by Peggy Gillespie. Amherst: University of Massachusetts Press, 1997.

Patterson, Jodie. *The Bold World: A Memoir of Family and Transformation.* New York: Ballantine, 2019.

Pollack, Sandra, and Jeanne Vaughn, eds. *Politics of the Heart: A Lesbian Parenting Anthology.* Ithaca, NY: Firebrand, 1987.

Turner, Dawn. *Three Girls from Bronzeville: A Uniquely American Memoir of Race, Fate and Sisterhood.* New York: Simon & Schuster, 2021.

Wheeler, Elizabeth. *Handiland: The Crippest Place on Earth.* Ann Arbor, MI: University of Michigan Press, 2019.

Wilkerson, Isabel. *Warmth of Other Suns.* New York: Vintage, 2011.